CITIZEN-PROTECTORS

CITIZEN-PROTECTORS

THE EVERYDAY POLITICS OF GUNS IN AN AGE OF DECLINE

JENNIFER CARLSON

OXFORD
UNIVERSITY PRESS

OXFORD
UNIVERSITY PRESS

Oxford University Press is a department of the University of
Oxford. It furthers the University's objective of excellence in research,
scholarship, and education by publishing worldwide.

Oxford   New York
Auckland   Cape Town   Dar es Salaam   Hong Kong   Karachi
Kuala Lumpur   Madrid   Melbourne   Mexico City   Nairobi
New Delhi   Shanghai   Taipei   Toronto

With offices in
Argentina   Austria   Brazil   Chile   Czech Republic   France   Greece
Guatemala   Hungary   Italy   Japan   Poland   Portugal   Singapore
South Korea   Switzerland   Thailand   Turkey   Ukraine   Vietnam

Published in the United States of America by
Oxford University Press
198 Madison Avenue, New York, NY 10016

Library of Congress Cataloging-in-Publication Data
Carlson, Jennifer.
Citizen-protectors : the everyday politics of guns in an age of decline / Jennifer Carlson.
pages cm
Includes bibliographical references and index.
ISBN 978-0-19-934755-1 (hardback)
1. Firearms ownership—United States. 2. Firearms—United States. 3. Firearms—Law and
legislation—United States. 4. National Rifle Association of America. 5. Public opinion—United
States. 6. Gun control—United States. I. Title.
HV8059.C37 2015
363.330973—dc23
2014031629

11/13/15
OCLC

1 3 5 7 9 8 6 4 2
Printed in the United States of America
on acid-free paper

In Loving Memory of Michael B.
For those who chased their dreams so I could find mine.

CONTENTS

———————

ACKNOWLEDGMENTS

NO AUTHOR WRITES A BOOK alone. I am incredibly fortunate to have had the unfailing support and encouragement of many colleagues, mentors, friends, and family throughout the journey of researching and writing this book.

First, I would like to thank the gun carriers and instructors whom I met over the course of this research: you shared your time during interviews and your expertise during impromptu firearms lessons, and you introduced me to other "gunnies" and invited me to picnics, potlucks, and events. This book would not have been possible without you. I would like specifically to thank Mark Cortis and Brian Jeffs; I am indebted to your initial openness to my project and your support as I carried it out. Mark: thank you for your calm and consistent generosity throughout; Brian: thank you for your unfailingly sharp wit on all things gun-related.

The vibrant community at the University of California, Berkeley inspired and shaped the dissertation that became this book. It is difficult to put into words my gratitude to the mentors who supported this project from the beginning: Raka Ray, Brian Delay, Jonathan Simon, Ann Swidler, and Loïc Wacquant. Thank you for kindly but consistently challenging me; for giving me the space to develop my voice while relentlessly drawing that voice back into the realm of sociology; and for teaching me that every intellectual act is also an ethical one. To Raka, my adviser and intellectual compass: From the start, you believed in me more than I could believe in myself. You showed me that sociology is a scholarly project and a deeply personal one, and because of you, I speak confidently and with my own voice. And to Kathryn Lively and Dawne Moon, thank you for providing me rich lessons in intellectual creativity and methodological and theoretical rigor during my undergraduate and early graduate school years, which served as signposts throughout this project.

This book benefited enormously from scholars who meticulously read early drafts of chapters and articles; who pushed me into better thinking; who shared wine and whiskey; and who knew when and how to tell me to stay true to my own compass, especially Abigail Andrews, Kemi Balogun, Dawn Dow, Fidan Elcioglu, Katie Hasson, Sarah Macdonald, Katherine Maich, and Jordanna Matlon. At Berkeley and beyond, Jessica Cobb, Kimberly Hoang, Katherine Mason, and Nazanin Shahrokni provided me with persistent deadlines, endless intellectual energy, and much-needed emotional support to move this manuscript forward. Jessica and Kimberly, I am especially grateful for your rare blend of sheer brilliance and loyal friendship. At every step of this project, you've been my first responders as I've struggled to make sense of unfamiliar data, entertain new angles of analysis, and learn to take intellectual risks. Sarah, thank you for lending a listening ear and reminding me to celebrate the small victories along with the large. I also want to thank Cal Morrill and Rosann Greenspan for providing a generative forum through the Berkeley Empirical Legal Studies fellowship program for discussing my work, and Hillary Berk, Veena Dubal, Margo Mahan, Tamera Lee Stover, Giuliana Perrone, and Genevieve Painter.

As this project developed from a dissertation into a book, I relied on several scholars who painstakingly combed through the pages of the manuscript and supported this process in too many ways to list here. Michael Musheno provided me with boundless mentorship throughout the book-writing process and particularly helped me in sharpening my analysis of how police and gun carriers think about, and approach, crime in strikingly similar ways and also face similar pitfalls. Josh Page also provided me with seemingly endless support and insight at all stages of the project. From its core theoretical contribution to the minutia of wordsmithing, this book would simply not be the same without Josh's meticulous engagement in the project. Mariana Valverde's sharp eye for empirical nuance, combined with staggering analytical rigor, helped immensely in fleshing out and bringing to the surface many of the subtle arguments surrounding race, gender, and class in the manuscript. David Yamane pushed me to hone my ethnographic voice, and his detailed understanding of gun culture combined with his knack for generative disagreement improved the arc of the book as well as the clarity of the argumentation. Feedback from Scott Melzer and Michael Messner significantly tightened my analysis of the links between masculinity and gun rights. Amy Cooter and Michelle Phelps also provided sharp insight and consistent motivation throughout the tedious revision process. Finally, I have been overwhelmed by the support I've received from the community of scholars at the University of Toronto, especially Clayton Childress, Hae Yeon Choo, Randol Contreras, Rosemary Gartner, Phil Goodman, Kelly Hannah-Moffatt, Anna Korteweg, Candace Kruttschnitt, Jooyoung Lee, Matthew Light, Paula Maurutto, Neda Maghbouleh, and Jamie Rowen. Thank you for your generosity during informal conversations over coffee, by commenting on drafts and rewrites, and through engaging my work in colloquium settings, especially at the Centre for Criminology and Socio-Legal Studies.

I am extremely grateful to those who provided a space to share my work beyond my home institutions, especially Margaret Dewar, Dagmar Ellerbrock, D'Lane Compton, James Messerschmidt, and Claire Renzetti. This book also greatly benefited from the anonymous reviewers and editorial support at *Gender & Society*, the *British Journal of Criminology, Feminist Criminology*, and Oxford University Press, especially from James Cook, Joya Misra, Pat Carlen, and Jana Jasinski. James and his team have brought superhuman levels of diligence, sharpness, and know-how to the publication process, and their detailed engagement with this book significantly changed it for the better. Jessica Cobb's and Letta Page's meticulous editing considerably enhanced the book as well. Portions of this book appear in *Gender & Society*, the *British Journal of Criminology*, and *Feminist Criminology*.

Finally, I am indebted to my friends and family. Especially Bradley Coffman, Chessa Rae Johnson, Selby Mashakova, and Jaime Tollefson, your friendship and irreverence carried me through the toughest periods of this project. Brittany, my little sister, you've earned your spot as an honorary sociologist: you've been by my side from the beginning to the end of this project, and despite our difference in ages, I have always known I could go to you for thoughtful advice, commiseration, and mustard. My little brother, Chris, you have given me a lifetime of steadfast laughter and friendship, and I greatly relied on you and your smile during the final stages of the manuscript for much-needed moral support. Last but not least, to my parents, Steve and Patricia Carlson: you gave me the conviction that anything is possible and the support to make any possibility a reality, and both of you, in your own ways, taught me important lessons about the power of will, without which this book would not have been possible.

CITIZEN-PROTECTORS

I

American Dreams, American Nightmares

AN AFTERNOON A FEW YEARS AGO, Corey,[1] a white man in his late thirties, was working the cash register at his family's corner store in Flint,
Michigan. The store had stood on the same block on the east side of
Flint for almost forty years, stubbornly refusing to join the empty lots
that blighted the once-bustling area. Describing the neighborhood's
decline, Corey told me, "Before, it was all blue-collar, shop workers,
and a little bit of welfare. Now it's all welfare, and things are different."
As jobs left Flint, houses were abandoned, and then, Corey explained,
"the kids were having fun burning them down . . . two, three fires a
night down there." The arsons escalated in 2010, when the city of Flint
drastically reduced its fire and police forces. Flint attempted to deal
with the ongoing problem by bulldozing houses. "Where our store is,
they've torn down, like, four hundred houses," Corey told me. "It's like
open football fields."

Despite the loss of jobs and then buildings, the store still enjoys a
regular and diverse customer base: younger members of a local gang,
Flint city workers, police officers, and the elderly. On that March
afternoon, Corey had just finished ringing up a seventy-year-old
regular customer when he sensed that two more customers had come
in. Without looking up, he continued sorting the old man's bills.
Shutting the cash register, Corey raised his eyes to the barrel of a

gun. The young man holding the gun—a nineteen-year-old African American "with a criminal record" (as Corey described him)—demanded money, staring at Corey's right hand. In a flash, Corey reached for a five-shot revolver with his left hand. He aimed it and squeezed the trigger once and then again, hitting his assailant twice. As the nineteen-year-old's accomplice ran out of the store, Corey fired the gun in his direction but missed. He called 911 while the would-be assailant bled to death.

At first, Corey was concerned, because the man he killed looked young, maybe as young as sixteen: "It just would have been terrible to shoot a kid," he said. But after the police told him that the man was nineteen and had a criminal record, Corey reasoned, "he's old enough." When I asked him how he felt about the shooting, he said, "[It] doesn't bother me." And it didn't seem to bother his customers, either: "It's been both Black and white [customers] that say, 'Good job.'" Even the police in Flint seemed unshaken by the incident and quickly declared it a justifiable homicide; Corey was never arrested or held in jail. A few days after the shooting, a police officer visited the store: "I had a cop stop in the other day, and he said, 'Are you the guy who shot him? Good job!' And he shook my hand!"

Explaining his decision to purchase a gun and obtain a concealed carry permit, Corey told me that he had been held up "a dozen" times with various weapons. He could "usually put up a fight if I find the opportunity is there," but recently, he decided that it was "just time" to start carrying a gun: "I just thought it was time, I guess. Crime's bad, cops are low. I think this is what we come to. Cops are low everywhere. They always lay them off first, and it doesn't make no sense why they lay those guys off first." Countless other businesses in Flint and Detroit installed thick bulletproof glass in front of the register to combat stick-ups, but a gun made more sense to Corey: "We don't really want to get glass. It's so impersonal. Who wants to talk to somebody behind glass? You can't shake nobody's hand, you can't talk to nobody."

As we talked in his kitchen, his wife laughed from the living room as she interrupted with one-liners about Flint's dismal condition: "Murder City, USA!" But despite Flint's abysmal crime rate, Corey mocked the financial barriers to leaving. He laughingly told me, "Soon as we hit the big game, we're gone!" But Flint was home: "I put my application out there every once in a while. But that's all I know—the store."

* * *

Jason, an African American man in his thirties, decided to take a walk one night around his hometown of Detroit. Reflecting back on that evening during our interview, he recalled holstering his .45 caliber handgun and openly carrying it as a deterrent to crime, as had become his routine over the past few months. Open carry designates the practice of carrying a holstered handgun in plain view. Most open carriers wear their guns holstered on a belt in a way that resembles the way that police officers wear theirs. Jason also strapped on a recording device; he never carried his gun without it.

As he walked along one of Detroit's major thoroughfares, a group of police officers with their hands on their guns approached him. Jason recounted, "You know . . . me being Black, I have to think, *don't make any sudden moves*, or, you know, I'll be dead . . . You should have seen their eyes . . . I thought I was Frankenstein or something!"

On Jason's audio recording, which he shared with me, the police acknowledged that his actions were legal, if unusual. Jason was not in one of the handful of areas in Michigan where firearms are strictly forbidden, his handgun was properly registered, and he even had his valid concealed-pistol license on him, although he was openly carrying his gun. Explaining the reason for stopping Jason and seizing his gun, one police officer simply said, "You don't see this every day, man."

After confirming that Jason's handgun was properly registered, the police returned it, along with his other belongings. On his recording of the stop, the police audibly drive off, and then a crowd starts cheering before the audio cuts out. Jason explained, "I was deep in Detroit when I got stopped. And people were at a bus stop, and they were looking like, *oh my God! Another Black man going to jail for a gun.* So when . . . they [saw] the officers let me out of the car, they handed me back my pistol . . . people were cheering . . . they couldn't believe it! I walked over to them, and I explained, 'Look, you know open carry is legal . . .' That's the whole point. They need to see you can carry."

Jason explained that he started carrying a gun because "the economy was going bad and everything" and because "I said, you know, my number's coming up." But, as with Corey, Jason's turn to gun carry seemed to go beyond personal protection; connecting his decision to carry a gun with the decline of Detroit, he said, "That's what I'm trying to do: take my city back one day at a time, one step at a time, and show the thugs, *look, that's right, I have a gun too.*"

In "taking back" his city, Jason saw himself as engaged in something bigger than self-defense. He was also a model for others in Detroit to emulate:

> When they learn I'm not a cop, they just become so animated, because they see it's real. It's not just something I heard about, that open carry is something you can do north of 8 Mile [the dividing line between Detroit and its suburbs] . . . There's a Black man here in my presence, open carrying, and he's confident. He's not a thug, there's no police, he's walking out of a door, and he's not trying to cover it. So when they see that, they're like, "I want to do that too."

Alluding to the legal restriction that forbids felons from owning or carrying firearms, Jason told me, "I wanted to walk over to them and be like, 'You want to do this? Stay out of trouble. Keep a clean record, and you can do the same thing I'm doing.'"

The Gun Carry Revolution

Corey and Jason are part of a major shift in America's gun landscape. Since the 1970s, more than three-dozen states have significantly loosened their restrictions on Americans' ability to carry guns legally. The US Government Accountability Office estimates that there are at least eight million licensed concealed carriers, while a more recent estimate by the conservative think tank Crime Prevention Research Center places this figure at over 11 million. The increased popularity of gun carry reflects changes in why Americans say they want guns in the first place: one survey shows that Americans are much more likely to own and carry guns for protection today (48%) than they were in 1999 (26%).[2,3] Gun owners and carriers are overwhelmingly men.[4,5] In Michigan, men are four times more likely than women to have a permit to carry a gun. The racial breakdown of gun carriers in Michigan may also surprise some. White and Black residents are equally likely to have a permit, at 1 in 25 residents, and in Detroit and its suburbs, African Americans have higher rates of concealed carry licensees per capita than white residents.[6]

The National Rifle Association (NRA) plays a key role in shaping this new brand of gun culture that is centered on gun carry. As the leader of the national gun lobby, the NRA sustains grassroots initiatives aimed at changing gun policy at the local, state, and national levels, often coordinating state-level and local organizations with national efforts. Soon after the NRA's legislative "lobbying" arm—the Institute for Legislative Action (ILA)—was established in 1975, the NRA began turning its attention to passing "shall-issue" concealed carry laws. Under a shall-issue system, all applicants who meet the basic criteria set forth by the state (e.g., no criminal record, over the age of twenty-one, a resident of the state, and, most of the time, having passed a fire-arms training course) and pay the application fee will receive a license to carry. The NRA advocated shall-issue in place of existing may-issue systems, which involve an extra step: applicants must convince licensing officials of their need for a license to carry. Officials may be generous or stingy in granting licenses, but it is at their discretion. Shall-issue legislation removes this discretion.

When Georgia passed its shall-issue law in 1976 with the help of the NRA, it began a gun-carry revolution: only four other states had similar systems. A few additional states quietly passed similar laws, and in 1986, Florida garnered national media attention for its shall-issue legislation, which galvanized more than two dozen additional states to follow suit in the 1990s and 2000s. In Michigan, the NRA coordinated with the Michigan Coalition for Responsible Gun Owners, a state-level organization that had been working to pass shall-issue legislation since 1996, to write the legislation and lobby elected officials. Michigan passed its concealed carry law in 2001. Today, most states now allow residents to obtain a permit to conceal a gun on a shall-issue basis (or, in some states, to do so without a permit at all). There is much variety among the states with shall-issue legislation, spanning the western, southern, midwestern, and even eastern regions of the United States. More Americans in every region of the United States are now licensed to carry guns than at any other time in history.

A second type of legislation has deepened this gun-carry revolution. Stand Your Ground laws apply the "No Duty to Retreat" doctrine to public space, which means that citizens have no duty to give up ground to an assailant, whether in the home or in public. While the "No Duty to Retreat" doctrine has long applied to the home,[7] which is commonly understood as a person's retreat, states' positions vary as to whether a person must demonstrate that she was unable to retreat safely from a threat in order to use force in self-defense in *public*, rather than *private*, space. Standardizing the legal rules of engagement for self-defense, Stand Your Ground laws extend the "No Duty to Retreat" doctrine from inside the home to public space. The proliferation of these laws shows a trajectory similar to that of shall-issue laws: Florida enacted its Stand Your Ground law in 2005 with the support of the NRA, and about two dozen more states followed, including Michigan in 2006.

Shall-issue and Stand Your Ground laws, aimed at expanding Americans' ability to use guns for self-defense, show that the NRA is not just a lobbying organization but also a proactive shaper of gun culture. These laws allow Americans to exercise their gun rights by integrating guns into their everyday social lives. In short, these laws allow gun carriers to put gun politics into practice.

If the NRA sets the stage for a new kind of gun culture centered on gun carry, it is Corey, Jason, and millions of other American men who navigate this gun culture. Indeed, the sixty gun carriers I interviewed and many more whom I met during my research alert us to the social significance of guns in a way that numbers and laws cannot, because while guns are about self-protection, they are also about much more. As these gun carriers' stories illustrate, gun use and ownership represents complex responses to economic decline, social disorder, and inadequate police protection. Owning and carrying a gun is a way of practicing a particular civic duty, a way to "take back" one's city. Corey's actions—to shoot dead a nineteen-year-old who was threatening him—were exceptional among the gun carriers I met while doing research for this book. His actions are, indeed, exceptional among Americans more broadly: according to the FBI, American civilians commit just over two hundred justifiable homicides with firearms each year.[8] However, Corey's concerns about vanishing economic opportunity, his abiding worries about crime and police cutbacks, and his descriptions of community collapse speak to a broader narrative of American decline.

Likewise for Jason: his action—the choice to openly carry a gun—was relatively rare among gun carriers, but his concerns about the economy and his "number coming up" are commonplace in the larger US context. Corey's and Jason's worries resonate with much more ordinary, even unremarkable, anxieties about American decline associated with persistent fears regarding crime and social control, the restructuring of the economy from manufacturing to the service sector, and the erosion of community. For Corey, Jason, and millions of other American men, these concerns are not abstract worries about American decline; they are concrete, practical worries about their own declining access to an idealized, outmoded version of America, one with well-paying jobs and safe and secure communities. Corey's and Jason's stories suggest that what is at stake in contemporary gun politics is not simply the affirmation of conservative social values (as scholarship on gun politics often suggests) or heroic narratives of self-defense (as pro-gun interests maintain), but something much broader and more complex: what is at stake is a story of American decline told as a problem of urban and suburban disorder.

American Gun Violence

Gun violence is an epidemic in the United States: gun deaths are on track to outpace motor-vehicle deaths, and in twelve states and DC, they already do.[9] A 2013 Center for Disease Control (CDC) report[10] on firearms-related violence details the disturbing statistics of the nation's gun problem: in 2010, there were 31,672 gun deaths (mostly suicides) and 73,505 nonfatal gun injuries. Of the 12,664 homicides reported to the FBI in 2011, 8,583 were firearms-related, and of these gun-involved homicides, 72% were carried out with handguns; this represents just under 50% of all homicides. Importantly, gun casualties are not equally distributed: the CDC reports that economic conditions and geography shape who is harmed by guns and how. Black men are most likely to be killed by guns. Poor youth of color in urban areas are most likely to be the victims of homicide; white, rural, middle-aged men are most likely to commit suicide. These are compelling, crisis-level statistics that are unmatched in the rest of the industrialized Western world—no one disagrees about that. But what should they compel us to do?

One answer is to strictly control guns and their circulation by strengthening restrictions on who can purchase guns, regulating the sale of certain kinds of guns, and perhaps even banning certain guns. Doing so, gun-control advocates maintain, will put a meaningful dent in the level of gun violence in the United States and help prevent sense- less mass shootings, suicides, homicides, and injuries and deaths from negligent discharges. Treating gun violence as a public health problem,[11] scholars argue that preventative measures such as background checks are easy to implement and effective. As evidence of this effectiveness, some point to the 1993 Brady Bill, which instituted background checks and a five-day waiting period,[12] while others emphasize the effects that gun buy-back programs and aggressive gun policing have had on urban gun violence.[13] And many look to Canada as a model: despite its proximity to the United States and the porous United States–Canada border, the country's gun-related homicide rate is just over a sixth of the US figure.[14] Canada does not ban guns altogether, but it does heavily restrict handguns; they are difficult to purchase and almost impossible to carry legally. Public health scholars therefore contend that Canadian legislation provides a practical framework for balancing the right to own guns with measures that decrease gun violence.[15]

But in the United States, gun control is not the only answer to the problem of American gun violence. Gun rights provide the other answer, and based on Americans' persistent opposition to a handgun ban, it is quite a popular one.[16] Gun rights proponents maintain that given the preponderance of guns already in circulation, people should have the right to defend themselves against gun violence with equal force—that is, with guns. Whether guns are effective tools of self-defense has been the subject of much debate among scholars. Arthur Kellermann's widely cited, and hotly contested, reports[17] suggest that the presence of lawfully owned guns increases the risk of homicide, whereas Gary Kleck and his colleagues[18] maintain that not only do people use guns often in self defense, but also that when they do, they have a lower risk of injury during criminal victimization. As the 2013 CDC report notes, even though gun owners report greater feelings of safety, "additional research is needed to weigh the competing risks and protective benefits that may accompany gun ownership in different communities."[19]

Many Americans are not waiting for more research to make up their minds about guns, however. Millions of them have already decided that guns are a solution to the problem of gun violence rather than its cause. While gun carriers do not comprise the majority of Americans or American men, carrying guns is an increasingly prevalent practice—and it is a practice that provides much insight into the everyday meanings that Americans attach to guns.

This book is not about the public health consequences of guns, nor does it attempt to advocate for specific gun policies—whether they be gun rights or gun control measures. This book does something different: it examines a world in which guns are a sensible, morally upstanding solution to the problem of crime, a world in which the NRA is not a hard-line lobby that distorts the political process in Washington, DC, but rather a community service organization that serves middle America, and a world in which guns are attractive not only to white men but also to racial minorities. Drawing on interviews and participant observations with Corey, Jason, and other men in Michigan who carry guns regularly, this book dissects the complex ways in which guns come to figure as the solution and analyzes the problems that they purport to solve. It raises questions about how, as social objects, guns work to address real and imagined[20] social, economic, and physical insecurities. And it argues that what lies at the heart of gun politics is a critique of the state's ability to secure social order, a critique that becomes particularly appealing within a historically specific, postindustrial context of decline.

Michigan, particularly Metro Detroit and Flint, brings into focus the impact of socioeconomic decline in this regard. The loss of blue-collar jobs has been felt most acutely in Michigan, but the shift from stable union jobs to more precarious work is a national problem. This economic transition has been accompanied by fiscal stresses in municipal budgets and declining faith in the state among the citizenry, particularly the state's capacity to provide police protection. In Michigan, these factors combine to make guns appealing to diverse groups of men, and as they turn to guns, they also remake ideals of citizenship. Sometimes alarmingly exclusionary, sometimes surprisingly inclusive, this politics of gun carry stipulates new moral codes for how a responsible citizen should behave in a context saturated with socio-economic insecurity and aggravated by the state's failure to adequately provide security.

In this book, I foreground a sociological analysis of gun culture that represents neither a wholesale endorsement nor flat-out condemnation. When I use words like "moral," "dignity," "rational," and "sensible" to describe the social life of guns, I am using these words to explain how guns become meaningful to the gun carriers I studied. I am not saying that guns always carry these meanings, especially outside the context and historical moment I studied, nor am I attempting to provide a value judgment on guns themselves.

Rather, I focus squarely on documenting how guns are used by men to navigate a sense of social precariousness. This requires thinking about guns in terms of three registers of decline. First, the appeal of guns must be situated in a context of changing economic opportunities that have eroded men's access to secure, stable employment. Second, the urgency of guns must be understood in terms of abiding fears and anxieties surrounding crime and police inefficacy, concerns that encourage men to embrace their duties as protectors. Third and finally, the celebration of guns must be understood as a response to growing feelings of alien-ation and social isolation, such that guns come to represent not simply an individual's right to self-defense but also a civic duty to protect one's family and community.

By taking this line of analysis, I argue that the consequences of this turn toward guns are far more profound than what either the statis-tics on gun violence or concealed carry licensing rates can tell us. Specifically, this turn toward gun carry has transformed the meanings of American citizenship for the men who carry guns. Embracing a model of citizenship that I call the "citizen-protector," gun carriers use firearms to actively assert their authority and relevance by embracing the duty to protect themselves and police others.

Mourning Mayberry

How do gun-carrying men of diverse backgrounds understand firearms as a means of keeping people safe, rather than making us less safe?

When and how does a gun make you a better person, rather than a criminal or vigilante? In short, what are guns doing for the men who carry them, and with what consequences?

These questions aim to shed light on the significance of guns for the millions Americans who carry them on their person as part of their everyday lives. I argue that their answers lie in part in the perceptions and realities of American decline, a decline that is particularly acute in places like southeastern Michigan. Examining men of diverse racial and class backgrounds, I argue that the proliferation of guns in everyday life is more ambiguous and multifaceted than often acknowledged: Gun-carrying men are not just motivated by crime and insecurity but also by a loss of American values, a loss of masculine dignity, and a loss of confidence in the state. For some, gun carry signifies the recuperation of respectability, rights, and safety; for others an assertion of authority; and for still others—such as Jason—a heightened risk of criminalization.

I use "Mayberry" as shorthand—as Frankie, a retired African American welder from Detroit, did when he justified his decision to carry a gun by telling me, "Shit, if this was Mayberry, I'd be all right! But it's not." Rich in cultural imagery, Mayberry expresses a nostalgic longing for a "state of mind," as one Andy Griffith tribute maintained, about a particular version of America. A fictional small North Carolina town on the long-gone *Andy Griffith Show*, Mayberry represents, in the American psyche, an idyllic space of single-family homes, nuclear families, community cohesion, and safety and security. It has no urban troubles, like crime or poverty—at least, none that cannot be solved with a few laughs and a half hour's time.[21]

As historian Thomas Sugrue's[22] landmark study of Detroit shows, the real-life emergence of Mayberry depended on white flight en masse from American cities to the suburbs in the 1950s, '60s, and '70s and a manufacturing-based economy that offered men a breadwinning wage to support the nuclear, single-family household that it idealized. While white, middle-class Americans chased the socioeconomic security of the white picket fence, their mass divestment from urban centers helped to further concentrate and isolate poor people of color, who were left behind in America's so-called "urban ghettos." A denial of the troubles plaguing poor communities of color, Mayberry represents refuge, a "haven in a heartless world."[23] Yet, decades later, the elusive promise of tranquil suburban life remains just that for most Americans: an unfulfilled promise. As the American middle class dwindles and the problems typically associated with urban life extend out into the suburbs, the pristine dream of Mayberry is marred by the realities of racial inequality, economic insecurity, and declining community.

Crime

The first sign of the frailty of American suburban life came in the form of racialized fear: legal scholar Jonathan Simon argues that the 1960s represented the beginning of a period characterized by "the problem of criminal violence and the widespread and enduring fear among Americans that our systems of public security, primarily our criminal justice system, could not protect them from becoming victims."[24] Fear of crime was originally sparked by urban rioting in the 1960s, spiking violent crime rates in the 1970s, and high-profile cases in the 1980s, like the Central Park jogger rape of 1989. These fears were inflamed by the "tough on crime" politicians chasing votes, on the one hand, and the sensational news coverage by media outlets chasing profits, on the other.

The moral panic[25] surrounding crime had profound, if racially divergent, effects on Americans' relationship with crime and the criminal justice system. In addition to being disproportionately the victims of violent crime, men of color are also disproportionately targeted by the criminal justice system for nonviolent offenses and stereotyped as criminals more broadly in American society. While African Americans and Latinos in America tend to view the criminal justice system and its gatekeepers—the police—with suspicion, white Americans have also become increasingly concerned with the state's ability to control the problem of crime, particularly in terms of police efficacy.[26] As a result, many Americans have invoked their power to purchase, fueling a massive private security industry that markets home alarm systems, private police, and even cell phones and SUVs as security-enhancing commodities.[27] Guns are part of this push.[28]

As sociologists Gary Marx and Dane Archer[29] presciently noted just as the NRA began implementing its strategy of pushing for shall-issue

legislation in the 1970s, Americans "responded to recent law enforcement problems through increased fear, estrangement from one's neighbors, avoidance behavior, increased receptivity to law-and-order politics
and—as the rising fortunes of the private security industry suggest—
increased purchases of protective devices such as better locks, alarms
and weapons." This sentiment fits with scholars' findings that stipulate guns as a response to perceptions of increased crime and decreased
police efficacy.[30] Although crime has plummeted over the past twenty
years in many places, both anxieties about crime and the bloated criminal justice system these anxieties helped to sustain persist more than
fifty years after Nixon's call in 1968 for a "war on crime."

Economy

As Mayberry seemed to be threatened by crime *from the outside*, a
second dynamic threatened to undermine Mayberry America *from
within*: the shift from a male-dominated, single-income-earner, manufacturing-based economy to a service-based economy that lacked the
benefits, like reliable healthcare, retirement, and even paid sick leave,
that characterized men's jobs in the 1950s and '60s. More men are out of
work than before: forty years ago, about 6% of men of prime working
age—between twenty-five and fifty-four—were without work, but in
2009, that figure ballooned to 20%.[31] And fewer men are sole breadwinners. In 1960, 70% of families were headed by a sole male breadwinner,
but today that figure is 31%, according to a Pew study on breadwinning
moms.[32] The erosion of the breadwinner model places strain on men's
roles within families by undermining traditional gender relations that
posit women as homemakers and men as breadwinners. With Mom
needing to work alongside or in place of Dad, men are increasingly
unable to assert their masculinity as productive workers and providers.
The erosion of the breadwinner model therefore has both economic
consequences (given the loss of breadwinner jobs and the employer
obligations that used to accompany them) and social impacts (as family
relations and definitions of masculinity within the family come to be
redefined). The effects of these changes are particularly devastating for
Americans who have already been shut out of middle-class America,
particularly poor urban racial minorities[33] and poor rural whites.[34]

Community

Faced with fear of crime and their own economic precariousness, many Americans feel disconnected from their own communities and estranged from a country that no longer represents (or never did represent) them and their interests. Long associated with the ennui of American suburban life, these feelings of disenfranchisement and disenchantment also characterize American urban life, which has been rocked by the intrusion of the criminal justice system, poverty, and persistent crime.

Robert Putnam[35] addresses this decline in community in his famous argument that Americans are increasingly "bowling alone." This is due, he says, to a withering of "social capital," meaning that Americans are increasingly withdrawn from their communities, forming weaker ties than generations past. This pattern is visible in a number of ways: decreased voter turnout, growing distrust in government, and increasing rates of divorce. Though describing a general social trend, Putnam's findings are particularly applicable to those Americans most invested in traditional values and social institutions, such as the nuclear family. Indeed, among white conservative Americans, this alienation has given rise to a version of politics aimed specifically at defending and resurrecting Mayberry America.[36]

Yet, as Putnam shows, these feelings of alienation and decline are intertwined with but not reducible to white conservative backlash. Indeed, they are indicative of a broader decline in community engagement, and they are concerns felt by groups other than white conservative Americans. When Corey, a Democrat who voted for Obama, resists putting up bulletproof glass, despite his fear of crime, because "you can't shake nobody's hand," he's communicating these broader concerns about community. Getting a gun was not his initial response to increased social insecurity; after all, he told me he had been victimized several times before he finally turned to a gun. But a gun was also not a last resort for him; it was an appealing alternative to something that he saw as more destructive of community: bulletproof glass. So too is Jason concerned about community when he insists that his decision to carry a gun openly is a way to "take [his] city back." Here, his gun allows him to model to onlookers a kind of armed citizenship typically off limits to

African American men, especially when he publicly compels police to recognize his right to carry a gun.

The stories of Jason, Corey, and other gun carriers suggest that if Americans are increasingly disconnected from their communities and worried about the economy and crime, they are increasingly *carrying guns* as a response to this decline—in other words, to "mourn Mayberry."[37] Yet in mourning Mayberry, they are also reproducing its exclusionary politics. Mayberry is not for everyone. With firearms, gun carriers are able to stake out community boundaries by policing those who do not belong. In Corey's case, it's a nineteen-year-old African American pointing a gun at him, and for Jason, it's the "thugs" to whom he can say "I have a gun too." The broad appeal of guns to men of diverse backgrounds suggests that this may be an inclusive moment in gun politics, but guns are inherently exclusionary objects in the sense that they are about aggressively policing others—in this study, (suspected) criminals who are always imagined as hyperaggressive men and often (but not always) imagined as economically precarious people of color involved in drug dealing or gangs. This exclusion is further troublesome because gun carriers can—and, indeed, sometimes do—misinterpret threats and overreact to them, endangering the innocent life, including even their own, that they profess to protect with their guns.

Michigan

Decline is the focus of this book, but it is not the only driver of pro-gun sentiment in the United States, or even in Michigan. Gun proponents may be interested in hunting, in target shooting, in protection; they may be driven by ideology or by practicality, or something in between. American gun culture is far from monolithic. There is frontier gun culture in the West that has taken root in less populated states like Montana, Utah, Arizona, and Wyoming; in many of these states, gun advocates have managed to push through legislation that removes licensing requirements for concealed carry as well as pass the Firearms Freedom Act, which maintains that guns banned under federal law can be manufactured within the state in question, as long as they do not cross state lines. Meanwhile, southern states like Louisiana, Georgia, and Alabama also have a distinct gun culture, more squarely rooted in the so-called "culture of honor" documented by sociologists Richard Nisbett and Dov Cohen.[38] Then there are the "anti-gun" cultures of coastal states like New York, Massachusetts, and California, where gun control has enjoyed much more popularity than in other states. Finally, there are the urban and suburban gun cultures found in once-bustling manufacturing hubs in midwestern Rust Belt states like Michigan, Ohio, and Pennsylvania. Hunting traditions throughout the United States, the culture of honor in the South, and Manifest Destiny in the West—all of these factors have uniquely enhanced the appeal of guns in the American psyche.

But the question of decline—and decline in multiple registers, affecting diverse groups of American men—has not received sufficient attention in popular and scholarly debates surrounding guns. To understand the links between decline and guns, therefore, we must examine an exceptional case within the United States, where America's nightmare of decline is reality. We must go to places like Detroit, Flint, and the suburbs that link them in southeastern Michigan.

This book uses the postindustrial state of Michigan to unpack contemporary gun culture and think about guns as a response to contemporary concerns about decline. In this regard, Michigan can tell us something different about contemporary gun culture than Texas, Arizona, or Montana can. Portrayed as America's nightmare in several recent popular books and films on Metro Detroit,[39] the state may be a harbinger of what may lie ahead for much of the United States as the country adjusts to a new socioeconomic landscape following the 2008 recession. Michigan's gun culture is situated in these broader trends of economic instability and elusive recovery, with roots that go back to the 1960s. This is why the state provides a useful—and extreme—window into the appeal of guns amid contexts of economic decline, unraveling public services, and rampant fear of crime.[40]

This book focuses on gun carriers in Michigan because they help to reveal a much-overlooked aspect of contemporary gun politics: how the politics of decline shapes men's turn toward carrying guns for protection. Amid a decades-long process of socioeconomic decline, Michigan passed a watershed concealed carry law in 2001. The shall-issue law allows residents to carry a gun concealed on their person provided they can demonstrate that they legally own the gun, have taken a qualifying firearms course, and have paid the state a $105 processing fee. As of May 2013, there are more than 425,790 residents with concealed carry licenses; the vast majority of the license holders are white (320,194, or 75%), while African Americans make up 21% (or 88,990) of license holders (they make up 14.3% of Michigan's population, based on 2012 US Census data).

I primarily draw on interviews with sixty male gun carriers (fifty-one white; seven African American; one Hispanic; one multiracial) and ethnography to examine the appropriation of guns by men. Most interviewees were in their forties, fifties, and sixties, and about a quarter were retired. The vast majority of interviewees were from southeastern Michigan, including Detroit, Flint, and Lansing and these cities' suburban and rural surroundings. Based on their own political identification and the political views expressed during the interviews, the vast majority were right-leaning conservatives and libertarians. The men I interviewed were blue-collar workers in professions like welding or trucking (46%); white-collar professionals, like lawyers, IT specialists, and administrative staff (37%); and security specialists, such as current or former police officers, self-defense instructors, and bouncers (12%[41]). While the bulk of my interviewees were men, I periodically draw on interviews I conducted with eleven women for the purpose of highlighting gender differences.

In addition to interviewing gun carriers in Michigan, I also participated in their social world, conducting around 150 hours of participant observation at shooting ranges, activist events, and firearms training classes. I went to indoor shooting ranges and outdoor rifle ranges, as well as the unregulated "Pit" near Lapeer, Michigan, where gun owners often let me try out their firearms—the "James Bond" gun; the infamous AR "Michigan Pistol"; a fully automatic 9 mm Uzi—and where they lectured me on proper grip, trigger control, and recoil. In addition to shooting, I attended several pro-gun "potlucks," where gun carriers gathered to share food, firearms expertise, and conversation. We chatted about a range of topics: the appeal of pocket guns, the practicality of ankle holsters, and the importance of backup guns. From these impromptu lessons on the range and off, I learned to appreciate the raw texture of guns and their use—the dependable but snappy Glock, the smooth trigger pull of the 1911, and the comfortable hand grip of the 9 mm Smith & Wesson M&P.

As I moved through these spaces, I knew that my age, race, and gender (a white female in my twenties when I conducted the fieldwork) allowed me to present myself as an eager-to-learn novice to the men I met. I always introduced myself as a researcher, and I never disguised my affiliation with UC Berkeley. Although this affiliation elicited some raised eyebrows among the generally conservative gun crowd, I found gun carriers welcoming and willing to participate in the study, especially when I told them that I was open to shooting and even carrying a gun. And indeed, after attending firearms training courses that stressed the everyday practices that make a person a gun carrier, I decided that I could not understand the universe of gun carriers unless I took gun carry seriously not just as something that people believe in but as something that people *do*.

Eventually, I purchased my Smith & Wesson M&P, and I obtained a concealed-pistol license to carry it. While I already owned a small .22 caliber pistol, it never occurred to me to carry it: this was a target-practice gun, not a defensive handgun, and besides, concealed carry was effectively illegal in the San Francisco Bay Area, where I lived before moving to Michigan.[42] I didn't grow up in a pro-gun household and had few pro-gun friends or relatives. But as I prepared for Michigan, I became curious about experiencing gun carry firsthand: I wanted to understand what it was like to go through daily life—grab a cup of coffee, run errands, grab a quick bite—while armed. My desire to understand gun carry ultimately led me to continue my training, and I became a certified NRA instructor.[43] After I obtained my license, I carried a gun every day of my fieldwork, often concealed but sometimes openly. Though I never used my gun in any kind of defensive capacity, my gun, at least when openly carried, instigated both curious conversation from the public and attention from the police.

I conducted this research while living in Metro Detroit. I stayed a half-mile north of the infamous 8 Mile boundary between Detroit and its suburbs, which gave me a firsthand sense of the barriers that are etched into Metro Detroit's social geography. For example, just days before concluding my fieldwork and leaving Michigan, my 2010 New Year's Eve celebration was punctuated by a torrent of gunfire—the loud booms of shotguns and rapid fire characteristic of fully automatic guns—as the clock struck midnight on the border of Detroit and its suburb. Many times, I received admonishments from locals and gun carriers about how to navigate this borderland: 8 Mile is fine, but don't go too far south; Royal Oak Township is not too dangerous, except that everyone knows there's no functioning police force, so if you're over there, you're on your own; Ferndale cops only care about arresting African Americans coming from Detroit, but if you're white, you shouldn't have a problem; never open carry a gun in Warren, otherwise the police will mess with you. Bluntly and directly, I was told in so many words that my presentation as a young, white woman meant that I could move through some spaces with little trouble, while I would be pegged as someone who "looks like a victim" in others. Alongside my interview and ethnographic data, I used these admonishments and experiences as a window into how locals parsed out Metro Detroit and its complicated geography of race, socioeconomic decline, and crime.

While this research on Michigan is not generalizable to all states, my analysis of these interviews and ethnographic observations provides insight into how Americans may negotiate socioeconomic decline against a backdrop of dwindling public services and fear of crime. For this reason, Rust Belt states can offer unique insights into how guns and gun carry become meaningful to Americans, particularly American men, even though this region has been overlooked in studies of gun culture. As other states follow similar paths as Michigan in terms of the reformulation of public services and economic decline, we might expect to see similar patterns in terms of gun politics—both in terms of Americans' reasons for turning to guns and the social consequences of those guns. In Michigan, a central social consequence of this turn, I argue, is the reformulation of citizenship to center on policing and protection. The citizen-protector model of citizenship calls attention to the moral politics that positions the act of killing to protect oneself and others as morally just, warranted, and respectable.

Citizen-Protectors in a State of Decline

This book argues that the everyday practice of gun carry sustains a model of citizenship—the citizen-protector—that celebrates the protection of

self and others as an everyday civic duty that is particularly compelling in contexts where alternative ways of asserting masculinity (such
as being the sole financial provider for one's family) are eroding and
the state's capacity to protect (through policing, for example) appears
precarious. This is a particular kind of citizen who is willing to take
(criminal) life in order to save (innocent) life, a moral duty that scholars
have explored mainly only as it relates to the police role rather than as
a generalized basis of citizenship.

Notions of citizenship have long been at the heart of American gun
politics. As Kristin Goss, author of *Disarmed*, summarizes in a 2013
op-ed:

> Gun politics is not simply about differences on policy proposals. Gun
> politics is about what it means to be a good American. It's personal.
> Even gun owners who don't belong to the NRA believe, as my dad
> did, that gun ownership is a civic virtue, a hallmark of American
> self-reliance and duty . . . For gun owners, ownership is evidence of
> their civic spirit.

Varying across time and place, citizenship is defined by both
rights and duties. In both regards, the United States provides fertile
soil for gun-centric citizenship. The gun has historically served as the
medium to exercise a right to self-defense and to enact a duty to ensure
broader social order, oftentimes in revolt against the state. The Second
Amendment as well as state constitutions stipulate the gun as a tool of
citizenship. The Second Amendment maintains that "the right of the
people to bear arms shall not be infringed," and it connects this right
to the militia—an armed body of citizens—in its preamble, "necessary
for the functioning of a well-regulated militia." Michigan's constitution,
written in the early 1800s, is even more explicit in connecting guns to
both self-defense and civic duty: it proclaims the right to "bear arms for
the defense of himself and the state." Here, guns reflect long-standing
features of the so-called "American mind" by bringing together two
distinct strains of citizenship—one centered on an individual right, the
other on a collective duty.[44]

These two strains appear in a variety of ways in contemporary gun
culture: in the 1984 Bernhard Goetz case,[45] in the text of the Stand

Your Ground laws[46] passed in roughly two dozen states since 2005, and in the "insurrectionist ideology" that legal scholars Joshua Horwitz and Casey Anderson[47] identify in some pro-gun arenas. These strains are also evident in the texts that dominate pro-gun politics. Regarding the right to self-defense, the NRA's "The Armed Citizen" is a long-running column (dating back to the early 1900s) that features accounts of armed self-defense. In cultural anthropologist Kevin O'Neill's[48] analysis, the column emphasizes the valiant heroism of men, women, elderly people, and even children who defend themselves against faceless threats. The narrative is privatized (many of the incidents happen within the sanctuary of the home) and individualistic, showing the inefficacy of the state and emphasizing an individual need for the means to self-defense.

Yet, regarding the collective duty to promote social order, other texts suggest a more proactive dimension of pro-gun politics: John Lott's popular *More Guns, Less Crime*,[49] another hotly contested statistical analysis of guns, posits that the more people carry guns, the safer society will be for everyone. *More Guns, Less Crime* has been embraced by gun advocates to justify an individual right to self-defense as well as to make the case that guns are good not just for those who carry them, but for everyone. In other words, Lott suggests that gun ownership and carry are not simply expressions of the right to self-defense but are also collective duties that aim to promote social order more broadly.

This book argues that in the context of Michigan, these individual and collective duties come together into the citizen-protector model. I argue that a major, but overlooked, accomplishment of the NRA has been to promote this version of citizenship from the ground up in its training programs. Acknowledging the prowess of the NRA's lobbying arm and the firearms industry that backs it in shaping American gun politics and, by extension, American gun culture, this book takes a slightly different approach from previous studies of the NRA:[50] I focus primarily on the NRA's service initiatives, which train more than 750,000 Americans every year. My goal here is neither to provide a history of the NRA nor to analyze the organization's impact on policy-making. Rather, I examine how the NRA becomes a meaningful institution for many Americans by zeroing in on the organization's training programs, and I argue that these programs are important spaces in which the NRA shapes the political rights and moral responsibilities that gun carriers attach to their firearms. As such, this book is concerned more with understanding the consistently favorable public opinion the NRA has enjoyed for over a decade among everyday Americans than with the organization's ability to steer gun legislation in Washington, DC, and state capitols across the country.

I argue that the NRA continues to enjoy favor among many people because they view the organization as empowering Americans with a basic community service (firearms training). This understanding of the NRA requires a bottom-up look at what is actually happening in NRA training courses, and it cannot be gleaned from analyses that focus on NRA lobbying efforts alone. My goal is to show how this service aspect is critical in reproducing the NRA's power, and how we can't understand the broader appeal of the NRA without understanding this service aspect. I take this angle because this book is ultimately not about the NRA per se; it is about the gun carriers who turn to the NRA.

Placing gun carriers, rather than the NRA, at the center of analysis reveals a new perspective on gun politics and gun laws. Even though the language of "rights" saturates popular debates about gun politics, understanding guns in the context of an NRA-approved version of citizenship—including both rights and duties—suggests that recent gun laws expand much more than the right to self-defense. They empower Corey, Jason, and the other gun carriers I met to do something they simply could not have done before: to perform some of the duties traditionally associated with police and even to "act" like a police officer. Both can carry concealed guns, thanks to Michigan's 2001 shall-issue legislation, which allows residents to obtain a license to carry a concealed gun provided they meet a set of predefined criteria. Moreover, Michigan's 2006 Stand Your Ground law allows citizens to use a gun to protect not only themselves but also others—family members, friends, and even strangers—against the threat of death or grave bodily harm. As police departments are defunded and gun carriers trade stories of police inefficacy and, especially among men of color, police aggression and harassment, gun carriers see themselves as performing a necessary social duty—the duty to protect.

This emphasis on policing as a generalized civic duty—something that gun carriers *do* when they carry their guns—is at the core of this citizen-protector version of citizenship. From Corey's point of view, his gun was a response to the police's ineffective capacity—"crime's bad, cops are low"—to combat crime alongside eroding social controls, including the breakdown of Flint's automotive industry, rampant unemployment, notorious spikes in violent crime, and the bulldozing of huge swaths of the city. But far from providing an alternative approach to public law enforcement, Corey seemed to mimic it: if he held a badge alongside his gun, his justifiable homicide would have been far less noteworthy. Indeed, Corey acted out a familiar story that pitted gun-wielding men (police officers) against poor men of color (repeat offenders "with a record"). It is no coincidence that Corey borrowed the logic of the criminal justice system to justify the unworthiness of the nineteen-year-old he shot: rather than a youth and a fellow citizen, he is an adult offender with a criminal record, "old enough" to be held responsible for his actions.

Like Corey, Jason supplemented police inefficacy and negotiated a broader context of socioeconomic decline with his gun. But, as a Black man, he did so from a very different position than Corey. Rather than playing out a stereotypical story of Black criminals and white victims, Jason's actions upset this narrative by throwing into question the presumption that armed Black men are necessarily criminals, and he acknowledges as much when he characterizes the police's perceptions of him as "Frankenstein." Jason asserts his rights before both public law enforcement *and* the public at large, as suggested by the attempts of police officers to arrest him for his lawful behavior and the cheers of the crowd when they let him go. In doing so, he sees himself as a role model in his community based on his capacity to self-police. And as a model for his community, Jason extends an invitation to those willing to follow his actions: "You want to do this? Stay out of trouble. Keep a clean record, and you can do the same thing I'm doing." Yet, in doing so, he draws a thick boundary between himself and the "thugs," reinforcing the division between "criminals" and "law-abiding citizens" that drives the police to stop him in the first place.

As this book will show, gun carriers' attitudes and ideas about policing and public law enforcement play a central role in the meanings they attach to their guns. That said, gun carriers are not police officers; while some told me stories of performing citizens' arrests or intervening in crime (or being willing to do so) in ways that moved their understanding of their guns away from mere protection tools and toward policing tools, they were not involved in police bureaucracy and paperwork, in enforcing laws beyond citizens' arrests, or in coordinating raids and SWAT operations. I use the term policing not to suggest that gun carriers replace police officers but rather to call attention to how they assert their decision to carry guns—and their professed willingness to use them—as a civic duty. Embracing this duty to protect themselves and others, the men I met in Michigan reinvented themselves as citizen-protectors in a context in which their relevance and authority as financial providers and productive workers was undermined. Centered on a particular kind of citizenship promulgated and enacted in different ways by different kinds of gun carriers, this politics is not simply an ideological stance; it is a deeply felt, everyday politics. In fulfilling what they see as a duty, gun carriers do not just respond to the threat of crime—they reclaim a sense of dignity.

Carrying Guns, Claiming Dignity

For the men I studied, guns are convenient and attractive tools with which to embrace this version of citizenship and, in doing so, assert one's masculine dignity in contexts of declining access to Mayberry America. Dignity takes different forms in different contexts: Michelle Lamont's[51] *The Dignity of Working Men* shows how American working-class men define themselves as morally upright, rather than economically successful, by emphasizing themselves as "disciplined" (particularly white workers) and "caring" (particularly Black workers). Likewise, Victor Rios[52] rethinks the social ecology of young boys of color in Oakland, California, arguing that petty acts of delinquency (such as stealing a twenty-five-cent bag of chips) should be read *not* as crimes but rather as acts of reclaiming dignity; they are ways of asserting agency in a context of widespread and intensive criminalization, even if these acts lead to the greater policing and surveillance of these boys.

Claiming dignity can be a "weapon of the weak,"[53] that is, a humble enterprise undertaken by the socially marginalized. But the pursuit of dignity can also be a way for the privileged who feel anxious about their position in the status hierarchy to reassert their authority. Because of their race and class positions, the men I studied had different relationships to Mayberry America, and this in turn shaped the way they deployed guns to "mourn Mayberry." Thus, their quest for moral respectability took on multiple expressions—as relevance, as authority, or both—depending on their social location. In contexts of economic decline, fear of crime, and crumbling community, men turn to guns from different positions of privilege and marginalization that shape how they both understand and use guns to pursue a particular form of dignity.

On the one hand, working-class men of color and working-class white men tended to live in higher-crime neighborhoods, more often reported direct experiences of crime, and had more precarious work situations. For them, carrying a gun was both instrumental and symbolic. Gun carriers attempted to address an immediate threat of crime, but they were also performing a particular kind of masculinity[54] that "includes protecting the family from threats, at times literally putting [their bodies] in the line of fire on the street," as Elijah Anderson[55] describes fathers in "decent" families in West Philadelphia. And they performed this against the backdrop of a particular understanding of policing: these men are more likely to be affected by the overpolicing/underpolicing paradox. This paradox refers to how the communities most underserved in terms of police protection—often poor, urban communities of color—are also those most intensively targeted for intrusive police attention. This paradox has many consequences, including the normalization of everyday harassment that poor minority men face from the police and a deep distrust of public law enforcement across broad sectors of America. My analysis suggests that one more consequence should be added to this list: the joining of gun politics with police mistrust and cynicism about the legal system. For some gun carriers, carrying firearms becomes a protest against public law enforcement.

On the other hand, more privileged gun carriers—especially whites living in the suburbs—often experienced decline more as anxiety than as immediate threat. They tended to hear about crime mainly through newspaper headlines, local television broadcasts, and personal stories about crime and victimization. These men were also more likely to identify with public law enforcement, even as they acknowledged that law enforcement, though well intentioned, tended to be overburdened and ineffective. Although these men were economically secure in the context of broader US economic statistics, they often lost sight of their security within the context of Michigan's economic decline. This was partly because they understood themselves in relation to their parents' class positions, whose working years occurred during a period of much greater economic stability in both the United States and Michigan. For these gun carriers, it was often not their own personal decline but their perceptions of decline more broadly that led them to embrace guns and masculine protectionism.[56] Here, guns are more symbolic than instrumental, at least insofar as one can make such a distinction.

As I lay out this argument about the appeal of guns, readers may be reminded, on the one hand, of theories of "status anxiety" that stipulate that conservative backlash erupts when the power of the privileged is called into question or undermined—as happened during and after the civil rights era in the wake of gains by racial minorities, women, and sexual minorities. Threatened by these changes, conservative Americans—disproportionately white men—embraced the politics of the rising New Right and the Reagan Revolution. In this way, scholars[57] have analyzed guns (and conservative politics more generally) as a reactionary response to white men's declining status within the United States.

Readers may also recall a related but distinct theory that explains not the anxieties of relatively privileged Americans but those of more marginalized Americans. Here, I am talking about "strain theory"—the theory that at least some people turn to crime because they experience alienation and anomie from "mainstream" society and are furthermore shut out from "legitimate" channels for upward mobility. Like the image in a camera obscura, strain theory is status anxiety upside down: it talks about the strain that people at the bottom of the social hierarchy—for example, urban African American men or the working poor—experience amid rapid change and declining opportunity, particularly deindustrialization in major American cities like Detroit, Chicago, Philadelphia, and Oakland. If status anxiety describes those who are desperate to hold on to their place at the top of the ladder, strain theory describes those who are desperate just to step onto the ladder at all.

My formulation of the citizen-protector bridges and broadens these theoretical perspectives to better understand the appeal of guns as tools of protection and policing. Legal guns can and do serve as a symbol of a lost America once available almost exclusively to white Americans. For status-anxious Americans, the carrying of a gun may be a symbolic reclamation of white, masculine authority, a throwback to a time when "white" equated to both "right" and "might." But guns are also a way for American men to assert themselves as relevant, useful protectors, an assertion that becomes particularly appealing in contexts of declining employment opportunities and insecure communities. As social objects, guns are tools to assert dignity in the form of authority or relevance and to contest both declining status and dreams deferred.

But guns do more than address social contexts of decline. They also transform those social contexts in which they are carried. In his "crime as social control" thesis, legal scholar Donald Black[58] argues that crime is justice by another means. Under American gun laws, one might flip this script, as many critics did in the wake of the Trayvon Martin shooting, and argue that in the case of justifiable homicide, justice is crime by another means. With or without the good intentions of gun carriers, the version of citizenship I describe in this book brings with it novel, and potentially devastating, opportunities for lethal mistakes and mishaps that in another context would be treated as crimes rather than acts of protection. Indeed, national gun debates focus so much on whether criminals have access to guns that we've failed to interrogate how gun laws themselves have redefined what counts as criminal versus upstanding behavior. This shifting landscape of armed self-defense thus creates both instrumental opportunities to supplement diminished policing capacity and symbolic opportunities to assert one's dignity in the form of authority or relevance amid economic decline, but it can also blur the line between licit and illicit and between protection and aggression, sometimes resulting in violent encounters with irreversible consequences. As such, it raises new kinds of questions that can only be asked of a heavily armed populace: What would have happened had Corey not decided to purchase that gun or bring it to the store that day? Would he have been the one bleeding his life out? Or would he have been able to defend himself without a gun, as he had done several times before? Likewise, how would the police have reacted if Jason hadn't been wearing his neatly tucked, button-up shirt and dress pants and instead opted for "saggy" jeans and a hoodie, which are commonly associated with urban criminals? What if Jason hadn't gone out of his way to politely comply with every request the police made—even those, such as showing legal identification, that he had no legal obligation to follow? Analyzing contemporary gun-carry culture from the ground up to understand why Americans carry guns and with what consequences, this book opens up space to ask new kinds of questions and, ultimately, to imagine a different kind of debate about guns in the United States.

Outline

This book starts by situating Michigan's gun politics in the state's history of deindustrialization and economic decay, racial inequality, and violent crime. In chapter 2, "Criminal Insecurities," I examine gun carriers' articulation of decline within Michigan's political economy, which is experienced as a breakdown in social controls and in turn articulated as a crisis of crime. Situating in-depth interview data within the socio-economic transformation of Michigan since the 1950s, I show how gun carriers imagine and articulate crime using narratives of race and class that resonate with broader insecurities associated with postindustrialization and neoliberalism.

I next turn to the process by which people become gun carriers by examining the NRA courses required to obtain a concealed-pistol license. Chapter 3, "NRA Training and the Everyday Politics of Gun Carry," shows how the NRA attaches a particular set of civic rights, duties, and responsibilities (that is, a model of citizenship) to the lawful carrying of guns. While the organization is often associated with its role as the leader of the gun lobby, this chapter calls attention to the NRA's service side to show how NRA gun training reshapes gun culture from the ground up by presenting and promoting an alternative model for citizenship—the citizen-protector—that centers on the moral capacity to use lethal force to protect both self and others.

This book then considers how this version of citizenship presented in NRA training courses is enacted in everyday life by different kinds of gun carriers. In chapter 4, "The Right to Self-Defense, the Duty to Protect," I revisit the historical relationship between the state's power to police and masculinity to examine how gun carriers use firearms to address concerns about public law enforcement by claiming the right to self-defense. I show, however, that gun carriers embrace firearms not just to protect themselves but also to *protect others*: their families, friends, and even strangers. In a context of decline, this "duty to protect" provides an appealing basis upon which men assert their utility, relevance, and authority to their families and broader communities.

In chapter 5, "Policing Guns, Profiling People," I examine how experiences of racial profiling and other kinds of intensive police attention intersect with gun carry to produce a distinct gun politics among men of color and open carriers. Attending to the meanings that guns take on in relation to the race and gender identities of their carriers, I show how these gun carriers use firearms—sometimes in confrontation with police—to assert themselves as lawful citizens and to compel public law enforcement to recognize their rights as such.

In chapter 6, "Jumping the Gun," I explore how this version of citizenship—the citizen-protector—opens up the possibility for mistakes and misunderstandings that can place gun carriers in legally risky situations and put innocent lives at risk. Focusing on one gun carrier who was arrested, charged, and convicted for pulling his gun on an unarmed woman, I explore how his actions suggest an overzealous commitment to—rather than deviation from—a model of citizenship that emphasizes the moral duty to protect innocent life, especially one's family, with lethal force.

The conclusion summarizes my findings and their implications for scholarship as well as gun policy. Focusing on how the politics of armed self-defense intersects with masculinity, race, and socioeconomic decline, I argue against the current terms of the contemporary gun debate, which focuses largely on whether guns and gun-related practices should be legal or illegal. Gun rights advocates have largely won this debate: guns are here—more than three hundred million of them—and politically and legally speaking, they are here to stay for the foreseeable future. And they have won because the gun lobby offers something tangible and concrete—the ability to own and carry a gun—to Americans who are fearful about crime, concerned about police inefficacy, and anxious about decline. A more productive—and even, perhaps, less divisive—debate would focus on how guns can be made not illegal but less socially relevant by addressing some of the root causes of contemporary demand for firearms, at least for Americans turning to guns for self-defense. This is an objective that gun control and gun rights advocates, if they are sincere in their concern about the American problem of gun violence, should both embrace.

2

——◦◦◦——

Criminal Insecurities

"I GREW UP IN DETROIT. It was a different era back then. It's not anything like it is today," Frankie, a retired African American welder said as he cut his chicken-fried steak at a greasy spoon. I was asking about his hometown of Detroit. At first he hesitated, chewing thoughtfully and then getting the waitress's attention and asking for some extra napkins. When I questioned what exactly he meant by "back then," he began to narrate a complex story of Michigan's decline. It flipped between nostalgic past and bleak present: "Back then" referred to a time before the 1967 Riot in Detroit, before the automation of the automotive industry, a time when he "got a job at General Motors, and they were hiring people off the street with zero education, and they could work twenty years, and they could make a living. You can't do that shit now. What killed all that was automation." "Back then" was a time when people knew how to "enjoy themselves"—playing "the numbers" (a version of the lottery) in underground bars. "Back then" was a time when crime was petty, because people were too busy "having a good time." Now, with jobs gone and crime rampant, Frankie has a handgun on his hip, because Detroit is not Mayberry: "I don't carry a gun to kill people, I carry a gun to keep from being killed! Pure plain and simple! Shit, if this was Mayberry, I'd be all right! But it's not." Frankie says that he carries one on him at all times.

Frankie is part of a new kind of gun culture, one centered in suburban and urban areas. Every year since 2001, when the restrictions on concealed carry licenses were loosened, the number of concealed carriers in Michigan has increased,[1] and of the roughly four hundred thousand concealed-pistol license holders in Michigan as of March 2013, more than one hundred eighty-five thousand reside in the three counties that comprise Detroit and its suburbs (Wayne County, where Detroit is located, has the most license holders, at almost eighty thousand). Frankie references crime to explain his turn toward guns, but his anger at Detroit's transformation suggests that this turn is more than just a calculation of crime's likelihood. As he recalled his feelings about Detroit upon his return from the Vietnam War, he told me, "Hell yeah, I'd like to blow it up! Wouldn't be no doubt in my mind. And have a big, thirty-foot-high fence so that whatever survived could not get out." Yes, crime is a central element of the story, and Detroit regularly ranks as one of the United States's most dangerous cities. But Detroit and other postindustrial cities in Michigan and beyond represent something much more. Key sites of the demise of the American dream, Detroit and Flint are specters of two American nightmares: one centered on socioeconomic decline, the other on racial fears and anxieties.[2] For Frankie, crime is an idiom to express his resentment, anger, dejection, and disappointment with a dream that betrayed him.[3] He carries a gun to protect himself against crime—and to protect whatever other dreams he might still hold.

This chapter unpacks the social factors that drive gun carriers to view Detroit and Flint as epicenters of a crime wave and themselves as at ever-present risk of victimization. Among the gun carriers I interviewed, crime was the most common articulation of decline, but this view gained currency from a complex urban and suburban process of economic restructuring, chronic unemployment and underemployment, and racial segregation. While the men I met during my research often emphasized the threat of criminal victimization, they were also threatened by their own economic precariousness.[4] The complexity of these narratives, along with the appeal of gun carry to whites and African Americans alike,[5] suggests that fear of crime and men's turn to guns in the context of Metro Detroit cannot be reduced to a simple story of racism: race does matter for gun carriers—not unlike Americans in general—but the way that it matters is shaped by broader contexts of decline. As opportunities shrink and anxieties grow, the narrative of crime provides a persistent, explanatory thread that links together a story of social breakdown that reflects and aggravates social inequality. Overall, violent crime has steadily declined in most of Michigan since the early 1990s (though there are important exceptions, like Detroit and Flint), but the economy remains the big story of decay.

Like Americans in the mythical Wild West, gun carriers turn to guns for enhancing their security and safety, but they live in a different kind of frontier than the one that figures in what Scott Melzer, in his study of the National Rifle Association (NRA), calls "frontier mythology."[6] In contrast to a frontier marked by rural imagery and rugged individualism, the gun carriers I interviewed articulated a frontier embedded in suburban and urban life—marked by 8 Mile, 7 Mile, or any number of streets that Michiganders use to parse out spaces of varying degrees of safety and insecurity. Frankie's story illustrates this new gun culture, centered on gun carry, not simply because he lives in a context of crime, but because of the way in which crime comes to express the feelings of despair, loss, and being "under siege" that are associated with the broken promise of southeastern Michigan in particular and the declining American middle class in general.

Motor City Dreams

In December 1936, three thousand men gathered inside a General Motors factory in Flint, Michigan, to demand safer working conditions and better wages. The autoworkers halted production and stayed barricaded inside the facility for almost a month and a half. After the strikers faced off with the police and cost General Motors millions in lost wages, the automotive giant succumbed to their demands on February 11, 1937. The strike resulted in new safety standards, higher wages, and benefits.

Winning this battle, these workers also won the war—at least until the 1950s. General Motors recognized their organization, the United Auto Workers (UAW), as the exclusive representative of its workers. Over the next several decades, the UAW expanded to cover autoworkers throughout the state and the country and fought for access to the hall-marks of middle-class American life: healthcare, housing, family wages, and pensions.

Buttressed by the seemingly unstoppable engine of American industry, workers helped to forge the American dream in south-eastern Michigan in the 1950s. This manufacturing sector was at the center of an American era of consumerism, single-family households, nuclear families, and suburbia. This is where the fantasy of Mayberry America—an idyllic, crime-free, suburban refuge—could take root. Michigan workers earned some of the highest wages in the United States, and because of their union-backed job security, they qualified in unprecedented numbers for mortgages. In 1950, Michigan led the country in homeownership, and Detroit became a spread-out, low-rise city of single-family housing. Even the most historically marginalized in American society—African Americans—were comparatively well off in Detroit: despite mortgage discrimination, red-lining subpar housing, and employment discrimination (factors that historian Thomas Sugrue shows put Detroit on a path of decline as early as the 1940s and 1950s), African Americans there still had the highest rate of urban Black homeownership.[7,8]

Michigan's prosperity and prominence in labor struggles helped create an idealized version of American citizenship: the male bread-winner model, through which men could claim a privileged position as head-of-household, sole providers for their nuclear families.[9,10] The family wage sustained this version of masculinity because it allowed one worker the financial security to support an entire family. This is one reason why being an automotive worker held a certain status for men. As employees, Frankie told me, each autoworker received a badge, which guaranteed not only their employment but also enabled them to get dates: "On the weekend, the guys would have their shirts and their suits, and they'd put their badge where their tie should be, and the women would just flock to them. Because they had a source of income, see what I mean? And women loved them!" As productive workers, men proved their worth to their families and their country, putting food on the table and fueling American industry. Their ability to provide made them good men, good fathers, and good citizens. With crime relatively low, guns were predominantly used as tools of provision or sport (i.e., hunting) rather than of protection.[11]

Reflecting on this bygone era, the gun carriers I met in 2010 recounted nostalgic narratives. Life felt different then, gun carriers maintained. Christopher, a white gun carrier from the suburbs, waxed nostalgic, emphasizing idyllic family dinners, parental involvement, and community: "When I grew up—it was family dinners, it was a lot of family interaction, that type of thing, and there was always family involvement. Now, because of the economy, because of keeping up with the Joneses, you have two parents [each] working one job, twelve-, fourteen-plus-hour days, five to six days a week, and the kids are coming home and playing Xbox 360, then living on the Internet. It's a complete breakdown . . . Nobody knows their neighbors."

Fred, a white gun carrier who lived in a rural area outside of Flint, also spoke of a halcyon past. Laughing ironically as he explained the origins of the idea of the "doughnut-eating cop," he emphasized an earlier era of tranquility and safety by presenting a fabled account of public law enforcement: "It was really kind of an Ozzie and Harriet country, everybody was getting along, and cops were sitting in the doughnut shop because there wasn't anything else to do." Although the stereotype of cops as doughnut eaters most likely began because doughnut shops were convenient late-night spots for cops to congregate on cold graveyard shifts—a stereotype that today is popularly associated with lazy cops—Fred provides a different explanation. He took the stereotype as an indication that there was once a time when police officers had nothing better to do than have a cup of joe and relax in the doughnut shop.

Gun carriers—Frankie, Christopher, Fred, and others—articulated their nostalgic visions from different racial and socioeconomic positions. Frankie's view of social breakdown grows out of a context that concentrates poverty, crime, and violence in predominantly African American urban centers.[12] Meanwhile, Christopher articulates a white, middle-class experience, emphasizing the struggles of an isolated, single-family household and calling attention to a narrative of suburban decline represented by decreasing civic engagement and lack of community.[13] Finally, Fred emphasizes a bygone era of tranquility and safety typically associated with small-town, white America, before urban crime and, eventually, public defunding began to stretch police resources thin.

Despite their different vantage points, each of these men's tales converged on a nostalgic rendition of Michigan's past: good jobs and crime-free, close-knit communities. A time when the American dream—promising upward mobility and even equality—was within reach.

"Our Own Katrina"

Soon, however, the promise of Michigan's American dream began to wane. Jobs became scarcer as factories began to close, and entire neighborhoods that had been built up around them soon declined. Although the collapse of manufacturing would not fully take effect until the 1990s, there were harbingers of decline in the 1940s and 1950s, when Michigan's factories pioneered a new approach to manufacturing that would transform the industry's reliance on human labor.

In 1946, the Ford Motor Company invented what has come to be known as "automation," which replaced human assembly lines with machine assembly.[14] Billed as a way to ramp up productivity, this technological innovation ultimately could not keep Michigan manufacturing afloat, and consumer demand fell (not least because workers had lost their factory jobs). Chasing the bottom line, companies relocated factories to places in the United States and abroad with lower taxes and fewer unions. By the end of 2012, this process had come full circle: decades after the bloody fights in Flint that resulted in the founding of the UAW, Michigan became a right-to-work state.[15] As the economic situation grew bleaker, the state cut social safety nets. Welfare rolls dropped by more than half from 1996 to 2001, and in 2011, then-Governor Rick Snyder signed into law a lifetime cap on welfare cash receipts, effectively banning eleven thousand families (and counting) from receiving welfare. In July 2013, Detroit, the city that once called itself the manufacturing capital of the world, filed the largest bankruptcy case in US history.

Michigan has witnessed a "tsunami" of job loss since the early 1990s,[16] which was described as "our own Katrina" by then-Governor Jennifer

Granholm in 2009.[17] It was the only state with a statewide decline in employment from 1990 to 2009, with manufacturing positions declining from 2000 to 2009 by a total of 435,000 jobs.[18] Michigan reflects a larger process of restructuring in the United States: from 2000 to 2010, the country lost almost six million, or about a third, of its manufacturing jobs.[19]

This restructuring is also visible in union membership rates—one way to measure the quality of jobs in terms of stability and benefits. Overall, US union membership dropped dramatically, but Michigan's drop was even more precipitous: while 26% of Michigan's employees were union members in 1989, in 2012, union membership rates fell to 16.6%.[20] And while US median household income dropped about 5% between 1999 and 2009, Michigan's median household income declined around 20% over the same period.[21] Though Michigan once boasted incomes above the national average, in 2012, the state's median household income was $46,859, compared to $51,371 for the country as a whole.[22] Adjusted for inflation, median household income in Michigan was actually *lower* in 2008 than it was in 1980. The state has been hit harder than most.

Previously celebrated as the epicenter of a thriving manufacturing-based economy, Detroit is a living ruin of the once-vibrant automobile industry. As Reynolds Farley, Sheldon Danziger, and Harry J. Holzer note, "Detroit, the Motor City, was once the symbol of our national industrial prowess, the home of an innovative automobile industry that played a key role in the development of the middle class . . . [now] Detroit no longer symbolizes industrial might or technological innovation. Rather, the city is frequently seen as leading the nation in unemployment, poverty, abandoned factories, empty office buildings, high crime, and bitter racial strife."[23]

Industrial oasis is now urban wasteland. Majestic buildings pockmarked with broken windows and loosely attached plywood line the streets of Detroit, eerily evocative of the city's former glory. The once-monumental, but now abandoned, Central Station has been stripped of its plaster and brass by vandals, and shattered glass and broken tiles now cover the floor as dramatic arches inside cast shadows across the vast building's interior. Wander around Detroit, and you'll see the empty houses and lots of a zombie-like city, simultaneously living and dead.

Schools are closed down and abandoned; only 65% of Detroit's students graduate high school.[24] Quaint houses are uninhabited and dilapidated, mocking the middle-class lifestyle promised to new migrants back in the early 1900s. Detroit ranks last among large cities in median home value, trailing Cleveland by almost $30,000.[25] A far cry from the Five Dollar Day advertised by Henry Ford in 1914 to attract new workers to the city, today's Detroit maintains an unemployment rate of around 19% and a poverty rate of 39%.[26] Life expectancy in Detroit is lower than in any other major American city.

Eight Mile marks the northern boundary of Detroit. Cross this road, perhaps traveling up the thoroughfares of Woodward Avenue on the west or Gratiot on the east, and you'll find a cacophony of suburban spaces: Ferndale, Royal Oak, Warren, Roseville, Eastpointe, Southfield, Dearborn Heights, Clawson, Madison Heights. With few exceptions, these are historically white areas, where first aspiring, but then panicked, white homeowners fled as African Americans began populating the city of Detroit in the 1920s. Life in the suburbs promised not only home ownership but also refuge from the problems that blighted urban centers, including crime. In other words, for white Americans, suburban life has historically served as a form of social security, as legal scholar Jonathan Simon[27] shows.

These predominantly white suburban areas are no longer immune to the socioeconomic decline brought on by the processes of deindustrialization that have gutted Detroit. Some suburban strongholds—Bloomfield Hills, Grosse Pointe, and Rochester Hills, for example—remain economically secure, but, for the most part, the presumed safety of the white suburb has been eroded by economic insecurity. The miles and miles of mom-and-pop shops that used to thrive off of Michigan industry have closed, one by one, leaving suburban Michiganders with fewer and fewer employment options. Ernie's, a famous local deli near Ferndale that still manages to sell its hearty, high-calorie sandwiches, used to cater to factory workers in the early and mid 1900s. Now, it's more of a kitschy relic.

Passing through this suburban sprawl during the ninety-minute drive up I-75 from Detroit to Flint, you eventually arrive at a dead end—both literally and figuratively, as the interstate had been closed down and eerily turned to dirt during my fieldwork. The birthplace of GM and the UAW, Flint has lost twenty thousand residents since 2000. Despite attempts to reindustrialize the city after GM closed its last factory in the 1980s, Flint was declared a "financial emergency" in late 2011. According to the US Census, over 40% of its population lives in poverty.

Deindustrialized, depopulated: southeastern Michigan is a broken dream, a place where hardworking, industrial Americans had risked life and limb—while working, while striking—only to end up stuck in one of the worst regional economies in the United States. Now, Michigan is a popular symbol of neoliberal decline. Scholars use the term "neoliberalism" to trace the multifaceted social system[28] of state policies, market practices, and values that organize society according to competitive, free-market logic. Neoliberalism can be seen in Michigan in the dwindling of its social welfare system and the erosion of the rights of its workers, which displaces the collectivist politics of unionization and social welfare for individualized, market-oriented responses to social problems. It can be seen in the corporate pursuit of low wages, which ultimately displaced Michigan's factories. Although Michigan is often touted as an exceptional case, the indicators of Michigan's decline—manufacturing job loss, union membership losses, declines in median income, and more—are reflected in national statistics. As the United States experiences long-term fallout from the 2008 recession, the key difference between Michigan and the rest of the country is one of degree, not of kind.

* * *

The economy loomed large throughout my interviews. Each of the men I interviewed had something to say about the economic precariousness they saw around them. Nate is a white, middle-aged, middle-class man from the suburbs. A white-collar professional whose job hasn't been replaced by automation, he makes a good enough living to invest in a variety of specialty firearms. And yet, he sees the economy as an overarching factor shaping "every family's" life. "The economy's sucked for such a long time that so many people have to survive—and you know, they'll grow a victory garden to try to keep their grocery costs low. They'll commute and carpool and stuff like that to keep their costs low. Because every family, it seems, is suffering in some way through the economy."

Often, gun carriers spoke of their own experiences. Austin and Brent both described a lack of access to well-paying, stable blue-collar jobs. They told me stories of being laid off, re-employed, and forced to relocate. When I asked Austin, a white gun carrier and father, to identify his hometown, he joked, "I've moved over fifty times, so I don't really know." Tattooed with his daughter's name, Austin seemed to value his identity as a father, and he explained that he first turned to guns for protection when he moved to Flint with his daughter. There he carried a handgun on his person, even at home, and "after dark in Flint in that area, I would not even go off my property." While he no longer lives in Flint, his situation still seemed precarious. When conversation turned to "Obamacare"—the Affordable Care Act, which had just been passed as I conducted these interviews—he told me he opposed it: "to force people to buy something they can't afford? I mean, I can't afford it. And for them to fine me for not having it, I think, is a joke. They want to penalize me." He said that he couldn't afford health insurance, let alone a fine for not having it.

Brent also told a story of long-term instability. He went through several marriages and moved many more times in search of work:

> I was laid off from General Motors, I worked at the plant in Ypsilanti, and I was laid off, I finally was able to get a job in a plant up in Flint. So, I was out there, and I was riding with another guy, and he had to do a one-hundred-mile trip to Flint every day for work. And, uh, then I moved up into Flint, yeah. [Flint was] on the list of dangerous cities to live in at that time. There were dead people here, there, and everywhere. We were right in the middle of it. Got a 12 gauge. Had to pull it out a couple of times because people were running up and down the streets, yelling and screaming.

Austin and Brent's stories are indicative of the lack of opportunities for working-class men as the manufacturing bases of Michigan moved first south and then overseas. That constraint had gone beyond job security to housing and even personal safety. Nothing was safe.

More economically secure gun carriers referenced a changing experience of what it means to be middle class, particularly in comparison to their parents. Though not in financial trouble himself, Nate also intimated that his parents were sheltered from violence because they were just "peaceful, middle-class folks":

> I grew up in a lower-middle-class income, middle-class neighborhood. My dad worked in a shop, and he had an eighth-grade education. He worked in a factory that made machine parts, like airplane parts and automobile parts. My mom was a former judge's secretary. Her background was far different from my dad's. Neither one of them related to guns or the use of force—they were really protected from that kind of thing. Or at least felt that they were protected from that thing generally, because each of their backgrounds was a nonconfrontational background. Nobody got into fights or arguments or anything like that. They were just peaceful, middle-class folks.

While Nate is a middle-class professional, he does not have the same middle-class life as his parents: the stark contrast he draws between his parents' "peaceful" lives and his own turn to guns for self-protection suggests that his sense of security—articulated through a class narrative—has eroded.

While gun carriers often used terms like "sheltered," "liberal," and "anti-gun" interchangeably to deride gun control advocates, only when discussing their anti-gun or gun-ignorant parents did they use these terms to highlight *classed* contrasts between their parents' "middle-class" or "upper-class" sensibilities and their own. For example, Anthony, a white gun carrier who was kicked out of his house as a teenager and worked three jobs while he was finishing high school, told me that his parents were "very liberal," "anti-gun," and "upper-class, all prim and proper." In my conversation with him at a gun-rights picnic, Ted told me that his parents, a social worker and a middle school teacher, were "goody two-shoes" and "middle-class" people with "sheltered" ideas about the need for guns. These narratives provided a contrast between gun carriers and their parents: while their parents may have been "protected from that thing [violence] generally" (as Nate notes), gun carriers themselves no longer can count on the peaceful middle-class life available to their parents, just as they can't count on the stable jobs once afforded to their parents.

Economic decline is a core element of Michigan's predicament, and it's true that, as Nate notes, everyone has been hit hard, including white workers. Compared to those elsewhere, Michigan's white workers were the second-hardest hit by the 2008 recession, trailing only Nevada in the number of quarters that white workers faced an unemployment rate greater than 9%.[29] Yet it is African Americans who bore the brunt of socioeconomic decline: comprising the highest African American unemployment rate in the United States, almost one in five African Americans in Michigan is officially unemployed (18.7%).[30] The 2011 median household income in Detroit, a predominantly African American city, was just $25,193, while the poverty rate for families in Detroit was 35.5% (compared to 11.7% in the United States).[31] Thus, there is another side to the story of Michigan's decline, one that centers on the region's stark racial inequalities.

Both of sides of this story—economic decline and racial inequality—are necessary to understand how gun carriers of diverse backgrounds think about and respond to crime.

"Shoot Me, I'm Already Dead"

Michigan has experienced extreme economic decline, but this has paralleled a separate, if related, dynamic: a long-standing history of racial segregation, discrimination, and inequality. This history is revealed in the current unemployment rates facing African Americans in Michigan, who have been hit much harder than white workers in the current recession, but its roots go back much further. It is reflected in Detroit's treatment of African Americans from the South as second-class citizens in the 1920s and 1930s; in the decades-long process of white flight, starting in the 1950s and accelerating after the 1967 Detroit Riot; and in the aftermath of the Riot, in the 1970s and 1980s, when heroin and crack markets arose as men searched for economic opportunity in a city with few prospects. And, most importantly for understanding gun carriers and how they think about crime, this history is reflected today in how Detroit, Flint, and other cities serve as not just examples of economic decline but also as powerful symbols of violent crime and urban unrest.

Though Detroit had a relatively small Black population prior to 1910, because of both Black and white migration from the South,

Detroit was the United States's fastest-growing metropolitan area in the 1920s.[32] African Americans were lured by promises of higher wages, better housing, and less racial animosity, but many found that the problems that beset them in the South followed them northward. The slums that housed the influx of new residents, though the result of racist housing practices, were seen by white Detroiters as evidence of the degeneracy of the new African American residents.[33] As Elizabeth Martin[34] writes, "whites responded to the influx of 'uncivilized' Blacks with restrictive covenants and segregation . . . [and] the presence of white migrants from the South intensified racial tension in Detroit." Crime, poverty, moral laxity—all of these problems were attached to Black southerners, whose customs, lifestyles, and mannerisms seemed offensively foreign to Detroiters, particularly to white and Black elites, the latter of whom "generally agreed with white Detroiters 'that the southern Negro is more criminal by nature than his northern brother.' "[35] The next thirty years would be marked by abusive police practices, the formation of violent all-white homeowners' associations aimed at keeping Blacks off all-white blocks, the dwindling of economic opportunities for African Americans and (to a lesser extent) whites, and the fleeing of white residents and white-owned businesses from the city, as historian Thomas Sugrue[36] describes in detail in *The Origins of the Urban Crisis*.

One of the most notable cases of white-on-Black violence in Detroit during this era occurred on September 8, 1925, and involved Ossian Sweet, a Black doctor who had purchased a house on Detroit's all-white Garland Avenue (he paid a substantial markup because of his race). Recalling the lynchings he witnessed during his youth in Florida and knowing that there had been recent increases in violent assaults on Blacks aiming to move into white neighborhoods, Sweet decided to stockpile several firearms to defend his family and property. Within hours of moving in, he and his family were surrounded by a white mob. After several projectiles had destroyed windows, shots rang out from the house, and a white man was mortally wounded (another suffered a shot but did not die). Once police entered the Sweet residence, one officer asked, "What in the hell are you fellows shooting about?" Unsatisfied with Sweet's explanation that he was being threatened, the officer continued, "What have they done? I have been here right along.

I haven't seen anyone throw anything and I haven't seen no disorder. I don't know what you men are shooting about."[37]

The famous trial that ensued, which centered on Clarence Darrow's insistence that "a man's house is his castle," ended in a mistrial, and was then followed by another trial, in which one of Sweet's acquaintances was acquitted. The NAACP wondered, "Does the Black man have the white man's right to defend his home?" Less than two years later, the Michigan state legislature passed Public Act No. 372 of 1927, requiring the registration of all firearms. Although Sweet did not need a permit to stockpile firearms in his own house in 1925, after the PA 372 registration law, he would have had to present the actual firearms to local authorities for a "safety inspection" before being able to legally possess them.

The gun carriers I met often cited the gun registration law inspired by the Sweet trial as evidence of the "racist roots" of gun control. However, it wasn't just gun control that was racist: the whole of Michigan's social fabric—housing, law enforcement, education, employment, and, yes, even gun laws—functioned as a two-tiered system that privileged whites and put African Americans at a disadvantage. The system was bound to burst. When it did, it erupted into violence.

First, there was the interracial riot in 1943, the bloodiest riot in the country to that point.[38] And then the 1967 Riot happened. Although the complex and long-term problems besetting Detroit have their roots in social arrangements that unfolded decades earlier,[39] the 1967 Riot is widely understood—in the press and in the popular imagination—as the turning point for racial politics in Detroit and the decline of the city.[40]

The Riot began on July 23, 1967, early in the morning, when police raided a blind pig (an illegal liquor establishment) on Twelfth Street. It had been serving alcohol after hours. A number of circumstances made the raid noteworthy, though not out of the ordinary: because of joint welcoming and farewell celebrations for Vietnam War soldiers, the blind pig was particularly crowded that night; a split-second decision to arrest everyone in the establishment meant that the police required additional reinforcements; safety concerns with the alley behind the establishment led the police to parade arrestees on Twelfth Street, thereby bringing the raid out in view of the public; the slow arrival of additional officers provided time for a crowd to gather; and finally, the politicized messages screamed by arrested African Americans as they were brought into police vehicles added an immediate element of protest to the raid. Initially, the police seemed to take a rather apathetic attitude toward the gathering crowd. Aiming to contain the riot area around Twelfth Street, they did little to stop the looting and vandalism that had already started.[41] The atmosphere initially seemed jubilant. Referring to the diminished police presence in the early hours, one rioter noted, "For the first time in our lives we felt free."[42]

But the Riot soon turned violent, on the part of the rioters and the responders. The National Guard was called in by Mitt Romney's father, George Romney, then-governor of Michigan, and Detroit turned into a war zone, suddenly populated with three thousand police officers, five hundred state troopers, two thousand members of the Michigan National Guard, and five thousand paratroopers from the Eighty-Second Airborne. Representative John Conyers of Detroit said later, "what really went on was a police riot," with "federal agents . . . restrain[ing] Detroit police . . . [who were] unbelievable in their determination to visit excessive violence upon the population."[43] In all, the official numbers reported seven thousand people arrested, forty-three dead, and 1,189 injured, with the vast majority of fatalities due to police and National guardsmen shooting African Americans.

The Riot had long-lasting consequences for the social ecology of Michigan. For whites,[44] it solidified popular images of African Americans as ruthless, even animalistic criminals—what criminologist Esther Madriz[45] calls the "ideal criminal" image for its dehumanizing portrayal of poor men of color and its encouragement of racial divisions by marking off entire groups of people as fearsome, savage criminals. The evocative imagery of the "ideal criminal" helped justify various expansions in punitive social control—from the growth of the criminal justice system to aggressive policing practices. Whereas African Americans in Detroit viewed the Riot at the time as a protest against long-standing police abuse, whites in the suburbs of Detroit and in America more generally saw the Riot (and other examples of Black civil unrest—from the uprisings in Newark and Watts to the public actions of the Black Panthers) as signs that ever-increasing brutality was justified. New police initiatives (such as the FBI's COINTELPRO)[46] at both the federal and state levels led to the dismantling of the Black

Panthers and the continued repression of inner-city Blacks more generally. In Michigan, the Detroit Police Department's repressive Stop the Robberies, Enjoy Safe Streets (STRESS) program, implemented after the Riot, led to the murder of a plainclothes Black officer after white officers decided he looked suspicious and failed to recognize that he was a fellow officer.[47] These new policing initiatives would have long-lasting effects on criminal justice in America by increasingly targeting street crime in low-income, Black areas. Notably, it was the 1967 Detroit Riot that inspired the watershed 1968 Safe Streets Act that inaugurated the War on Crime,[48] unleashing an expansive carceral apparatus that has ravaged Black communities, even as overall crime rates have dropped since the 1990s. Today, there are more Black men under the control of the criminal justice system than there were enslaved in the mid 1850s, and Black men are now more likely to go to jail than to college. On some blocks in Detroit, at least one in seven Black men is under the control of the criminal justice system—either incarcerated or under community supervision.[49]

The Riot also further exacerbated the socioeconomic conditions in which the criminalization of racial minorities—particularly Black men—could become a self-fulfilling prophecy. While Detroit's Black population already faced difficult socioeconomic conditions, the Riot accelerated the exodus of white residents and white businesses from the city. Detroit's suburbs, cultural historian Amy Kenyon[50] argues, depended on the "mystification" of white privilege:

> In Detroit as in other rust belt cities, middle-class whites were able to follow and add to the flow of investment away from the city. Many white workers had the means to move into tract houses in the blue-collar fringe developments located near suburban manufacturing plants . . . suburbia held out the possibility of sustaining social divisions based on the consumption and distribution of space . . . distinctions within suburbia rested on house size and style, yard size, and distance from the city . . . suburban space was increasingly consumed by a cross-class segment of white Americans . . . but regardless of their social position, all suburbanites could differentiate themselves from inner-city dwellers.[51]

Back in Detroit, conditions of poverty, discrimination, and segregation had long since blocked legitimate forms of work and mobility for poor people of color. But the Riot and white flight that followed only aggravated the situation. Young, industrious Detroiters had to look for alternative means of financial gain. Put simply, they turned to criminal enterprise, pioneering what scholars have called the "postindustrial" gang. Smart, profit-oriented organizations comprised of members trying to "figure out how to survive in a postindustrial world,"[52] these gangs are not solely driven by pride, turf, or honor. In a 1986 ethnography of Detroit gangs, criminologist Thomas Mieczkowski[53] finds that quite unlike individual "hustlers" who are interested in protecting territory, runners (those who sell heroin and are not allowed to work while high) had a strict work ethic, and the organizations were kept in line with violent social control (usually exerted by the crew leader—or "the gun").

As the 1980s came to a close, gangs were credited with making Detroit one of the epicenters of the crack epidemic. Public officials in nearby cities in Indiana and Ohio blamed their own crack problems on "crack mobs" and "criminal entrepreneurs" "spreading" from Detroit to seek new markets "in communities of all sizes."[54] Rather than alluding to the long history of urban decline, popular media reports made sense of growing violence in Detroit by sensationalizing it: Detroit was famously captured in the 1987 *Village Voice* headline "Kids Killing Kids: New Jack City Eats Its Young." The article's author, Barry Michael Cooper,[55] ends his exposé with a disturbing image: a teenager dressed in "sweats, trench coat, and Ellesse gym shoes . . . [and] a black cap with a white stencil that said, *Shoot me, I'm already dead.*"

The fallout from the 1967 Riot reveals the other side of neoliberalism, the second nightmare. Highlighted in the work of Loïc Wacquant,[56] Bernard Harcourt,[57] and Joe Soss, Richard Fording, and Sanford Schram,[58] punitive social controls emerged as the solution to the twin problem of massive contractions in social welfare provisions and the exclusion of huge swaths of Americans from the labor market. There was too little aid and too many people who needed it. Thus, the War on Crime was much more than an attempt to subdue crime rates. Rather, it was an aggressive, neoliberal version of poverty management that garnered populist support by creating a moral panic[59] centered around fears of the urban Black criminal.

Together, these histories of economic decline and racial inequality shape the social reality of gun carriers as well as the ways in which they make sense of that social reality. These histories are living in terms of the material conditions they produce, and they are also living in terms of the cultural narratives they foster, particularly with regard to ideas about crime and criminality. I now turn to the powerful narratives—of race, of economy—that gun carriers use to make sense of crime.

Murder City, USA

Richard was a white gun carrier and instructor with whom I often drank coffee, late into the night, at a diner just off 12 Mile. He grew up in Detroit but later relocated to the suburbs. A seeming jack-of-all-trades, he made a living by dint of his involvement in a variety of entrepreneurial enterprises: an adult care facility; a car shop; a bounty-hunting enterprise; and his own firearms school. He always arrived at our coffee meetings before I did and sat facing the door (a habit I noticed dozens of other gun carriers repeat). He wanted a clear view of anyone who might come into the diner, and he never wanted his back turned to a potential assailant. At one of our first meetings, he let me in on the self-defense scenarios that played in his head, telling me that if someone came into the diner pointing a gun, he knew exactly which of the three firearms[60] he was carrying that he'd pull, and in what order, in order to protect himself and the other diners.

The first time we met, I asked Richard why he began carrying firearms in the first place. Turning back the clock, he told me:

> When I was 18, I was nearly beaten to death by a gang. I sustained really serious injuries. I was able to break the hold that somebody had on me—there was nine of them. When I got away, I called 911. A police car finally rolled up, and I told them I needed to get to the hospital. They weren't all that concerned, but they let me in the car. [Then they left me at] a bus stop, and when the bus came, I staggered onto it and said to the driver, "I have to get to a hospital somehow, I can't see, I don't know where I am." And he took me to another

intersection and gave me a transfer so I could take another bus and eventually end up at the hospital. I had a couple of surgeries, a couple months of rehab. About six months later, I was able to return to work, and it cost me thousands of dollars.

When Richard was victimized in the 1980s, he was part of a wave of crime that gripped the American imagination and increased the appeal of "tough on crime" policies that would ultimately result in the highest incarceration rate in the free world. While rising crime rates were not the only factor shaping "tough on crime" policies and politics,[61] crime provided a powerful, and powerfully simple, narrative of social disorder.

Detroit was one epicenter of this pandemonium. From the late 1960s to the 1990s, Michigan, particularly Detroit and Flint, became known more for violent crime rates than for the grit, ingenuity, and creativity that had formerly characterized the area. Murder rates in Flint and Detroit increased sharply in the 1970s and 1980s. In 1987, Detroit reached an all-time annual high of 686 homicides (or 63.5 per one hundred thousand residents). The character of crime also changed during this period: while 40% of homicides were committed with a gun in 1963, by 1973 this figure was 76.2%.[62] According to a 1984 *Time Magazine* article, guns were starting to resemble "household appliances" in Detroit, "with an estimated 1.5 million firearms in a city of only 1.2 million people."[63]

In that era, Detroit and Flint earned their reputations as "murder capitals" or "murder cities." As crime across Michigan and the United States dropped dramatically starting in the early 1990s, Detroit's rates still outstripped its surrounding suburbs as well as the aggregated rates for the US.[64] According to FBI data in 2012, the city experienced its highest homicide rate since 1993 (54.6 murders per one hundred thousand residents), reflecting both its persistently high number of homicides *and* its dwindling population.[65] The only city in the United States with a higher homicide rate than Detroit in that same year was Flint, with 64.9 murders per one hundred thousand residents—the highest ever recorded in that city.[66] There were 15,011 violent crimes committed in Detroit, or 2,123 per one hundred thousand residents, and in Flint, there were 2,774 violent crimes in a population of just 101,632.

About half of the gun carriers I interviewed shared concrete first- and secondhand experiences of victimization, providing close-to-home examples of specific crimes that demonstrated their physical insecurity. Take Victor, an African American gun carrier who lives in Detroit, who said, "I was never pro-gun, I was never anti-gun. It was something that I felt I did not need. That happened all the way until I got robbed at gunpoint about five or six years ago. And then I realized, I might need a handgun." Or Connor, a white gun carrier from Eastpointe, who told me that, "like 99% of other people in the world, I thought nothing's gonna happen to me, I'll be okay," until a random kidnapping occurred at a local Subway sandwich shop that he frequented. The "it could happen to me" feeling caused him to obtain a concealed-pistol license thereafter.

Victor and Connor's sense of ever-present risk was not unique; interviewees frequently highlighted this sense of ever-present threat: "You don't know when it's going to happen. If you knew when it was going to happen, you wouldn't take a pistol. You'd take a shotgun or a rifle. [But . . .] a pistol [is] convenient to have with you"; "you know, anytime you're without, you never know when you're going to need [a gun]. So it's best practice to have it at all times . . . Just like carrying a wallet." Jeremy, a white gun carrier, said that there is no place he doesn't feel "at risk," and the only time he does not carry is when he is legally unable to.

While crime *could* happen to anyone, crime rates are structured by race, class, gender, and geography. Who you are, where you live, how much money you make, your race, your gender: all of these have a huge impact on your likelihood of becoming a victim (as well as how and where). Connor, for example, is 1.6 times as likely to be the victim of violent crime in Eastpointe as compared to national FBI statistics.. Yet there were no murders in Eastpointe in 2012.[67] Eastpointe's violent crime rate is a far cry from Detroit's and Flint's predicaments.[68] Aggregated across the United States, violent crime has dropped precipitously since the early 1990s, and it has plummeted in most of Michigan. According to FBI data from 2007 to 2012, most of the suburban areas where gun carriers lived saw meaningful drops in violent crime rates, including Dearborn (35% decrease), Eastpointe (16%), Grosse Pointe (61%), Royal Oak (59%), and Sterling Heights (22%). A few areas, however, saw city-level increases: for instance, Hazel Park (a 35% increase). Overall, Michigan has its share of crime, but it does not even make the top-ten list of the states with the highest crime rates in 2012. And this is true of many states where concealed carry is booming: in Pennsylvania, Ohio, Utah, Arizona, Wisconsin, and roughly three dozen other states, concealed carry licensing has spiked alongside dropping crime rates.

All of this serves to suggest that crime rates do not necessarily map onto how people *experience* crime: a murder or mugging that happens on one's block or that happens to a close friend or relative, especially if this experience is reinforced by television and other media reports suggesting that crime rates are high or increasing, is likely to have a bigger impact on one's experience of crime than reading aggregate crime rates for a state, a city, or even a neighborhood. Furthermore, gun carriers do not stay put in one neighborhood, city, or even region but rather navigate through varying contexts of crime and insecurity.

In Michigan, crime matters in at least two ways: first, as a social reality informed by first- and secondhand experiences of crime, and second, as a lens through which to make sense of decline. Jonathan Simon explains how crime acts as a social lens in his book *Governing through Crime*. He argues that the War on Crime transformed crime into a central social problem in the American psyche, which has in turn organized how we see and understand other social issues—from poverty to education to health. As Simon and others argue, since the 1960s, crime in America has reached the status of a language or an idiom to describe deeper phenomena, such as economic restructuring and racial divisions, and it has become a way of diagnosing, and developing solutions to, social problems that have little to do with crime, such as school discipline. The persistence of crime's designation as a central social problem, despite marked drops in crime, is a testament to this bigger role crime plays not just as a social reality but also as a social lens. How you think about crime affects how you think about the world.

This lens is evident through local media depictions of crime. Almost daily, the *Detroit Free Press* and other news outlets broadcast stories of horrific crimes: a beat-up grandma; an unidentified burned body inside a torched SUV; gas station carjackings; and random shootings. Viewed through the lens of crime, Detroit and Flint become more than just cities with particular demographic trends and historical lineages: they became tropes by which to vocalize fears and anxieties associated with postindustrial decline. Detroit and Flint are not just cities; they're specters. Gun carriers within and outside of these two cities imagine Detroit and Flint as "dead ulcer[s]," as Sam, a white gun carrier, put it. He said that he felt relatively safe where he lived, about a forty-five-minute drive from Detroit, but exclaimed, "People in Detroit—for the love of God, carry something! Anything! It's the only way that the predators in society are going to learn!" Other suburbanites said that they worried about "roving gangs of criminals" that presumably traveled from Detroit to terrorize surrounding areas and render suburban homes—the space of middle-class security[69]—vulnerable.

No longer the promising urban centers of the early 1900s, Detroit and Flint are popular symbols of crime, poverty, and urban decay. Paralleling the twin nightmares unfolding in Michigan—one centered on race, the other on the economy—gun carriers provided two distinct explanatory discourses on Detroit's and Flint's crime problems: a *moralizing* discourse centered on gangs, drug dealing, and other markers of "Black violence" and an *instrumental* discourse centered on economic desperation.

Race

Racialized tropes of crime were almost unavoidable in a social ecology that overdetermined criminals as Black. Several gun carriers described crime with racial code words—the gangbanger, the drug dealer, the crackhead—that suggested gang- and drug-related activity. For example, Paul, a white gun carrier who lives in Flint, said:

> Let me get this straight. Somebody whose lifestyle revolves around selling hard drugs and violent crime and shooting whoever wears the wrong color hat—[they] are going to worry that you made it illegal for them to have a gun? Who is going to suffer from that the most? The gangbanging thug who lives that lifestyle anyway and has no respect for human life, or you know, my wife, who is no physical match for that thug who has decided that she looks like an easy mark tonight and is going to bust in her door?

This vision of crime connects it to gang activity ("selling hard drugs and violent crime and shooting people" and wearing "the wrong color hat") and justifies guns (we hear about the "gangbanging thug who . . . has no respect for human life"—are they "going to worry that you made it illegal for them to have a gun?"). As such, Paul provides a moralistic understanding of the gangbanger: he is sociopathic in his disregard for human life, and only good guys with guns could face him down.

Many gun carriers alluded to the criminals of Detroit and Flint as "thugs," "crackheads," "fellows perhaps of a darker skin with britches down to their knees," and "gangbangers" who wore "hoodies" and "droopy pants." In stipulating (some) Black men as particularly aggressive, some gun carriers echoed popular caricatures that link hypermasculinity, aggression, and blackness.[70] Importantly, these images were not limited to white gun carriers: African American gun carriers also used racialized language— "thug" and "ghetto"—as they made sense of crime, criminals, and criminality.[71] In Michigan in particular, and in the United States more generally, poor men of color provide the image of the "ideal criminal," even for other poor men of color.[72]

But there's something more than just criminal imagery at play here. Detroit is not just a symbol but an ongoing threat against which whites and "good Blacks" must protect themselves. Consider how Ben, a white gun carrier who lives just outside of Detroit in an upper-middle-class neighborhood, talks about Detroit:

> We are still in Wayne County, though we are on the very edge out here—right on the Washtenaw border. We still have reason to be concerned about the city of Detroit and its residents. I mean, you heard it—years ago—white flight! Then it became good Black flight. And now it's just—the bad of the bad are leftover and leaving. [Detroit] had such an admirable reputation in its day. It's just so sad to see what's become of it.

Though he admits that he lives moderately far from Detroit, Ben says that he still has "reason to be concerned about the city of Detroit," pinning his own insecurities on the "bad of the bad" Black Detroiters, who, as he told me earlier in the interview, "are migrating out this way to do their dirty deeds."

This racial imagery shapes how threats are evaluated and imagined: as political scientist William Rose[73] suggests, we should not confine racial profiling to public law enforcement, but rather consider it a generalized way of "seeing" (that is, a lens for interpreting social reality) justified by the criminalization of racial minorities within the contemporary American criminal justice system, but hardly confined to that system.[74] Race, here, acts as an everyday mechanism to assess and appraise both persons and places.[75] In this way, race and racialized criminality can be mobilized as interpretive tools[76] by gun carriers (not unlike Americans more generally) to make sense of their perceived social insecurity.

Economy

Race is, however, not the only narrative used to explain crime's rise and fall. Despite the economy's complex effect on differing crime rates,[77] Americans also turn to economic narratives: prolonged poverty breeds criminals; unemployment makes people desperate enough to steal; economic instability makes people anxious, stressed, and even violent. Among gun carriers, I found that the economy provided a separate narrative to understand crime at different turns alongside, intertwined with, or without explicit reference to race. Many gun carriers—like Michiganders more broadly—saw "the economy" as a catch-all explanation for crime that had hit people in Detroit and Flint especially hard, but not exclusively so. Gerald, an African American who lives in the suburbs and travels throughout Detroit for work, connects a rise in unemployment and decay in social institutions to crime rates:

> We have 30% unemployment. [A] 75% high school dropout rate in Detroit. And I think they're down to, like, a third of the schools: two thirds of the schools are closed down. So it's sad . . . people that got all these different skills and education. And we just—fell off like that. But that's a whole 'nother conversation. If people would just educate themselves a little bit more, [crime] wouldn't be so bad. But when people are poor, they can't eat—I don't know. You or I can't say we wouldn't do it [commit a crime]! Know what I mean?

Gerald presents a mixture of empathy and blame. He blames Detroiters who turn to crime by doubting their work ethic: "If people would just educate themselves a little bit more, it wouldn't be so bad." But he also states that he *understands* why people commit crimes: they need to survive, and they need to eat. He cites a number of statistics that suggest he is blaming the broader socioeconomic system, and concedes, "you or I can't say we wouldn't do it!"

Others emphasized, as a vague but definitive truth, that "the economy" has made people more "desperate." For example, Darius and Henry tell me:

> We live in an arguably [pause]—some people are desperate, and our society has become—I don't have any facts, but it seems to me that it's been pretty violent. (Darius, white gun carrier)

> Some people, no matter what happens—they are not going to commit crimes. They're going to work, they'll dig up their yard and plant vegetables. They'll do whatever they can so they don't commit a crime. But then you have other people where, as soon as things get hard, they're out there trying to take somebody's property or something. (Henry, African American gun carrier)

Juxtaposed here, these two statements suggest the extent to which the economy is seen as an overarching stressor in people's lives—whether they are law-abiding ("growing a victory garden to keep their grocery costs low") or criminal ("it's been pretty violent").

In addition to discussing crimes committed for economic gain in a flailing economy, white gun carriers in particular talked about economically motivated crimes best captured by the phrase "going postal." Popularized after a series of shootings involving current or former employees of the US Postal Service, the phrase has since gained currency as an expression of workplace rage.[78] Marlin, a white gun carrier, described what he views as a "typical" crime scenario. He alluded to a guy "who had a bad day at work" to demonstrate the variety of criminal threats gun carriers may face:

> Say you're walking through whatever mall right now. A guy had a bad day at work, lost his job, grabbed his deer rifle, and he decided to

have it at the mall manager and whoever was at the mall. And now you've got three-hundred-plus people [at risk].

The criminal described in this passage is implicitly white: he owns a deer rifle (whites are significantly more likely to own guns for sporting or hunting purposes), he lives near a mall (thus is likely to be suburban), and he has (or had) a job. Like the "gone postal" worker, Marlin's hypothetical criminal is driven to violence by his economic situation—he "lost his job."

Gun carriers also saw long-term low wages—even in a steady job—as connected to criminal behavior. Rusty, a white gun carrier who had been laid off at General Motors, told me he understands the incentives of crime, emphasizing *low pay* rather than *un*employment. He explained:

You know, a cop on the street makes forty grand a year, maybe, if you're lucky. So, a drug dealer wants to pay you more than they make in a year to look the other way. Yeah, take it, right? They'd be stupid not to. Even I can see that—my practical ass can see—you're going to put your kid through college on a drug dealer's money? More power to you, buddy.

In these conversations, gun carriers highlighted different moments of economic insecurity: joblessness and unemployment (Gerald); job precarity and underemployment (Marlin and Rusty); and a more generalized sense of the pressures resulting from economic hard times (Darius and Henry). Intersecting at times with racialized narratives of crime, these different economic perspectives emerged out of the social positionalities of gun carriers themselves; white, middle-class and working-class gun carriers tended to emphasize job precarity and underemployment, whereas minority gun carriers were more likely to highlight unemployment and joblessness. Despite their differences in social background, however, gun carriers converge on the narrative of crime as a means of imagining—and explaining—the impact of economic decline on the social fabric of Michigan.

Conclusion

Michigan is a case study in what scholars have come to call "neoliberalism": deregulation, deindustrialization, and the criminalization of poverty. Understood as the crossroads of two nightmares—one about race, the other about the economy—Detroit and Flint serve as flashpoints for the neoliberal and punitive developments in the United States over the past fifty years. In the 1960s and 1970s, spiking violent crime, urban upheaval, and political unrest gripped the American imagination. For the gun carriers who mourn the passing of a particular kind of social life (access to breadwinning jobs, family values, crime-free communities), their concerns about broad decline and generalized insecurity overlap. Making sense of Michigan and its problems, they marshal crime as a concrete reality and a discursive lens.

Simultaneously exclusionary (crime is concentrated in "bad areas" like Detroit and Flint) and inclusionary (anyone can be a victim), gun carriers participate in and help reproduce a popular discourse surrounding the ever-present threat of crime emanating from Detroit and Flint. Crime is something strongly associated with the "bad of the bad" in Detroit and Flint, with desperate economic times, with gang life. And because of these powerful associations, crime is never understood as neatly contained. Conversation over coffee or a dinner with friends could always be interrupted; you always have to have your guard up.

On the politics of neoliberal punitiveness, Jean and John Comaroff note that "criminal violence is taken to be diagnostic of the fragility of civil society."[79] Similarly, it is through crime that gun carriers in southeastern Michigan express broken American dreams as tragic nightmares. In this context of economic insecurity and decay, on the one hand, and racial inequalities and anxieties, on the other, guns become appealing tools with which to assert oneself as a moral, upstanding person against a backdrop of decline.

3

NRA Training and the Everyday Politics of Gun Carry

SO, I GUESS WHAT EVERYONE has to ask themselves is where you draw that line. You are going to defend yourself—but are you going to pull your gun to protect that woman over there? Or that guy?[1] Griff asked between bites of his BLT sandwich, pointing to a middle-aged woman seated in a booth and then a gray-haired man at another table. As Griff chomped on his sandwich, Brenden piped up: *I really hope I never have to kill anyone. No one wants to do that. I hope I never, ever have to pull my gun.* As I ate at a greasy spoon across the street from a Metro Detroit firearms school, I listened to Brenden and Griff, both white gun carriers who looked to be in their late thirties, pontificate about self-defense and taking the life of another human being. Brenden, Griff, two other men, and I were participating in a training course to become National Rifle Association–certified instructors. Tucked into an industrial area in the suburbs of Detroit, the firearms school consisted of a windowless room with fluorescent lights (the "hands-on" portion of the training would take place at an off-site shooting range). The room felt sparse but not unpleasant, its odds and ends more functional than fashionable. Firearms paraphernalia—gun-cleaning supplies, NRA booklets, spare magazines—was stacked on filing cabinets that lined the room, and the only decoration affixed to the wall was a sign reading "We don't dial 911!"

We arrived at 8 a.m. While I came in order to find out what it takes to become a certified NRA instructor, the men came hoping to start their own firearms training businesses. NRA-certified instructors do not work directly for the NRA but are self-employed (hence, I do not refer to them as "NRA instructors"); they are certified by the NRA to teach NRA-approved courses. In seeking out NRA certification, these future instructors wanted the name recognition that the NRA logo could provide to their firearms schools, and they also wanted to be able to tap into the growing market for concealed-pistol license training. After all, with rare exception, it was NRA-certified instructors who provided Michigan residents with the training certification necessary to apply for their concealed carry licenses. NRA-certified instructors were the gatekeepers of gun carry.

As I would soon find out, I was "outgunned" in that small classroom: for the first full hour of class, there was lively back and forth about these men's backgrounds, their firearms proficiency, and their formal and informal training. As we went around the room introducing ourselves, they dropped acronyms and firearms terminology—SWAT,[2] IDPA,[3] simunitions[4]—that conveyed their tactical proficiency, quipped about their preferred guns, and shared observations of people "doing it wrong" at the range. There were no firearms skills covered in this class—the instructor admitted—that these four men did not already know. But that didn't matter much, because the topic of the day so far was not practical skill, but the morals and ethics of self-defense: How should instructors address the uncomfortable possibility implicit in self-defense training—the possibility of using lethal force against another human being?

The first day of instructor training and the impromptu discussion of the ethics of self-defense over lunch reinforced what I witnessed in firearms training courses both before and after I became an NRA-certified instructor: the NRA courses required to obtain a concealed-pistol license in Michigan focus a surprisingly great deal on shaping the moral disposition of the gun carrier.

For those outside of gun culture, the NRA is usually not thought of as a service organization, let alone one involved in shaping the moral politics of life and death in people's everyday dispositions toward guns. Rather, many Americans—especially those outside of gun culture—associate the NRA with a no-compromise, hard-line gun agenda. That version of the NRA is captured by figures like NRA Executive Vice President Wayne LaPierre, who called federal agents "jack-booted thugs" in 1995, or former NRA President Charlton Heston, who famously told gun control proponents in 2000, "I'll give you my gun when you take it from my cold, dead hands!"[5] From its hard-line stance against universal background checks to its suggestion that the answer to school shootings is more, rather than fewer, guns, the NRA is portrayed in mainstream American media outlets (with the exception of Fox News) as a politically divisive organization more devoted to the multibillion-dollar firearms industry than to its professed objectives of "safety, education, and responsibility."

Like all caricatures, there is some truth to this one: the NRA has ridden the wave of the rising American New Right since the 1970s,[6] and its lobbying efforts, its ties to conservative politicians and the firearms industry, and its ability to command votes and dollars have shaped it into one of Washington's most powerful lobbies. Galvanizing Americans with fears of gun bans and government overreach, the organization has dealt significant blows to the Democratic Party and leftist politics more generally. It has managed to block the bulk of state and federal gun control efforts.

But caricatures can also conceal. The NRA is much more than a group of talking heads badgering Americans about the inherent evils of gun control and liberals. In addition to preventing guns from being taken from the "cold dead hands" of Americans, the NRA is deeply concerned with expanding Americans' rights to holster guns on their bodies and, ironically, stipulating the terms under which Americans enact their "God-given rights." The political lobby of the NRA works alongside its training operation—a collection of some eighty thousand NRA-certified firearms instructors who train around 750,000 Americans every year.

In Michigan, would-be gun carriers usually have no choice but to take NRA training to obtain a concealed carry license. Michigan is not unique. Throughout the United States, most concealed carry laws implicitly or explicitly require NRA training courses. This means that even though the NRA takes a hard-line, no-compromise stance on gun rights as "inalienable," individuals wishing to exercise these rights by carrying a gun must often go through the NRA to do so. Drawing on the courses I observed and the instructors I interviewed, I found that much of the time in concealed-pistol licensing courses was spent on the moral and legal dimensions of gun carry—not hands-on firearms skills applicable to self-defense encounters. Rather than prioritize hands-on defensive training, these courses teach gun carriers that they are a particular kind of person—a law-abiding person willing to use lethal force to protect innocent life if faced with a violent threat. NRA training encourages gun carriers to affirm their "love of life" and provides them with the tools—visualization, situational awareness, and repetitive practice—to put this affirmation into practice in everyday life through gun carry. In this way, the NRA not only profits off of Americans wishing to exercise gun rights[7] but also shapes new norms and expectations of citizenship. I argue that NRA courses encourage gun carriers to be "citizen-protectors," marked by their willingness to take criminal life in order to save innocent life.[8] Thus, I examine the NRA's political project from a very different angle than most previous scholarship:[9] from the perspective of the NRA classroom.

A Brief History of the NRA

"We must build the NRA into such a strong force, no politician in American will dare intrude on our rights." Those are the words of Harlon Carter, former NRA president and executive vice president in the 1970s and '80s, who transformed the NRA into the powerful political lobby group that it is today. Despite its present-day power as a lobby, however, the NRA was founded in 1871 as a service organization. Its stated goal was to promote rifling skills among Americans after the Civil War revealed most Americans' dismal shooting skills. Within a few years, the NRA's target competitions had become extremely popular,[10] and after World War II, the organization focused almost exclusively on hunting and sports shooting until the 1960s. While lobbying efforts sometimes crept onto the organization's agenda, these efforts were few and far between during this period.[11] When it did engage in lobbying, the NRA oftentimes supported gun control measures (e.g., the 1938 Federal Firearms Act), but the organization remained, for almost one hundred years, primarily a service organization dedicated to firearms safety, training, and recreation.[12] In other words, it was "a sportsmen's league" that attracted boy scouts, police departments, and the Olympic rifle team.[13]

The better-known side of the NRA as a bulldog lobbying organization emerged only in the 1960s, when political assassinations and urban upheaval placed crime—particularly gun crime—at the center of US public debate.[14] After the assassination of President John F. Kennedy in 1963 (with a mail-ordered firearm), the NRA's leadership was split in its response to legislative initiatives. The US Congress put forward bills that would outlaw certain types of guns and place further restrictions on the purchase of guns. The legislation that was eventually passed, including the 1968 Gun Control Act, was endorsed by the NRA leadership at the time as "sane."[15] However, another contingent within the NRA, led by Harlon Carter, began to articulate a new "no compromise" position and treated any gun control as problematic in principle. After a series of conflicts within the organization (including the dramatically named Weekend Massacre and the Cincinnati Revolt, among others), the Carter contingent took leadership of the NRA. In 1975, they founded the NRA's Institute for Legislative Action (NRA-ILA).

Since the mid-1970s, the NRA's uncompromising approach to gun laws has proven wildly successful. Arguing that firearms are the solution to crime, rather than its cause, the NRA has organized countless successful campaigns at the national and state levels. Meanwhile, the NRA was instrumental in rolling back some of the provisions in the 1968 Gun Control Act with the 1986 Firearms Owners Protection Act, which prohibited the Bureau of Alcohol, Tobacco, and Firearms from creating a national registry of gun owners;[16] the organization helped defeat US Presidential Candidate Al Gore in 2000; and it has prevented a number of gun control measures—from the reinstatement of the Assault Weapons Ban upon its 2004 expiration to federal magazine restrictions and gun registration.[17] At the federal level, the NRA has suffered only two major legislative defeats[18] (the Brady Bill and the Assault Weapons Ban passed in the early 1990s under President Bill Clinton), and the NRA has used these defeats to further galvanize pro-gun Americans. After all, when Republican Newt Gingrich took over the Speakership of the House in 1994, President Clinton mused: "the NRA is the reason the Republicans control the House."[19]

Despite its newfound status as one of Washington's most powerful lobbies, the NRA never lost its service component. Service activities like hunting courses, competitive shooting events, and self-defense training continue to comprise much of the NRA's organizational focus.[20] Unlike other organizations within the gun lobby, such as Gun Owners of America, the NRA offers a systematic firearms training program that is recognized at the national level. It's best known for its marksmanship and hunting courses.

The NRA's lobbying- and service-oriented arms complement one another. Recent shall-issue concealed carry laws put forth at the state level by the NRA represent the nexus of the NRA's service and lobby arms: these laws expand both gun rights (Americans in most states can now carry guns concealed) and the organization's reach in terms of training (many of these laws effectively require training from the NRA, either because the NRA is either explicitly named or because it is effectively the only organization that fits the law's designated requirements for training). These concealed carry laws have been a lynchpin of the NRA's state-level lobbying success over the past four decades in states as diverse as Georgia, Minnesota, Oregon, Texas, Florida, and Michigan.

In the vast majority of states, before the 1970s, access to concealed carry permits was restricted and issued at the discretion of licensing boards (the so-called may-issue system). Under the passage of what is now called shall-issue laws—because states *shall* (that is, must) issue licenses to qualified applicants—state licensing bureaus are forbidden from denying Americans a permit on an arbitrary basis. In other words, the forty states[21] with shall-issue laws are required to issue citizens a permit to carry firearms concealed, provided that they have met a number of basic guidelines and criteria based on their residency, criminal record, age, and—most of the time—training.[22]

Even though the NRA opposes gun control, it has often supported training requirements for concealed-pistol licensing. For example, in Iowa, the NRA openly called for a training clause to be included in the state's 2010 shall-issue legislation (Iowa's law explicitly names the NRA), and the organization opposed an alternative, more pro-gun law proposed by state legislator Kent Sorensen that would not include training requirements. The NRA argued that without the training provision the law would not pass. Soon after the law went into effect, the NRA issued a "call to arms" on the organization's blog, NRAblog. com, to rapidly increase the number of certified NRA instructors in Iowa (the NRA counted only 145 of its own instructors in Iowa willing to teach the concealed pistol licensing course upon passage of the law— out of roughly eighty thousand instructors nationwide).

States that require training (more than three quarters of shall-issue states do) carve out a space for the NRA to train thousands of Americans who wish to obtain a concealed-handgun license. Not all states explicitly require NRA training, but in well over half of shall-issue states, licensing guidelines are stated in such a way as to de jure or de facto require NRA courses and/or courses run by NRA-certified instructors. For example, consider Michigan's shall-issue law, passed in 2001. This legislation[23] allows anyone who has completed a one-day training course, has no record of felonies, and has fulfilled a number of other requirements on age, residency status, and so forth, to obtain a concealed-pistol license (CPL). Michigan's Public Act 372, which outlines the requirements for a CPL, states that the training program must be "certified by this state or a national or state firearms training organization." Although there is room—legally speaking—to offer a non-NRA course, I found no concealed-pistol license training course in Michigan that did not in some way integrate NRA-sanctioned training elements into its classroom. Oftentimes, an NRA course—at the time of my research, usually Personal Protection Inside the Home[24]—was adopted in its entirety. This means that each of the four hundred thousand–plus Michigan residents who have a license to carry a firearm has likely entered a training space marked by the NRA.

The proliferation of gun carry and training requirements not only reflects the NRA's power as the leader of the gun lobby; it also helps to maintain and expand the NRA's political power. These courses help to generate revenue for the NRA from would-be concealed carriers,[25] but they do much more. They provide a critical space in which to shape gun culture from the ground up. This grass-roots effort to shape culture reflects a broad trend that sociologists have highlighted in other, mostly progressive and left-wing, social movements. For example, sociologist Elizabeth Armstrong showed that the success of the LGBT movement was tied to a fundamental shift from a gay-rights platform that emphasized political lobbying in the 1940s and '50s to one based on identity politics that emphasized the celebration of diversity in the 1960s and '70s.[26] The proliferation of gay communities and gay pride events in this latter era allowed the LGBT movement to bring together a broad range of queer sexual cultures under the banner of "diversity," while LGBT-friendly social spaces (bars, bathhouses, pride parades) helped further consolidate the movement. Although the LGBT movement has seen important gains in terms of rights, particularly regarding gay marriage, reducing the movement to rights-seeking misses the point that this movement's successes had as much to do with transforming culture as with seeking rights.

Although scholars have largely focused on how identity politics and cultural processes shape left-wing and progressive social movements, right-wing and conservative movements are also shaped by cultural processes. This is particularly true for gun politics, itself often inseparable from gun culture. Cultural anthropologists Joan Burbick, Abigail Kohn, and Kevin O'Neill show that the shooting range, the gun store, the gun show, and the gun magazine provide social spaces for gun proponents to come together to celebrate and practice a particular kind of cultural politics centered on self-reliance, individualism, and masculinity. But scholars and others outside of gun culture have generally not paid enough attention to the critical role that the NRA has played in shaping this culture—not just through ideological rhetoric but also through the everyday practices and meanings attached to guns.[27]

This is where shall-issue concealed carry laws come in: because shall-issue concealed carry laws generally require NRA training as a condition of licensing, these laws provide the NRA a space in which to shape a moral politics of life and death.[28] Specifically, they encourage gun carriers to think about their attitudes about life and its value, to consider whether they are capable of embracing an ethical code in which taking life—in order to save innocent life—can be a morally upstanding act and even a civic duty. Based on my observations, the objective of these courses is not the creation of sharpshooters but the cultivation of responsible, safety-conscious Americans—or what I call "citizen-protectors." This is how culture matters in the context of firearms training: at the grass-roots level, NRA shapes the moral politics that gun carriers use to define themselves as good citizens.

The Citizen-Protector

Seemingly apolitical, the NRA's training materials encourage the personal transformations of people who, to quote the title of one NRA program, "refuse to be a victim." I argue that NRA firearms training encourages gun carriers to become citizen-protectors—a term I use to capture the moral worldviews of gun carriers.

First and foremost, the concept of the citizen-protector refers to a moral disposition regarding life and death. Citizen-protectors consider using deadly force against another human being, under certain circumstances, to be a morally upstanding response to a violent threat. They view their decision to carry a gun as a commitment to this moral politics and, by extension, a celebration of life. They probably will never use their gun in a defensive or protective situation, but they see their willingness to do so as placing themselves on a different moral plane than victims or criminals. When faced with the threat of violence, citizen-protectors believe themselves to be capable of making and executing a courageous moral call about life and death—all in the name of protecting innocent life.

What I refer to as the citizen-protector is often described colloquially as the "sheepdog" by gun carriers. Parsing people into the heroic, the cowardly, and the wicked, many gun carriers explicitly identified themselves as "sheepdogs" who protect the "sheep" from the "wolves." Randall, a white NRA-certified instructor who lived in a suburb of Detroit, told me that he introduces these categories to his students:

> We're all either sheep, we are wolves, or we are sheepdogs. And you got to ask yourself—which one of the three are you? Obviously, we're not the wolves. We're not the evil people. The wolves want to attack the sheep, but they don't want no resistance, obviously. So that means we're either the sheepdog or the sheep. And the sheepdog is there to protect the sheep, and that's how I look at it. We're one of the three. Sheep, wolves, and sheepdogs.

Likewise, Jonathan, a white gun carrier from a rural area, connected his decision to carry a gun with a willingness to kill in order to save life:

> I see gun rights as an issue of life . . . It matters not your political affiliation. This goes with life and keeping life in here. [My brother would say], "I have no interest in killing anyone; however, I have no interest in being killed, either." And that just so succinctly explains it. It just goes with life.

As a daily gun carrier, Jonathan highlights a basic premise of gun carry: he professes a fundamental determination to protect innocent lives and assumes that it is his responsibility to do so. Gun carriers describe themselves as responsible, independent types who refuse to be "sheeple," as several gun carriers told me. More than just an American pastime, firearms provide a proactive way to enact a particular moral politics of life and death.

This leads to the second core aspect of the concept of the citizen-protector: it generalizes a moral disposition often associated with police and soldiers as a basis of good citizenship. To people outside of gun culture, the idea of training oneself to injure or kill in order to celebrate life may seem like an oxymoron. It is, however, a common moral dilemma: soldiers in the military and police officers on the street face the same quandary, and they navigate it by developing a code of ethics in which the willingness to take life is tantamount to a civic duty.[29] In gun carry culture, however, this civic duty is not just the prerogative of a public servant; it is the mark of a full citizen. As a blueprint for a particular brand of citizenship, the concept of the citizen-protector therefore includes a set of rights, duties, and obligations associated with full participation in the public sphere and a sense of cultural belonging.[30] In gun culture, full participation in the public sphere means fully exercising one's gun rights, while cultural belonging means blending the self-made individualism long celebrated in American culture as a marker of full citizenship with the moral imperative to protect innocent life (with deadly force, if necessary).

It is important to remember that this embrace of individualism within gun culture reflects deep-seated cultural dynamics, both old and new. On the one hand, American culture has historically placed a high premium on rugged individualism, individual responsibility, and anti-statism. On the other, since the 1960s, American society has undergone a broad reorganization under what scholars call neoliberalism (introduced in chapter 2), which has had a particularly profound impact on the relationship between citizenship and security. This is the third and final aspect: the concept of the citizen-protector is rooted in contemporary contexts of neoliberalism, even as it reflects historically long-standing aspects of American citizenship.

Under neoliberalism, a person's ability to participate in the market surpasses her relationship to the state (unlike under a social welfare system) in defining her rights, duties, and obligations as a citizen. In more practical terms, everyday people are increasingly expected to take on—and are celebrated for embracing—social functions formally or typically addressed by the state by turning, instead, to the marketplace. Criminologist Pat O'Malley[31] uses the term "responsibilization" to capture this shift of responsibility from the state to citizens and the redefinition of social functions as personal responsibilities. The blooming private security industry provides a good example: from private police to home alarm systems to cell phones, Americans turn to the market to purchase a degree of security that they believe the state cannot, or will not, provide.

Likewise, gun carry shifts the social responsibility for crime control away from the police patrol car and into the holster of a licensed gun carrier,[32] with the explicit expectation, according to pro-gun rhetoric both within and beyond the NRA classroom, that gun carriers are "responsible, law-abiding citizens" capable of self-governance. Declaring the Second Amendment "America's First Freedom," NRA course materials (as well as their magazines and membership brochures) suggest that Americans are better off relying on themselves and their personal guns than the police for protection against crime.

But guns, especially when carried, *are* different from other security commodities, such as gated communities or home alarm systems. Gun carry is an unmediated and individualistic form of personal security. It is directly performed by the same individuals who purchase guns and practice with them. It requires the cultivation of particular manual skills and mental capacities (while one could install a home alarm and forget about it, the same could not be done with regard to carrying a gun on a regular basis). And finally, it is embedded in a particular moral politics surrounding life and death.[33]

As I will show, the NRA trains Americans to *perform* security—rather than just purchase it. NRA courses help shape gun carriers' "habitus," what Pierre Bourdieu defines as a set of "taken-for-granted" bodily capacities and practices.[34] Such capacities and practices are patterned by people's access to different resources; their identities along lines of race, class, gender, sexuality, and other lines of difference; and their varying positions within social institutions like the family or the workplace—or what, in short, sociologists call "social structure." If Bourdieu's concept of habitus can be described as "society embodied,"[35] then the effect (if not the intent) of these courses is to turn gun carriers' capacities and practices into "gun culture embodied." Without understanding how gun carriers embody a particular set of duties and obligations, we miss a huge swath of meaning-making that goes on between Americans and their guns, meaning-making that is mediated, at least in the firearms classroom, by the NRA.

Inside the NRA Classroom

In Michigan, the NRA's training courses represent one of the first steps in becoming a concealed-gun carrier.[36,37] These classes often take place inside commercial shooting ranges, but not always: I attended training in outdoor shooting clubs, in sports outfitters like Gander Mountain and Bass Pro, at privately rented office space earmarked for firearms training, and temporarily repurposed office space (one course I attended took place in a real estate office after hours). Regardless of where you live, you can find someone willing to train you to carry a pistol: the website of the Michigan Coalition of Responsible Gun Owners, a Michigan-based gun rights organization, lists hundreds of "preferred" NRA-certified instructors, from urban Detroit to rural western Michigan. Some firearms instructors rely on word of mouth to advertise their courses, especially if they have managed to get an exclusive deal with a shooting range. Others have an elaborate social media presence, with websites, Facebook profiles, and Twitter accounts. Some advertise through highway billboards, T-shirts, and bumper stickers. Throughout my fieldwork, I couldn't help but notice how difficult it was to drive in Metro Detroit *without* seeing evidence of gun culture—the storefronts of shooting ranges on Woodward, 8 Mile, and other major thoroughfares; the billboards advertising concealed-pistol license training on I-75; or the pro-gun bumper stickers on an SUV in front of me as I drove to an interview.

Firearms students usually spend most of the day in a classroom, and depending on the location, walk or drive to a shooting range for a few hours, usually at the end. The number and composition of students varies. Some instructors offer training on an "on-call basis" and are willing to teach classes of two or three. Their classes take on a more conversational tone, and students receive direct, personalized attention. Other instructors move hundreds of students through their courses every month; peaking at around forty students, these classes have more of a lecture quality, and their instructors rely on a team of range officers to assist in the classroom and range portions of the class. The courses generally cost between one hundred and two hundred dollars (although Web-savvy firearms instructors may advertise discounted courses on social media sites like LivingSocial and Groupon.) For the most part, the students are mostly men, but "women's only" classes are gaining in popularity.

Location largely determines the racial composition of students: the farther from Metro Detroit, the whiter the classroom. Age-wise, students range from almost twenty-one (the minimum age for a concealed carry license) to the elderly. And their reasons for attending the course vary: based on polls taken by instructors in some of the courses I attended, many are motivated by a direct or secondhand experience of victimization and worries that where they live or what they do for work makes them vulnerable to crime. Then there are those students (almost always men) who want to obtain a concealed-pistol license to make a political statement against the Obama Administration—"I'm sick of the direction this country is going in." Others offer up vague reasoning: "It was just time." Some are dragged to the courses: one woman, who looked to be in her sixties, when asked why she wanted to obtain a CPL, simply pointed at the man next to her and flatly said: *He made me come here.*

Only two or three hours of the eight-hour course take place on the shooting range—and according to the NRA guidelines, students shoot less than one hundred rounds of ammunition, using marksmanship drills that focus on the ability to proficiently hit a target from a comfortable standing position with no time constraints. These drills never require students to draw from a holster, shoot from behind cover or while prone, or to use rapid fire. This may be good training for new competitive shooters, but the application to defensive shooting is unclear. During my fieldwork, I did not meet a single NRA-certified instructor who believed that this amount of firearms handling was sufficient to develop the skills necessary to proficiently use a gun in a self-defense encounter.[38] Rather, they agreed—as did I, after speaking to dozens of gun carriers, attending courses, and spending time at shooting ranges—that while the NRA course used for concealed-pistol licensing conveyed basic marksmanship skills and firearms safety habits, it does not adequately teach the kind of skills needed to quickly respond to a possible threat that unfolds in a time, place, and manner not of the gun carrier's choosing. As I argue in chapter 6, this has real consequences in terms of gun carriers' ability to ascertain and handle potential threats. Their inexperience may lead to mistakes and misunderstandings that may ultimately threaten or harm innocent people as well as strip gun carriers of their gun rights or even land them in jail.

The rest of the required eight-hour course in Michigan is primarily classroom-based, and it includes topics like the Basic Firearms Safety; Legal and Moral Aspects of Violent Confrontation; Defensive Shooting Skills; Threat Assessment Techniques; Fundamentals of Marksmanship; Mental Preparation; and an Overview of the NRA. These are the main topics from the NRA training guide and covered in class, and while instructors may focus on some areas more than others—after all, they are certified but not employed by the NRA—my observations suggest that instructors tend to stay on topic.

The courses I observed often opened with a focus on moral training: *Can I take the life of another human being to save my own life or my family's?*[39] Some variation of this question is usually posed to students early in the course. Presented as a question with "no right answer" (to paraphrase the instructors I interviewed), NRA materials provided to students suggest that there *is* a right way to approach this question: people should be concerned about defending themselves against a threat, even if they are wary of the means that they are willing to use to do so. It is not enough to care about your safety and carry a gun because the NRA and NRA-certified instructors have told you that you should: you have to be the rare kind of citizen who is willing to use a gun to protect *innocent* life. Thus, the question that lies at the center of these courses is not whether one should or should not carry a gun but rather whether one is morally capable of using a gun.

NRA training materials explicitly ask, "Are you capable of using deadly force?" Students are expected to do some soul-searching here: they should identify the religious, moral, and social limits to their willingness to injure or even kill another person. As an invitation to ethical contemplation, these questions ask students to think concretely about the type of person capable of using lethal force. It is a self, NRA materials note, who is "religiously," "personally," and "morally permitted" to "take a life in self-defense" and who can "tolerate the judgment" of others.[40]

Following the lead of the NRA materials, instructors pose these same questions to students in concrete, relatable terms, asking them not only to imagine an "ideal" situation in which self-defense is sanctioned but also more ambiguous scenarios. Jimmy, a white firearms instructor, told me:

> Morals and ethics are a huge part of what I teach in my class. We go through the various religions, and I leave it up to the individual. You have to decide yourself what your rules of engagement are. What if it's four guys? What if it's four teenagers? What if it's a six-year-old pointing a gun at you? You need to decide—under what conditions will you use your firearm? I leave it very much up to them.

Jimmy emphasizes that students must make their own decisions and also live with the (potentially lethal) consequences of them. His line of questioning creates a division between the type of self that is capable of shooting in self-defense and the type of self that is not. The latter, he suggests, need not pursue further firearms training. Howard, a white firearms instructor, voices a similar sentiment, delineating those who are capable and incapable of wielding lethal force:

A lot of people will take the class, and one of the first things that the NRA tells us [as instructors] is if [a student] can't shoot [a perpetrator], [the student] shouldn't take the class. You have to set your own boundaries. We tell [our students] that if somebody is hurting them or hurting their child or something, and that child is in danger of its life, if you can't shoot [the perpetrator], you shouldn't take the class. We've had ladies who have taken the class say, "I couldn't shoot nobody! I couldn't shoot nobody!" And we'll give them a scenario. "Okay, let's say somebody is grabbing your grandchild and trying to put them in the vehicle. What would you do?" "I'd hit them with whatever I had!" Now, are you worried about killing that person if you're hitting them with your purse? No. So, you have to set your boundaries.

Howard's description of the scenarios he uses in his courses is illustrative not only because it echoes Jimmy's demarcation between those who can and cannot wield force but also because it suggests how one comes to understand whether one is capable of using lethal force. Rather than assuming a self-evident ability or willingness to use a gun in self-defense, Howard's role as instructor is to uncover and expose whether his students have this sort of mettle in the right context. Andy, also a white instructor, likewise suggests that pushing students to imagine scenarios under which they would use their gun helps them clarify their personal comfort with the deployment of lethal force:

I think it's important to develop scenarios as to where is the line in the sand drawn when you say, "This is when it is I must use deadly force." I think that everybody goes through that period of not being sure whether they should use deadly force. Or whether they even could. Because the taking of a life is a horrible, horrible thing. It's not like in the movies where somebody gets hit in the shoulder and then they stop.

Together, Andy, Howard, and Jimmy elaborate on the NRA's basic message: shooting another person in self-defense is a repugnant experience, and taking a class in armed self-defense does not mean that one is capable of using lethal force. Therefore, identifying the boundaries of one's capacity to use a gun in self-defense requires ethical contemplation—usually in the form of imagined self-defense scenarios. Gun instructors never drew this line explicitly for their students, instead placing the moral weight of this decision squarely on the shoulders of their students. Instructors simply "empowered" students; students bore full responsibility in choosing when and whether circumstances called for the use of lethal force against another human being.[41] Nevertheless, instructors still conveyed a code of ethics surrounding the valuation of life: if a gun carrier truly values her own life and the lives of others, then she will find it within herself to use lethal force when she finds it necessary. The NRA also reiterates this code of ethics in its training materials,[42]

> Those who include a firearm in their personal protection plans are affirming the value of their own lives and those of their family members. The ethical person does not ever want to use deadly force, but recognizes that there are times when it may be the only option to protect innocent lives.

The NRA's training materials thus include a powerful message about the moral demands of gun carry: a gun carrier must value innocent life to the point that they are willing to "use deadly force" against presumed criminals, even if the gun carrier "does not ever want to" do so.

My own decision to carry a gun as part of my research was informed by the weight of this moral politics among gun carriers. Prior to coming to Michigan, I had some basic familiarity with guns—I owned a small .22-caliber gun for target shooting—but the idea of carrying that gun, or any other gun, throughout my day seemed absolutely foreign. I had simply never considered it.

As I prepared for this research prior to arriving in Michigan—drafting research questions, developing my proposal—I spent much time anticipating and envisioning my discussions with gun carriers about *their* decision to carry a gun. I did not expect, however, that these discussions would turn to *my* choices as well. Nevertheless, soon after arriving in Metro Detroit, I began to understand that a person's CPL was not just a legal document indicating one's lawful capacity to carry, but also a certificate of one's moral character. As a researcher, obtaining my CPL was a necessary rite of passage that demonstrated my commitment to gaining a holistic understanding of the politics of gun carry. I learned that, to gun carriers, an unwillingness to carry would mark me as naïve and even cavalier about my safety and the safety of others. Meanwhile, a concealed-gun permit—and the act of carrying—would help demonstrate to gun carriers that I was a trustworthy researcher, not just another out-of-touch academic, ignorant and afraid of guns.

In the process of obtaining a CPL, I got more than I bargained for. In addition to establishing myself as a trustworthy researcher, my own decision to carry exposed me to the moral dilemmas that carrying a gun entails. I knew that I was physically capable of using a firearm if I was faced with, for example, the proverbial violent rapist often referenced by gun carriers to justify why women should carry guns.[43] What if I was, in fact, violently attacked at some point during my research, while I was carrying? What kind of person would I be if I *did* use a gun? And what kind of person would I be if I didn't? How I answered threatened to uncover how I valued my own life and the lives of others. With the weight of the gun heavy on my hip, I could not ignore these questions. Indeed, because guns are lethal objects, they have the power to reveal uneasy truths about their carriers, the social contexts in which they live, and the moral precepts they follow. This dilemma is not unlike the unique role that police play in maintaining social order, according to law enforcement scholar Egon Bittner: "the role of the police is to address all sorts of human problems when and insofar as their solutions do or may possibly require the use of force at the point of their occurrence."[44]

For those who find the moral politics of gun carry complex and challenging, the NRA simplifies these moral dilemmas into a clichéd narrative of "good guys" and "bad guys."[45] In its course materials, the NRA provides the moral language to help future gun carriers navigate these ambiguities and inconvenient truths, reminding them that their decision to carry a gun is a justified and morally upstanding one. The NRA explicitly reminds its students that they are the good guys, defined in opposition to the criminals:

If you do defend yourself, it is important in the aftermath to remember:

- You are a good person [. . .]
- You are a moral person

- Your attacker was the one who chose a lifestyle and sequence of events that led to this encounter
- You were morally justified in protecting yourself and your family
- You have quite possibly saved the lives of others by stopping this predator from harming future innocent victims.

This is a colorblind discourse that frames the question of criminality as fundamentally about moral turpitude:[46] criminals are morally flawed individuals. Eclipsing other explanations of crime (for example, the structural forces that marginalize, incarcerate, and disenfranchise predominantly poor men of color), this discourse individualizes the problem of criminal behavior and moves killing—in some circumstances—from an immoral act to a moral act. It spells out who is worthy or unworthy of life.

The Practice of Gun Carry

By encouraging students to see themselves as citizen-protectors, NRA classes sometimes create immediate experiences of "transformation" and "empowerment" for students. Gun instructors told me that watching their students "transform" was an especially rewarding aspect of their classes, and concealed carriers reiterated this sense of transformation. Billy, a white gun carrier, explained how carrying a gun has changed him:

> Your demeanor changes. You're just all of a sudden become confident, more comfortable. You're not concerned about all of this petty shit that's going around.

Billy's words suggest a transformation now that he is concerned, as he told me later, with "staying alive." Men reported a number of personal benefits that resulted from regular gun carrying, including feeling calmer, feeling less likely to start a fight, experiencing less aggression on the road, and feeling safer. Frankie, an African American gun carrier, maintained that having a gun "lowers my stress level" and "helps you out to be a better person" because it makes him more aware of his surroundings. Meanwhile, Richard, a white gun carrier and instructor, emphasized that guns conferred a responsibility on the gun carrier to "keep things cool . . . because you have that power":

> If you know you can clear a whole room in less than three seconds, what do you really need to argue with anybody about? It puts a different perspective on things. Along with that comes the responsibility. Because you have that power, you have this tremendous responsibility to keep things cool.

Richard was not the only gun carrier who emphasized the power that comes along with carrying a gun. Expressing a similar sentiment, George, an African American gun carrier, told me, "I can destroy somebody, [but I won't] destroy somebody just because I can. I would take a lot of crap before I would defend myself. Because I plan on going home. That's my goal." Likewise, NRA materials caution, "the most important part of any personal protection plan comprises those steps to avoid having to use deadly force."[47] Gun carriers were well aware that guns gave them the ability to kill, but they maintained that this power motivated them to be less, rather than more, willing to react in a fight (a contention I examine in more detail in chapter 6).

Billy, Frankie, Richard, and George don't just assert a new approach to life in words; they put it into practice through gun carry and gun training. The courses required to obtain a CPL in Michigan teach students how to integrate an array of gun-related practices into everyday life—even as these courses generally do not directly drill students in hands-on defensive firearms skills. This integration of guns into everyday life accomplishes two things: on the surface, it promises students the practical, adaptive capacities to survive a criminal threat (even though the courses provide students with only basic marksmanship). On a deeper level, it allows students to embody the citizen-protector ideal that they embrace. In doing so, firearms classes encourage the transformation of students—in tangible, incarnate ways evidenced by the gun they now carry on their side. NRA course materials provided to students explicitly note that regardless of one's moral comfort or perceived willingness to use a firearm in self-defense, the ability to actually do so is a matter not only of will but also of training. Not least because of the "internal resistance" that "many people have . . . to inflicting deadly force on another person in a face-to-face encounter," "there is no way to determine ahead of time how you will react to a particular situation."[48] Therefore, "you must be prepared—through training, prior visualization and mentally playing out scenarios—to be in control of the situation and act decisively."[49]

As in the moral dilemma of using "deadly force" to save life, NRA course materials encourage students to navigate these more practical dilemmas of skills readiness by imagining a threat and practicing responding to it. As such, these classes do recognize and emphasize the importance of training regularly—even as they do not provide adequate hands-on skills to that end. NRA training thus becomes a place for future gun carriers to learn the types of practices and techniques (usually in the classroom portion of the class) that they can use to "continue to train, both mentally and physically": visualization, situational awareness techniques, and repetitive exercises aimed at developing "muscle memory." The cultivation of these capacities both assumes and anticipates that gun carriers will act as citizen-protectors should they be faced with a violent confrontation.

Visualization and Scenarios. NRA courses help students to navigate the more practical dilemmas of skills readiness by imagining a threat. Introduced during the classroom portion of training, visualization essentially involves imagining a crime scenario and then detailing one's response to it: "Visualization should be used to imagine defensive scenarios . . . [which] gives you a dry run of such situations, and helps reduce the surprise factor should any of these situations actually take place."[50] On the range, NRA materials encourage students, for example, to "visualize the [shooting] target not as a piece of paper or cardboard, but as a predatory criminal who is threatening your life or the lives of your loved ones."[51] Firearms instructors and gun carriers alike referred to visualization as key to their training; one gun instructor jokingly quipped that he visualizes crime scenarios so habitually that *I've already killed about a dozen guys since we've been sitting right here.* One instructor said that thinking through possible crime scenarios allows gun carriers to develop a "plan": "I talk to people about how regular training is important and about developing a plan so that the things that you may need to do are comfortable for you to do and easy for you to do. The assailants already have a plan, and you'll already be caught off guard when you are confronted by somebody against whom you may need to use deadly force."

Occasionally, I observed a more intense version of visualization, where instructors would improvise their own firearms drills and attempt to create feelings of anxiety and stress in students so they could better capture what it might feel like to navigate self-defense scenarios. In one course, to simulate the adrenaline rush that occurs in threatening situations, each student was paired with a range officer, who was supposed to increase the "anxiety level" of the student. As I tried to rapidly shoot downrange at a bullseye with a .38 revolver I had borrowed from one of the instructors, my range officer yelled—*Hurry up! What are you doing? Are you hitting him? What's going on? Come on!* For me, this caused more distraction than anxiety, but the point was to provide a window into the stresses I might face in an actual defensive scenario.

Another time, I was at an outdoor range during an informal training session when another shooter decided that as a training exercise, we should run a few hundred yards away from and then back toward the targets. It would, he thought, simulate the rush of adrenaline and elevated heart rate that would occur in a real gunfight. My hands shook as I pulled my 9 mm handgun from the holster after my sprint and aimed toward a large silhouette target. I hit it, but only because the target was so large and I was so close (a scenario, I was told, that reflects the close-combat nature of most self-defense scenarios).

As I describe further in chapter 6, NRA course materials do not explicitly detail what does and does not count as a threat. Nor do the NRA materials force students to simulate threat recognition during the hands-on firearms portion of the class. Rather, the NRA emphasizes visualization as a mental exercise for students to anticipate a threat. This is an important, if subtle, point: it suggests again that the effect of these courses is to create a particular disposition surrounding guns and gun skills rather than developing defensive firearms skills, which instructors assume will take place *after* the course has been completed.

Situational Awareness. The NRA course materials encourage students not just to actively imagine threats, but also to actively look for them. Students are instructed to modify their daily, habitual behaviors by practicing "situational awareness." Introducing a schema of "awareness" that encompasses unaware, alert, and alarmed, NRA materials advocate that students constantly survey their surroundings, remaining cognizant of any potential threats.

In this way, gun-related habits are not defined by what happens on the shooting range but rather are integrated methodically into everyday life. During my interviews with gun carriers, they often emphasized situational awareness. Matthew, a white gun carrier, told me about a time he almost drew his firearm; he was exiting the Detroit Opera House after a tie-and-gown event. His narration was shaped by the ways in which the NRA instructs students to use situational awareness:

> I just put my hand on [the gun] so that if anything happened I would be able to draw real quick. The biggest thing is situational awareness. If you walk out into a parking lot, look around, you know? See what the threats are.
>
> *What tips you off that it is a threat?*
>
> Something is just [off]—why are these two guys here? They're not wearing suits and ties? You know, what's the deal on that? This didn't look quite right. And they were following us pretty close. Just—if I didn't have to draw, I didn't have to draw. But I was aware.

Often speaking in abstract terms ("something is just [off]" or, as another gun carrier told me, "the hairs on the back of your head just stand up"), gun carriers use the language of "situational awareness" and "alertness" as they describe how they ascertain threat.[52] The actions of gun carriers seemed to confirm this vigilance. During my interviews, which mostly took place in restaurants and coffee shops, I would notice my companions visually scanning the area. When they arrived before me, it was not uncommon for them to choose to sit with their back against a wall to allow an unobstructed view of their surroundings. Perhaps an elaborate role-play undertaken in anticipation of a potential criminal threat, these actions brought guns out of the range and into everyday life, where they structured day-to-day habits.

Repetitious Exercise. The last set of techniques that NRA materials describe and NRA-certified instructors encourage is the repeated manipulation of firearms, including drawing, pointing, and shooting.

NRA course materials tell students they must practice, practice, practice to embody the moral readiness that gun carry requires:

> Your plan for responding to a potential threat should . . . be regularly practiced . . . There is nothing—no shooting sport, no motion picture or instruction manual, and no training regimen—that can fully prepare you for the experience of using your defensive firearm against a violent assailant. Nonetheless, those gun owners who avail themselves of every opportunity to prepare mentally and physically for a defensive situation will almost always fare better than those who don't.[53]

Interestingly, most of the defensive skills covered in the NRA handbook distributed to students—being able to comfortably and quickly reload ammunition under pressure or adaptively developing an exit strategy from a threat—are not practiced in the firearms-handling portion of the course required in Michigan to obtain a CPL. Effectively, these courses are more geared toward developing an everyday orientation to firearms skills rather than firearms skills per se. In other words, students should be focused on developing *habit*, which can only happen through repetitive practice. Habit is important, moreover, because it can protect gun carriers not only from the external threat of a criminal attack but also from the internal threat of their own potential inability to use force quickly and decisively. This emphasis on habitualized practice therefore adds—to reference Max Weber's famous argument on the Protestant work ethic[54]—a psychological compulsion to train diligently, methodologically, and habitually. It is impossible to know whether you have actually achieved the level of confidence or the type of mindset necessary to survive a gunfight until it actually happens, and this is emphasized during firearms classes. As Kenneth, a white instructor who "grew up fighting" in Detroit, told me, in his classes, "We're careful to point out to people that there are no guarantees to success. All that we can do is increase our chance at success."

This unknown outcome distinguishes defensive training from hunting or target shooting. Firearms handling requires a knack for manual dexterity.[55] However, in hunting and target shooting, the shooter receives a clear verification of his or her technical proficiency: Did you hit the game? Is there a hole in the bullseye? For the vast majority of Americans armed for self-defense purposes, there's no verification of their skill readiness.[56] NRA drills do not simulate self-defense encounters, and relatively few gun carriers will ever face an actual criminal encounter to find out whether they have the skills needed to survive. By then, it will be too late to modify their training regimen, anyway.

NRA-certified instructors encourage students to practice their shooting skills regularly—at least once a month at a minimum—to create muscle memory. One instructor I observed put it this way: *You need to develop skills that are automatic—you are going to be wetting your pants, with your heart beating at 220 beats per minute. You have to know what you are going to do.* This, of course, was discussed during the classroom portion of the course. Another firearms instructor encouraged gun carriers to practice every night, at home, drawing their (unloaded) gun and pointing it at an imagined threat.

Gun carriers, meanwhile, generally emphasized their training regimens, usually justified by concerns that they can never be "truly prepared" for "real" self-defense encounters. Although they disagreed on whether training should be a requirement to obtain a CPL (with hard-line gun proponents opposing any restrictions—including training requirements—on gun ownership and carry), they almost unanimously agreed that the training currently required to obtain a CPL was inadequate preparation for a real-life self-defense encounter. This line of conversation came up in a variety of contexts—from talking to people like Kenneth, the gun instructor who emphasized that there are "no guarantees," to formal NRA training classes and informal settings, such as at shooting ranges and on online forums. Outside of class, gun carriers deliberated over the intricacies of worst-case scenarios ad infinitum. They debated, developed, and shared an array of different kinds of shooting exercises aimed at simulating a real gunfight. Across these debates and drills, one consistency stood out: serious gun carriers must regularly practice in ways that simulate—as closely as feasible—the conditions of a real shoot-out, with the understanding that such simulations will never be quite like the "real thing."

Back in the NRA classroom, I found that students generally did not experience anything close to the "real thing," and that this, based on my reading of course materials, observations in courses, and interviews with instructors, was not the point of these courses. Indeed, the NRA student manual explicitly states that the course should be considered "the first step in the development of skills and abilities that will contribute to the personal safety of you and your family."[57] As such, visualization, situational awareness, and repetitious firearms drills provided gun carriers not with defensive skills as much as a practical way to integrate guns into their daily lives. Put differently, these practices help to create a new way of going about life. In this way, gun carry expresses more than a political ideology: it anchors a set of practices and moral dispositions associated with firearms into everyday activities, like a trip to the opera or dinner out.

This means that NRA courses, along with the training regimens gun carriers themselves undertake, help to shape the habitus of gun carriers.[58] Henry, an African American firearms instructor, hinted at how gun carry has become "taken for granted" when I asked him whether he thought concealed carry laws would ever be overturned: "It's here to stay. People like it because they feel safe, and they have a firearm, and it's a right that they never had before. Now, if you want it, you can go apply for it." Henry's straightforward words reveal how newly expanded concealed carry laws have created a "common place"[59] for guns. Embedded into everyday life, guns become commonplace objects to be worn and carried with purpose—rather than taboo "killing machines" that should be kept out of sight and out of mind.

The Practical Politics of Gun Carry

Scholars often emphasize the emotions of fear and resentment when analyzing gun politics,[60] but I found this to be a one-sided, partial view of the NRA. It misses how the organization helps to cultivate affective ties between a gun carrier and his or her gun by emphasizing the moral and lawful duties that this gun represents. NRA classes help to transform gun politics into more than mere ideology: gun carry is an embodied means of *doing* citizenship. It transforms how people think about gun rights: these are something people *exercise*, rather than something people simply believe in or abstractly have. For regular gun carriers, gun carry shapes their lived experience: carrying became second nature such that they maintain that they feel "naked" without their firearm.

The NRA uses gun training to recruit members; that is no secret. An entire unit in the NRA's Personal Protection Inside the Home course is dedicated to explaining the NRA's unique role in fighting for Americans' right to self-defense. After all, NRA course materials say that its basic goals "are to . . . promote public safety, law and order, and the national defense . . . [and to] train citizens and members of law enforcement agencies and the armed forces in the safe handling and efficient use of firearms," among other objectives.[61] Many instructors include an NRA membership in the cost of the course or sell it to students at a discounted rate. This, of course, provides the NRA with even more opportunities to situate itself as the primary "watchdog" looking out for Americans.

Still, these courses do more than celebrate and enrich the NRA. They also celebrate a certain vision of citizenship, and it is through this promotion of the citizen-protector that the NRA interjects itself into the practices and habits that millions of gun-carrying Americans undertake in order to maintain a sense of safety and order. NRA training provides insight into how gun rights are enacted in everyday life: far from the halls of Congress and even state legislatures, gun carriers are not just talking about gun politics. Rather, they are carrying guns as means of actively practicing citizenship. Pro-gun politics happen not just in the voting booths and not just in the vitriolic discourse often characterizing public debates on guns: pro-gun politics is also what happens when gun carriers strap on their handgun at the start of each day.

4

The Right to Self-Defense, the Duty to Protect

"WE HAVE TO PROTECT OURSELVES. It's up to us to take that personal responsibility," Connor, a well-dressed white man in his thirties, told me at an upscale lunch joint in a trendy suburb of Detroit. Our conversation had turned to the topic of public law enforcement and police efficacy—a hot-button issue in pro-gun circles. Connor's words referenced a common trope, captured by adages like "I carry a gun because a cop is too heavy"; "When seconds matter, the police are only minutes away"; "A gun in the hand is worth two cops on the phone"; and, simply, "I don't dial 911." These slogans appear on welcome mats, T-shirts, and bumper stickers; in the signature tags of gun carriers' online posts and emails; and all over National Rifle Association (NRA) paraphernalia. Gun carriers regularly shared these slogans and sayings during our conversations.

Connor went on: "So much of what our society has done in the past fifty years [is] shirk responsibility in everything to law enforcement." Recounting the armed holdup in his neighborhood that led him to carry a gun, Connor asked, "Do you really think that in the moment you need a police officer they're going to be within a stone's throw from you? That's just crazy. I don't understand the mentality of the people who think the police are going to save them in that situation."

Objectively, Connor's observation is true. Few people—even the most ardent gun control advocates—would agree that "in the moment you need a police officer," there's likely to be one nearby. And yet, most people do not feel as adamantly about police absence as Connor. In this chapter, I explore how his words reflect more than recited slogans and truisms: they zero in on how men understand themselves as citizen-protectors. After all, guns appeal primarily to men. Men are disproportionately more likely to own guns, disproportionately likely to have licenses to carry, and, based on news reports of justifiable homicides, they appear to use guns in self-defense disproportionately. According to Michigan State Police data, Michigan men are four times more likely to have a permit to carry a gun than women. And although racial difference is usually prominent in anything crime-related—in, for example, rates of victimization, criminal involvement, and incarceration—in the United States, lawful gun ownership for protection appears to be surprisingly equal among men across different racial groups.[1] Whites and African Americans in Michigan are equally likely to hold licenses to carry a gun concealed (at a ratio of 1 in 24).[2]

This chapter investigates why men, in particular, find the issue of police protection so problematic, as well as how the politics of policing and protection combines with gender to shape the meanings that men attach to guns. It examines how masculinity matters for gun carriers and how men use guns to assert themselves as independent from the police, on the one hand, and as protectors of their families, friends, and even strangers, on the other.

Connor's words reveal how gun carriers articulate their embrace of guns as both a right to self-defense and as a duty to protect. Gun carriers claim the right to self-defense by defining themselves with respect to the police—they assert themselves against a state apparatus that they see as incompetent, ineffective, and inadequate. Given gun carriers' acute concerns surrounding crime and insecurity, police inefficacy comes to be understood as a central problem that exacerbates social insecurities, and compels gun carriers like Connor to demand the right to self-defense. When Connor notes that he can't "understand the mentality of the people who think the police are going to save them in that situation," he's rejecting the state—and staking out his own identity as a responsible, self-reliant citizen. This is more than just a detached evaluation of the problem of policing: it's also a claim to a particular masculine status.

Connor also embraces a particular duty that has historically fallen on men—to take the "personal responsibility" to "protect ourselves." This is what the second half of this chapter examines: how gun-carrying men claim the duty to protect themselves and others. The moral worldviews of gun carriers revolve not just around the question of *self* protection but also the protection of *others*; in this way, gun carriers see themselves as enacting a civic duty as much as an individualistic moral stance. Indeed, amid Michigan's bleak employment landscape, guns provide men with a way to situate themselves as dutiful family men by embracing their role as protectors. Generalized anxieties about crime within Michigan and anecdotes about high-profile or close-to-home crimes (remember, crime rates in most places have fallen since the 1990s, though Detroit and Flint continue to have elevated violent crime rates, and a crime with personal ties will quickly skew how one feels about crime in general) shape men's embrace of protectionism as a civic duty. That embrace lets gun carriers assert themselves not just as self-reliant and independent men, but also as relevant fathers and community members.

Attending to the social life of guns as a right and obligation, this chapter unpacks how masculinity shapes the citizen-protector, revealing how civic duty, moral politics, and masculinity are intertwined in the practice of gun carry. By rejecting dependency on the state *and* embracing the responsibility to protect themselves, their families, and even strangers, gun carriers wage a double reclamation of masculinity, demanding the right to self-defense *and* claiming the duty to protect.

The Problem of Policing

In the summer of 2012, the Detroit Police Officers Association distributed flyers to baseball game attendees in Detroit's Comerica Park. Built in 2000 to replace the legendary Tiger Stadium, Comerica Park typically brings tens of thousands of Metro Detroit suburbanites into the city for every game. This time, however, attendees got a warning rather than a welcome. Calling attention to the underfunding of the city's police force, the Detroit Police Officers Association's[3] flyer warned attendees: "Detroit: Enter at Your Own Risk." The pamphlet informed them that "Detroit is America's most violent city"; "Detroit's homicide rate is the highest in the country"; and "Detroit's Police Department is grossly understaffed." Part of the pamphlet also compared doing police work in Detroit to being a fan at a baseball stadium, sarcastically suggesting that policing would be "more than exciting and beyond exhaustion."[4]

These statements seem to contradict a long-term trend of expanding criminal justice: from police to prisons, the American criminal justice apparatus has swelled dramatically. Police departments across the United States grew steadily from 1992 to 2008, resulting in 25% more sworn peace officers in just sixteen years.[5] In the months and years following the 2008 recession, however, about ten thousand to fifteen thousand officers have been laid off. In other words, even though the US criminal justice system has seen a massive expansion in the past decades, since 2008, there's been at least some contraction in states' capacities to police.[6] According to a report issued by the US Department of Justice Community Oriented Policing Services, "police agencies are some of the hardest hit by the current economic climate," and according to a survey of police chiefs taken in 2011, "94 percent of respondents agreed that they were seeing 'a new reality in American policing developing'" due to significant reductions in budgets and personnel since 2008.[7]

Though heavy on rhetorical alarm, the Detroit Police Officers Association's message to baseball fans reflected these shifts. Michigan police forces have been in decline, dropping from a peak of 28,596 officers in 2001 to just 23,744 in 2011. This 17% reduction is concentrated in certain areas of Michigan: from 2003 to 2012, Flint lost half of its force; Royal Oak and Ann Arbor lost about a third of theirs; Detroit, Troy, Roseville, and Lansing lost about one quarter of theirs.[8] Response times (fifty-eight minutes in Detroit in 2012) and rates of unsolved crimes (there were still more than eleven thousand untested rape kits in Detroit in early 2013) are used as flashpoints in the news and in everyday conversation, highlighting police impotence—even though crime rates across Michigan have shown a general downward trend since the 1990s.[9]

While some cities with significant police cuts have experienced increases in certain kinds of crime in particular years, it is unclear yet whether police cuts are systematically tied to an increase in crime across cities in Michigan. Still, gun carriers narrated these cuts as yet another indication of the broader processes of decline discussed in chapter 2. Tom, a white firearms instructor who lives in what he described as a "middle-class suburb," provided a stark now-and-then contrast between the well-funded police departments of the past and the defunded and overworked agencies of today: *When I was growing up, you had two police in a car. Then you just had one. Now police officers are peace officers who must take on multiple duties.*[10] He told me that during a big fire on his street, he was shocked to see the police officers changing into firefighting uniforms. As he pointed out, *This is not just happening in Detroit. People are starting to feel less safe, and they are coming to class [to obtain a concealed-gun permit].* Here, Tom makes sense of suburban insecurities by implicitly referencing Detroit as an extreme case of financial distress and a place where violent crime has recently spiked. Because of the generalized concerns about economic decline and public service defunding that Detroit inspires, people are starting to "feel less safe."

Fred, a white gun carrier living in a more rural area, echoed Tom's sentiments by highlighting the unlikelihood of receiving police help in a "bankrupt" Michigan. In doing so, Fred generalizes Detroit's dismal financial predicament far beyond its city limits (it was Detroit that declared bankruptcy, not the entire state of Michigan), and he reveals the intimate link between the anxieties of socioeconomic decline and insecurities about police protection:

The ultimate bottom line of it . . . always falls back to the dollar. Especially in Michigan. Michigan is bankrupt. And the police can't be everywhere. I don't recall the exact numbers, but in Michigan, for the number of on-duty law enforcement per capita, I believe you have 1 in a 2,600 chance of being the one who receives help if you need it. Sorry, I don't like them odds. You know, the amount of law enforcement just isn't there. [And some crimes are] automatically a two-car call. Now you have four officers tied up, and what happens to the person that's in the violent situation and needs the officer there? You got four of them tied up over there.

Practically speaking, police in Michigan (and beyond) have tended to address shortfalls in budgets and personnel by turning to the public, "shifting some of the duties typically reserved for sworn staff to civilian employees as a means of cost savings," as the US Department of Justice's Community Oriented Policing Services describes, and increasing use of volunteers.[11] This process of so-called "civilianization" chips away at public law enforcement's monopoly on policing and actively facilitates private citizen participation. Usually, this process has meant encouraging civilians to become the "eyes and ears" of the law[12]—not its "strong arm."

But in gun-rich Michigan, police are publicly embracing the idea of armed civilians, further reshaping how civilians relate to public law enforcement. Detroit Police Chief James Craig made headlines in January 2014 when he said at a press conference that "There's a number of CPL [concealed-pistol license] holders running around the city of Detroit. I think it acts as a [crime] deterrent." Acknowledging the role that public perceptions of police play in gun carry, Chief Craig admitted, "When we look at the good community members who have concealed-weapons permits, the likelihood they'll shoot is based on a lack of confidence in this Police Department."[13] Several gun carriers told me that they were specifically encouraged by police to carry guns and even to shoot. For example, Austin, a white gun carrier, said that while living in Flint, he called the police to report a "home invasion"— or burglary—that had occurred while he was gone: he found his door open and his house empty. After a long wait, an officer eventually arrived at the scene and repeatedly told Austin that he could legally shoot a home intruder on sight. "The cop showed up and just sort of glanced around, and he was very adamant in telling me to kill when they are in your house. And I said, 'I'm pretty well versed in that,' but he mentioned that *several* times."

Unlike Austin, most gun carriers do not receive such an explicit directive from police to carry and use firearms in lieu of public law enforcement. Nevertheless, they see the police as well-intentioned but underfunded, understaffed, and therefore bound to fail in their mandate to "protect and serve." Eschewing reliance on public law enforcement, these men embrace self-defense, particularly when law enforcement officers themselves aggravate a sense of ineffective policing.

The Right to Self-Defense

Jesse, a white gun carrier, sipped a tall glass of water as we waited for our breakfast. Leaning in over the empty table, he recounted how he became familiar with the "illusion of police protection." Reflecting on his years as an emergency medical technician (EMT) in Detroit, he said:

> I've treated thousands of people who were victims of violent crimes in Detroit, for fifteen years every day. EMT. So, all day long, gunshot, stab, gunshot, stab, beating, beating, gunshot, stab, beating, robbery, shot, robbery, shot—you know. I got the idea that the media put about one incident a day on TV, and I saw a dozen in one shift. . . . [This violent crime] is hidden from the public because the powers that be don't really want civilians to be aware of the crime. If you knew everything that happened in Royal Oak [a white, middle-class suburb] in twenty-four hours, you would probably stay home or move somewhere else. Because you have, in the back of your mind, the illusion of police protection. There isn't any police protection in America.

Jesse conveys a deep suspicion of police and their capacity to ensure the safety of the public: the "powers that be" sustain, he believes, the illusion of police protection by deliberately misleading the public about crime, despite the real threat that crime represents. Jesse saw others' reliance on the police as gullible and misguided: he later went on to quote the title of a well-known book in gun circles, *Dial 911 and Die*,[14] to suggest that people gamble with their lives when they look to the police as their primary source of protection from violent crime.

As Michiganders entertain the idea of carrying a gun, they learn from some police officers that gun carry is a sensible option and from the NRA and other gun carriers that the police have "no duty to protect,"[15] because they do not have a constitutional obligation to protect individual civilians—only to broadly protect social order.

While most of the gun carriers I interviewed were right-leaning libertarians and conservatives, gun carriers from all political persuasions and across all socioeconomic backgrounds voiced suspicions surrounding the state's capacity to protect. This ubiquitous suspicion resonates with penal developments that criminologist David Garland[16] traces back to the 1960s and '70s, when the American criminal justice apparatus was charged with the Herculean task of fighting a so-called war on crime. Shaped by the rise of "tough on crime" politics and the New Right, this era of American politics was sustained by contradictory attitudes and expectations surrounding the state: a deep distrust of the state and state efficacy (and support for small government) alongside a desire to crack down on street criminals (and therefore support for expanded government control). In the context of American citizens' long legacy of mistrust of the state,[17] the result was not an empowered state, legitimated by its capacity to protect, but a vulnerable state, undermined by a demand for safety and security it is incapable of satisfying.

One outcome of this deep distrust of the state was a generalized "culture of control": an impulse to minimize risk in all corners of the social world by embracing security not as a concern of the state, but as a personal responsibility.[18] Bolstering Garland's argument, scholars have found that support for armed civilian self-defense is particularly high in contexts where confidence in police is low.[19] In these contexts, those who act in self-defense are viewed not as rogue vigilantes but as citizens who are responding reasonably to the problem of state impotency.[20]

In an atmosphere already primed with stories of police inefficacy, gun carriers over and again saw people's willingness to rely on the police as naïve, if not ignorant. Greg, a retired autoworker, made this point hyperbolically: "You know, if you were going to call an ambulance, a policeman, or Jimmy John's [a sandwich shop], who would be the first one there?" Feigning more faith in sandwich delivery than the police to make his point, Greg treated police inefficacy as an obvious condition structuring his turn to guns: "That's a little far-fetched, but if you are counting on a police officer to show up and stop [a crime], it's not going to happen." Tom also mocked faith in police protection: *If you believe the police are going to come save you, you probably believe in*

Santa Claus, the Tooth Fairy, and the Easter Bunny. Dismissing confidence in the police as dangerously childish, he told me that about 10% to 20% of his students are victims of crime, while the rest *know what happens when you call 911.* Other gun carriers were more matter-of-fact, eschewing evocative metaphors for straight talk about police protection. Billy, a white machinist, said, "Cops don't show up until after the fact. They're not going to show up when guns are blazing and people are dying." And Henry, an African American who owned a restaurant and worked as a firearms instructor on the side, said of the police: "I think they'll be there late. Definitely. Their job is not to help you."

The sense that the police's "job is not to help you," that gun carriers "know what happens when you call 911," and that "there isn't any police protection in America"—these are broad indictments of American police power with a consistent message: reliance on the police is naïve. This emphasis on absence renders irrelevant the question of whether crime rates are going up or down: as long as one can entertain the possibility of becoming a victim, regardless of whether crime is very rare or very likely, then a gun is warranted. It's the only imaginable mechanism of protection against a criminal assumed to be armed and aggressive.

How often do gun carriers actually use their guns in self-defense? As noted in the introduction, scholars disagree vehemently on both the pervasiveness and effectiveness of defensive gun use. During my research, I did hear some stories of gun carriers using, or almost using, their guns defensively, such as Corey, who shot a nineteen-year-old African American who tried to rob him (described in chapter 1), and Matthew, mentioned in chapter 2, who had his hand near his gun, ready to draw, as he walked out of the Detroit Opera House. Other gun carriers, like Fred, described later this chapter, mentioned that they had either motioned toward or exposed their guns in a defensive manner. These gun carriers were in the minority; most gun carriers did not report having used their gun defensively, and virtually all told me they hoped they would never have to.

Even if never *used* defensively, a gun still served a purpose: to reduce gun carriers' reliance on police and allow them to assert their identities as self-reliant men who neither wanted nor needed the protection of the state. Guns helped men embrace a model of citizenship that places a moral premium on the willingness to make up for police absence with armed force. In other words, these men were not rejecting the *police* per se but their own *dependency* on law enforcement.

In American politics, where state dependency is treated as patholog-ical,[21] rejecting dependency on the state is also a way to stake claim to a particular masculine status. "Real men" don't depend on the state—for protection or for anything else. This puts a gendered spin on Garland's "culture of control" argument. An embrace of personal responsibility is not just an expression of state mistrust but also a rejection of state dependency, and insofar as state dependency conflicts with broader cultural demands on men to be self-reliant, inviolable, and indepen-dent, guns emerge as a way to reclaim self-reliance, independence, masculinity, and responsibility. It's not the man with the biggest gun who achieves masculinity (although see chapter 6)—it's the man who doesn't need the state. Guns matter because they help to demonstrate self-reliance.

Interestingly enough, many gun carriers saw themselves as helping the police with a job that police are no longer, and perhaps never were, capable of doing themselves. This assertion was made by both white gun carriers and gun carriers of color, and it fits well with US conservative ideology:[22] an emphasis on libertarian, statist alongside an embrace of law-and-order politics has characterized the American New Right since its ascent in the 1970s and '80s. One white gun carrier told me that police officers should be more "at ease" knowing that lawful Americans have obtained gun permits:

> If I was a state cop, and I pulled someone over, and I walked up to the door [of a car] with my hand on my gun, scared shitless, and the driver hands me his CPL and said, "I am also armed, here's my CPL," I would be completely at ease. It's the guy who stole the gun who is going to pull it out and shoot you . . . It's frustrating because people believe there is so much danger in it, but these are the most law-abiding people that we have! I give my CPL to officers if I get pulled over, even if the gun is not with me.

Occasionally, gun carriers cited abstract examples of how their guns would allow them to serve as "backup" for the police should a violent encounter escalate, and some talked concretely about helping the police in less-than-lethal encounters. For example, one gun carrier told me that he was asked to do "lookout" duties for a cop while a car blocked a local road. But during my research, I never heard of a specific incident in which a gun carrier provided "backup" for the police in terms of firepower.[23] More commonly, as described in chapter 5, I heard of many incidents in which legally armed men, particularly African American men, were treated with suspicion by the police.

Gun carriers might identify with the police (although many do not, as I explore in more detail in chapter 5), and they might even maintain that their choice to carry a gun actually eases the work of public law enforcement. Nevertheless, the very idea of trusting in law enforcement was not just a practical concern but also an affront to their own sense of personal responsibility, of self-reliance, and of independence.

The Duty to Protect

A few weeks into my research, I was supposed to meet a pair of gun carriers in a diner in a depressed area of Metro Detroit and then follow them to a friend's house. As I exited the freeway, I noticed graffiti, trash, abandoned businesses. The exit was less than a mile from the diner, next to what looked like a shuttered auto parts or tools store. From the outside, I could see the old-fashioned diner counter with barstools and a group of men. As I opened the door, I saw a "Gun Carriers Welcome" sticker, supplied by the gun carriers I was meeting, who had befriended the Albanian owner, who, incidentally, also agreed that guns were good for his business.

I sat down next to the men, and we chatted about gun rights, the city of Berkeley, and the economy over biscuits and gravy. As we finished up the meal, Adam, a white man in his fifties, warned me, *Just so you know . . . this isn't in all that nice of an area. So don't get scared.* As I wondered what "not all that nice of an area" meant by Southeastern Michigan's standards, an area nationally known for its violent crime, Adam interrupted my thoughts: *But don't worry. We have guns.*

When I returned to California and presented my research to other scholars, I was often asked whether I felt unsafe being around people like Adam, men who were armed with one, two, or even three guns. Motivated by curiosity about my fieldwork and perhaps by surprise that someone like me, who hardly fit the stereotypical image of a gun carrier, would have a concealed-pistol license, this question was generally posed by academics who lacked intimate knowledge of gun culture or prior experience with the mechanics of a gun to draw upon. For gun carriers, however, this question represents a moral affront: it implies that gun carriers are irresponsible or even threatening and that they ignore the duty that shaped their decision to carry guns. Not only was Adam not a threat, but he wanted me to know that he and his gun would protect me, if necessary. Gun carriers did not generally see themselves as a solitary "army of one," concerned exclusively with the asocial problem of personal protection. Seeing themselves as citizen-protectors willing to prioritize innocent life to the point of being willing to kill, they didn't view their choice to carry a gun as an action that benefited only them—they actually saw their guns as a way to claim their right to self-protection *and* as representing a duty to protect others.

Would or could Adam proficiently use his gun to protect himself and others? Would an attempt to protect me prove more dangerous than helpful? Thankfully, I was never in a situation that would reveal these answers (although see chapter 6). Rather, my research exposed the *moral* work that guns are doing for the men who carry. My experience with Adam and others opened a window to the flipside of the right to self-defense—the duty to protect, one that is informed by the gender politics of violence.

Adam was tapping into what gender scholar Iris Marion Young calls "masculinist protection": a set of moral codes that define men as "good" based on their willingness to protect others.[24] She summarizes this reasoning by noting that "the 'good' man is one who keeps vigilant watch over the safety of his family and readily risks himself in the face of threats from the outside world in order to protect the subordinate members of his household . . . [T]he role of this courageous, responsible, and virtuous man is that of a protector."[25] The capacity for protection situates men in a privileged position in the gendered hierarchy, not by advertising the threat of violence but by repackaging violence as a duty that men perform on behalf of women and children. Men who protect are not coercing their families into recognizing their raw authority—they are fulfilling what they understand as a necessary, honorable social duty to protect their households from outside, violent threats.[26] This is precisely what the citizen-protector model is meant to capture: the braiding of masculine duty with moral respectability that moves the use of lethal force from the criminal side of the moral ledger to the lawful and respectable side. In embracing this duty, gun carriers are tapping into a broader cultural symbolism, echoing images of armed men that populate music, movies, and television, men who use guns to heroically reclaim their masculinity as they save their families, communities, and—in the case of movies like *Independence Day* or *Rocky*—even the nation.[27]

Masculinist protection was illustrated in some of the targets I saw at shooting ranges. For example, one target I used depicted a cartoon rendition of a grimacing, racially ambiguous male clutching a scared, white female. On the one hand, it is a useful target for practicing firearms safety: Can you shoot well enough to avoid hitting your wife, girlfriend, or daughter? On the other hand, the target *extends* what gun carriers should be doing with their guns well beyond self-protection to the realm of *protection of others*, with particular race (a racially ambiguous hostage-taker, a white hostage) and gender markings (a male aggressor, a female victim). In doing so, it also makes assumptions about the person shooting the target. In its depiction of a "damsel in distress," this target situates the shooter as the protector of an "ideal victim"[28]—a role that has historically fallen on the husband, boyfriend, or father. As I show in the coming pages, not everyone is equally worthy of protection: men usually emphasized a deliberate willingness to protect family members alongside a more abstract willingness to protect strangers, particularly women and children, who are viewed as especially vulnerable, innocent, and helpless.[29]

The backdrops of police inadequacy in particular and broader socioeconomic decline in general help to deepen this gendered politics of protection. As the decline of manufacturing and a rise in the female labor force has disrupted men's privileged position as sole providers for their households, guns provide an alternative means of claiming masculine duty, authority, and dignity in the household—unrelated to the vicissitudes of the economy. In this way, gun-carrying men can blend "muscle and compassion"[30] and assert themselves as useful, relevant, and dutiful to their families and their communities.[31] Guns become symbols of manly self-reliance, responsibility, and independence[32] because of contemporary perceptions of inadequate police, socioeconomic decline, and the historically long-standing gendered politics of protection—not because of any inherent meaning attached to firearms.

Families

Butch is a veteran and staunch conservative who devotes his time to Second Amendment activism and gun instruction. In one of his classes that I attended, he began by introducing himself as a "proud stay-at-home dad." I did not expect that kind of self-introduction. Even though household care work is often stigmatized as "women's work," Butch—a strong supporter of Glenn Beck and avid fan of Fox News when I met him—openly embraced this identity. When I went to meet him at his home, he sat with his son, a toddler, on his lap, bobbing him up and down, as he answered my questions. He had been divorced a few times, and he is now married to the love of his life. While his wife worked upstairs, Butch described her employment as a "professional, upstanding job, well-paying," but pointed out that women lacked the "warrior mentality" that people (specifically, men) need to succeed in the workplace.

Though Butch referenced the specter of Detroit as a crime epicenter in a subsequent interview, he was relatively shielded from the city: living several hours away, on the very western edge of the state, Butch enjoyed a bucolic, rural lifestyle foreign to much of southeastern Michigan, free from crime and the breakdown of community. And yet, on that January morning, Butch had traveled to a Detroit suburb to lecture on the importance of the protection of self and others to a packed room of students, ranging in age from twenty-one (the legal minimum for concealed carry licensees) to retirees. Most—as in almost all of the classes I attended—were men, and Butch acknowledged the women attendees by cracking a joke at men who had managed to "drag their wives along." As he moved through the mechanics and legal intricacies of self-defense, he effortlessly shifted between self-protection and protection of others—citing Stand Your Ground to illustrate the dilemma of whether to intervene in an ongoing crime; promoting situational awareness as a means of not just keeping oneself safe but keeping others safe as well; and arguing that stopping a threat also meant controlling stray bullets that may endanger innocent lives caught in the crossfire of a self-defense encounter.

This slippage between the right to self-defense and the duty to protect ran through my conversations with gun carriers. As men spoke about the Second Amendment, their concerns about crime, and their worries about police inefficacy, they highlighted the individualistic cultural worldviews typically associated with gun proponents.[33] Indeed, gun carriers were very concerned with being independent, self-reliant, and individualistic—all characteristics voiced by Connor as he rejected the police as the primary guarantors of his safety. But, in line with what cognitive linguist George Lakoff calls the "strict father" model of conservative ideology,[34] they embraced these values not just to enhance their own safety but also to position themselves as protectors. In this way, guns augmented their status as men *and* as husbands and fathers. A recent Gallup poll found that married men were even more likely to own guns than single men.[35]

Among the men I met in Michigan, protection was an obligation and a responsibility—part of being the head of household. As Jeremy, a white gun carrier, told me, *when I'm with my family, I can defend them. I'm not a karate expert, so I never had that feeling of safety until I had a firearm.* When I probed Butch and Brad, both white gun carriers and fathers, about their decisions to purchase guns, carry them, and even become involved in gun politics, they told me:

> I would rather be home writing a novel rather than doing all this political stuff. I don't even like politics. But up until my kids were born, I didn't get involved in politics. That was kind of the wake-up call for me. Once I had a kid, I thought, man, I felt responsible. I have a responsibility now. I have to raise this kid. (Butch)

> The child's born. Mortgage, marriage. I have a kid. I'm paying for all this stuff on a truck driver's wage . . . she's [his wife] a stay-at-home mom . . . And it wasn't where I expected her to be in the kitchen, you know. We both knew right off the bat that we were equal, but we had different purposes. I was good at making money, and my wife's good at tending to the kid, and I wanted to protect them all, so then a firearm comes along. (Brad)

For Brad and Butch, their guns allowed them to fulfill a duty, a "responsibility" to their families. Not only were they providers; they were protectors. And it was a gun that provided them with this new capability. Brad, in particular, presents himself in terms of his dual role as a provider (he is "paying for all this stuff on a truck driver's wage") and a protector ("I wanted to protect them all"), together establishing him as head of his household. Brad exemplifies how men's role as protector does not *replace* their role as provider, but rather fortifies their claims to the position by bridging traditional breadwinner masculinity with citizen-protector masculinity.

From the perspective of gun carriers, guns confirmed men's utility to their families—both the guns that they carried and the guns that they encouraged women to carry. Men often told me stories about how they encouraged women in their lives to carry guns or how they were disappointed that the women in their lives chose not to carry. While, on the surface, this may seem to contradict men's narratives about masculinity and protection, it actually extends them. For example, Paul implicitly references his *wife's* gun as a way to fulfill his role as protector in absentia:

> I would hate to think that right now, while I'm sitting here at work, my wife is absolutely defenseless at home. If Hulk Hogan breaks into my house, my wife is going to stand in the hallway and blaze away until he falls. It doesn't matter that he could physically dominate her at any moment; she has an equalizer. The only thing that is going to protect my wife and my children from whatever he has in mind is a gun that she keeps next to the bed.

Likewise, Michael, a retired engineer, wanted his wife (and women more generally) to be armed:

> She [my wife] has a pistol that she keeps to the side of the bed, which is good. If she wants to get rid of me, it'll be handy [laughs]! But I don't want any woman to be in her own bedroom unarmed alone. I'm sorry. I don't think any woman should be on the highway alone without being armed.

As with Paul, the gun that Michael's wife has at her bedside seems to stand in for a missing (male?) protector: any woman who finds herself "alone" should have a gun. Men cannot always be there to protect women, but a gun serves as a virtual protector.

Another gun carrier told me he actively encouraged his wife to carry a gun, and insisted she carry any time she was with him during a short period when his CPL was expired. At first, I assumed that he embraced the idea of his wife defending him, and that he was a counter example to what I had observed with other gun carriers—that men believed they had a unique duty to protect their wives, girlfriends, and families, not the other way around. But I had misunderstood his intentions entirely. When I pressed him to explain, he told me that because his wife carried, if "anything happened," "you have it with you, and then I can use it." His wife's gun was a way of affirming *his* ability to protect.

I also experienced this encouragement firsthand. Before I had obtained a concealed-pistol license, several of the gun carriers I met instructed me to obtain one. For example, Michael, the white retired engineer, and Gary, a white lawyer in his early thirties, both ended our interviews by encouraging me to be armed, as my field notes show:

> *On the way out [Michael] gave me a short little pontification about driving alone—that as a woman, he wouldn't want to drive alone and unarmed at night on the highway, as it was just too dangerous. Armed, it seemed, would be okay, but not unarmed. [Michael]*

> *At some point, I realized that the interview had already gone on for almost three hours, and I had a ninety-minute drive back to Detroit. I told [Gary] I needed to start driving on the highway, and he replied back, "Not to be chauvinistic, but I wouldn't drive by myself if I was a woman on the highway and unarmed." [Gary]*

To these men, guns allowed women to be alone by affording them extra safety: Gary even admitted that it might sound "chauvinistic" to tell me that I should carry a gun: in his version of "chauvinism," the gun and the man appear interchangeable. A few men, usually younger men, did break this narrative: Jonathan, a mechanic in his thirties, relayed a lengthy story about an ex-girlfriend with whom he had reconnected many years after their relationship had ended. Upon learning that she had been physically assaulted by another woman, Jonathan took the woman to a shooting range for an impromptu lesson, filed an emergency CPL application, and helped her find a new place of employment. Casey, a paramedic in his late twenties, told me that he has taught each of his ex-girlfriends how to shoot a gun and encouraged them to carry as well; during our interview, he referenced Angelina Jolie's character in *Mr. and Mrs. Smith* to describe his ideal mate: "A girl who not only do I love and I want to be with, but she's got my back, too!" Opening the possibility that he might need a woman, and her gun, to defend him against a threat, Casey explicitly interrupts the formulation that men have an exclusive privilege to protect.

For the most part, though, men gun carriers, especially older men, encouraged women to carry as an extension of their duty to protect, and because of this they generally did not view armed women as a threat.[36] Echoing Sarah Palin's "mama grizzly" rhetoric,[37] gun carriers even emphasized "maternal instinct" to explain why women should be armed. For example, one gun instructor told me that he tries to spark this instinct in women who come to his class. Telling a story about a woman who "could not hit the broad side of a barn from the inside," he said he simply asked the woman to imagine that someone had kidnapped her child while she pumped gas and that her only hope was her gun. When he asked her what she'd do, she—a "Christian woman"—responded "I'd shoot that son of a bitch!"

A second gun instructor also told me that he purposely finds out whether the women in his class have children in order to "use [this] against them." He notes that once he taps into their maternal instinct, they turn out to be better learners than the men in his classes. As he explains:

> I see a lot of women every year in class. I am seeing more and more of them . . . They take instruction better [than men]. The women seem to respond better [than men to training]. The one thing that we usually use against them: we'll talk to them beforehand, we'll get more background [so] we'll get into their heads a little bit. [And then we'll] say, "You have this gun in your hand. It's three o'clock in the morning. They've kicked your front door in. They're going to probably tie you down, rape you, and probably rape your six-year-old

daughter that you just told me about. And God only knows what else they're going to do to you and your family. Unless you stop this situation now, immediately. Because you probably don't want to have your children see you killed and brutalized in front of them."

This emphasis on women's capacity to protect their children raises a question: are men promoting guns to women for women's *self* protection, or for the protection of *their* (that is, the men's) children? While men gun carriers emphasized women's capacity to protect *children* as a way to tap into women's capacity to shoot, the promotion of guns to women often seemed to buttress men's ability to act as protectors of their households. Consider my interview with Timothy, a white gun carrier and father. When I asked whether his wife carried a gun, he said:

My wife was robbed at gunpoint, but my wife still doesn't carry. She's not to that point where she's willing to do whatever is necessary to make sure she goes home [alive] . . . I hope that day will come, especially when she's out and about with my son. That really bothers me. You know, the fact that they're out there with no level of protection. So that kind of bothers me, but she's not ready for it. So I can't expect her to—but I hope.

This suggests the multiple levels on which men's promotion of guns to women is working. Timothy wants his wife to carry because he wants her *and* his son to be protected. His wife's unwillingness to carry, to his mind, jeopardizes the safety of *his* son and, by proxy, undermines Timothy's own duty to protect his family. Timothy *also* tries to be somewhat respectful of his wife's unwillingness "to do whatever is necessary to make sure she goes home [alive]." The bottom line is that what matters to Timothy is not so much whether his wife is protected (because she can *choose* to go unarmed) but whether his son is protected.

Ironically, men emphasized women's duty to protect others much more so than women gun carriers themselves did. The eleven women I interviewed[38] did not embrace the narratives that they should carry only in the absence of their male protectors or that they should primarily carry to protect their children. In fact, most of these women were divorced or unmarried, and most either did not have children or had adult children, making the issue of protecting children irrelevant to their everyday decision to carry guns. Veronica, a white-collar professional in her early forties, most directly questioned men's narratives:

> I really think women are socialized to believe that your life is valuable only in terms of other people's lives, like, "since I became a mother, I'm much more [interested in protection]." You know what? Your life, without children, is worth much more than that person who is trying to hurt you. And that's really good that you want to defend your children, but your life—not just your kids'—is worth it. I think a lot of women think, "I could kill somebody that was trying to hurt my kids, but if they were trying to hurt me, I don't know if I could do it." Bull!

Veronica insisted on the social worth of women's "life, without children" by asserting her right to defend her own life, not by embracing a duty to protect others. Other women emphasized an individualistic embrace of guns. Annie, a white administrative assistant, told me that guns were a way to *take the power back* and to *never be defenseless again* after an abusive childhood. Meanwhile, Cheryl, a white realtor who started carrying a gun upon the encouragement of her husband, told me, "It's funny. When you got the gun, you aren't scared." By emphasizing how guns make her feel less afraid, she primarily connected feelings of independence and self-reliance, rather than a responsibility to protect others, with her gun.

Veronica and other women's emphasis on an individualistic sense of empowerment highlights gender variation in the citizen-protector model. As Veronica suggests, the social expectation that women should sacrifice for their children is neither new nor feminist, and when women's guns are tied to a duty to protect others, women may well experience guns as disempowering, not empowering. This celebration of a "duty to protect," therefore, reflects *men's* approach to guns. As a gendered model of citizenship, the citizen-protector model—with its emphasis on protecting others—empowers men by providing them with a basis for recognition, privilege, and even power (their guns function, for them, as a means of demonstrating their social utility to others). It seems less relevant for women.

Strangers

I met Christopher, a white gun carrier, at a restaurant in a strip mall, deep in the suburbs of Detroit. We chatted about self-defense techniques, training requirements for the concealed-pistol license, and Second Amendment politics. He was in the middle of a long monologue about the importance of flexible firearm techniques when he decided to illustrate his point with a concrete example. He could have made up any scenario, but Christopher described a situation in which men's duty to protect their family is grafted onto a duty to protect their community:

> If you are driving by a schoolyard full of kids, and there's a guy standing there with a rifle, if you shoot him, the kids live. Do you have the skills and the ability to draw that handgun out and put rounds on that person effectively? Can you do that right this second? And that's a lot of chaos going on. That's a lot of movement going on. Are you going to stand there from thirty-five yards out and do it? Can you do it? Or are you going to move to get a better position and advantage?

This scenario reveals underlying assumptions about the duties of those who carry guns. Without pause, Christopher presumes that the armed, law-abiding citizen has a heroic willingness and even a moral obligation to intervene with force: "If you shoot him, the kids live." Christopher could have emphasized a variety of options that the armed passerby had—call the police, alert school officials, drive off. Yet, his resort to arms is instant and clear-cut. What matters is not the question of whether to intervene, but a set of technical concerns. The only thing preventing the armed citizen from taking out the "guy standing there with a rifle" is the former's firearms skills.

By emphasizing children's vulnerability, Christopher's story calls on gun carriers to act out their duties as citizen-protectors of innocent, vulnerable life. But in contrast to gun carriers' emphasis on protecting "loved ones," there's no familial relationship in Christopher's scenario—the armed citizen seems to be passing by the schoolyard by chance. Assuming that defending the kids is the right thing to do, the only issue for Christopher is whether the armed citizen has the skills to do so. Resonant with Adam's implied pledge to protect me (a young, white, unarmed female) from the imagined perils of a rough neighborhood, gun carriers often talked about their capacity to protect others—particularly women and children—even if they were strangers.

Generally, men's willingness to proactively protect others was bounded: gun carriers imagined guns mainly as a tool for protecting families and close friends. Nevertheless, they believed they had a right to intervene and protect others, including strangers, even if they chose not to. Sanctioned to protect and police their communities, gun carriers saw themselves as capable of a civic duty much broader than protecting self or family.

Frequently, gun carriers captured this sentiment by insisting that they "carry their castles with them." This phrase was meant to convey that their legal right to defend their property—a long-standing legal doctrine known as the "Castle Doctrine"—extended to the public sphere, thanks to Stand Your Ground laws.[39] Michigan's Stand Your Ground law reads:

> A person is justified in the use of deadly force and does not have a duty to retreat if he or she reasonably believes that such force is necessary to prevent imminent death or great bodily harm to *himself or herself or another or to prevent the imminent commission of a forcible felony* [emphasis added].

Stand Your Ground laws make it legally possible to achieve a kind of citizenship—the citizen-protector—willing to kill to defend oneself and to protect others.

This aspect of the duty to protect was most provocatively expressed by Timothy. I met Timothy in his home in an apartment complex on the more rural outskirts of Metro Detroit; while he discussed his involvement in gun culture and politics, his son periodically captured our attention—the boy was just learning to walk and string together sentences. Every so often, Timothy would plop his son on his lap. He had just let go of his son as he turned to the stereotype of gun proponents as racist "bubbas":

> You'll have your stereotypical bubba, with his two front teeth, that's gonna wanna "shoot any nigga that comes on his property." You've got that, just as with any other cross section of society. You've got your bad apples. But by and large a responsible firearms owner will stand back to back with another man, woman, or child of any race, nation, or creed to help them defend their own life.

Timothy admitted that some gun carriers are bigots (and even slipped in an illustrative racial slur), but maintained that gun owners, on the whole, were best characterized by their commitment to protect others. Timothy wanted me to know that the value he placed on life trumped anything else that might be used to divide people—"race, nation, or creed." Further, it brought people together, to stand "back to back" in their embrace of mutual protection.

While few were as explicit as Timothy, this general sentiment ran through my conversations with gun carriers. Sometimes, gun carriers unwittingly mentioned this broadened "duty to protect" as they made other points—for example, as Christopher illustrated a defensive scenario. Other times, it came out through men's inability to answer a simple question: "Do you carry a gun primarily for self-defense?" When asked this question, Travis, who lived in an inner suburb that bordered Detroit, recoiled, telling me it was too complicated to give "one reason":

> It's a right, it's self-defense, it's a deterrent against crime. It's letting other people know it's legal, it's also letting other people know that there are those who do this in the neighborhood, and so you might want to go do this [crime] somewhere else. It's all of it.

This interaction was instructive. I struggled to understand why Travis could not just answer "yes." He did carry for self-protection, but just as importantly, he carried for the more general protection of his neighborhood. In a similar vein, when I asked Billy how often he carried and why, he responded that he carries every day, everywhere it is legal to do so: "I'm going to stay safe. Whoever is around me is going to be safe."

This embrace of community defense was more symbolic than practical. Although acts of self-defense sometimes doubled as gestures of community protection (recall, from chapter 1, the police officer who said "good job" after Corey shot dead the robber in his store), gun carriers generally did not report intervening in ongoing crimes—even if they insisted it was their right to do so. There were two notable exceptions, both men who reported intervening in what they characterized as "domestic disputes." In each case, their guns remained holstered, but they used them as a threat against a man they saw victimizing a woman. Fred, an older white gun carrier, was one:

> A boy and girl were screaming and yelling back and forth. I still had my gun and everything on because I had just been home maybe twenty minutes or so. She's screaming all kinds of profanities, and she said, "You slap me again, and I'm going to call the cops."
>
> This is right in front of my house. So I step out on the porch, and he raises his hand back up to her, and she says, "I dare you to hit me."
>
> And I said, "So do I."
>
> And I'm standing there, wearing my 1911 [handgun]. And he looks up and says, "Who are you?" I say, "I'm the guy who's going to call the cops." I said [to the woman], "Do you want help?" She said, "Yeah, he won't leave me alone."
>
> So, I said, "You can step away from her, she's requested help, by law right now, I have the right to use deadly force to protect her." He just kind of shut up. I said, "Would you like the phone to call 911?" She said, "No, just keep him away from me until I can get out of here." I said, "Okay, if you don't call the police, then you go about your way. And I suggest you go up the hill, you go that way."
>
> So she took off running down the road, and he's just standing there, and I said, "Hit it. If I see you go that way, I'll call 911 while I'm running after you." So he took off, I went into my house and minded my own business. I never drew [my gun] on him.

Here, Fred is acting out masculinist protection[40] as he situates himself as a citizen-protector on behalf of a woman in distress and against an aggressive man, her abuser. Fred's story — particularly his prerogative to stand in for the strong arm of the law in the case of a domestic dispute—illustrates how gun carriers may claim a generalized duty to protect others that falls in line with a more targeted duty to protect one's family.

Not all gun carriers subscribed to this broadened duty to protect others—as Craig, a bus driver, said, "When you get the concealed-pistol license, you are not automatically deputized to go out and save the world." When they voiced reservations, they often highlighted conflicts between their duty to protect their own families and their duty to protect innocent life more generally. Even Timothy, the father who said that firearms owners will stand "back to back" with "another man, woman, or child of any race, nation, or creed," struggled with his professed duty to protect his family and strangers:

> Because you can't always help somebody. I mean, as much as I care about human life and well-being, you know, just because I see some woman being raped in the corner of a dark alley, I'm not necessarily going to give my assistance.
>
> If I can, and it's safe to do so, yes, I will do so. If it's just myself that's maybe going to be at risk, I'll be more prone to do what I can.
>
> If he's with me [referring to his son, now sitting on his lap], probably not. Not saying that I wouldn't or that I wouldn't try to if it was at all possible, but you can't always.
>
> And sometimes you can stop something like that by something as simple as walking outside, flicking your porch light on, and saying "Get the hell away from here." You don't even need a weapon. Most crooks are such cowards that as soon as you turn the light on, they run like a cockroach.

Here, Timothy highlights the nuances of this "duty to protect": Timothy wrestles with how the duty to protect innocent, vulnerable strangers (a woman being raped) contradicts the duty to protect one's own family (his son). Timothy realizes that sometimes, he can't do both: he might be in a situation where he has to choose whose life is more valuable, more worthy of protection. Wishing he didn't have to make such a decision (he clarifies, for example, that he is "not saying that I wouldn't try to if it was at all possible"), ultimately, Timothy's duty to protect his son trumps his duty to protect a stranger, even a stranger who is visibly victimized.

The most common reasons that gun carriers told me that they would not intervene in an ongoing crime were either that it would jeopardize their own safety or the safety of others, or that they might misinterpret a non-criminal encounter as a criminal one—for example, by misconstruing a risqué sexual tryst as a rape (this example of a "misinterpreted" rape came up over and again in conversations with the men I met). These contradictions and apprehensions demonstrate two core themes at work in men's turn to guns. First, the ability of Timothy and other gun carriers to imagine such dilemmas is telling. It demonstrates that men's guns implicate far more than personal protection or the protection of property—they elicit a politics of duty. Whether they ultimately decide to intervene in a particular incident should not distract from the finding that they believed that intervening was their prerogative. Second, this duty is gendered in multiple ways. Their willingness to protect a family member, a female rape victim (as per Timothy), or a child school-shooting victim (as per Christopher) resonated with men's embrace of protection as a moral duty—as a way to assert their relevance, their utility, and their authority within their families and beyond. These gendered meanings sometimes meant that gun carriers had to make a choice in terms of what kind of citizen-protector they would be. Faced with the decision to protect a stranger or a loved one, will a gun carrier choose to be someone who protects and defends his family, or his community more broadly? Almost all gun carriers who entertained this dilemma during their conversations with me ultimately chose their family.

Conclusion

Taking stock of the American obsession with crime and crime control, Eric Klinenberg makes an interesting update to Putnam's "bowling alone" thesis: he argues that if Americans are bowling alone, they are increasingly policing together.[41] In hopes of increasing police legitimacy and efficiency, public law enforcement agencies since the 1970s have encouraged citizens to participate as the "eyes and ears" of public law enforcement through neighborhood watch groups and community organizations. Klinenberg[42] argues that the contemporary brand of American community policing

> . . . marks a disturbing trend toward a society where distrust, suspicion and fear are organizing principles of politics and culture. If effective as a form of organizational reform for police departments and as a means for combating local crime problems, as a program for civic renewal collective policing represents democracy in its most desperate and depraved form. Americans may not be bowling together, but they are policing together with unparalleled enthusiasm.

Gun carriers do not necessarily police "together": with a few exceptions, gun carriers are not involved in community patrols or organized neighborhood watch groups, and the NRA organizes rifle clubs, not armed patrols. Nevertheless, gun carriers interpret their turn to guns in terms of larger constellations of policing and protection as well as of family and community. If community policing elevates *dis*trust as an organizing principle of society, as Klinenberg maintains, gun carry channels that principle into deep suspicions surrounding the state's ability to police and protect, alongside a celebration of men's duty to protect. In doing so, gun carriers not only help to reshape the ties that bind Americans but also the gendered forms of good citizenship that Americans—at least, gun-carrying Americans—hold in esteem.

Gun carriers braid together a "right to self-defense" with a "duty to protect," and their ability to do so is embedded in two broader social dynamics. The first is a loss of confidence in the police, reinforced by police layoffs and self-effacing statements by police about their own capacity to protect citizens. Police themselves tell citizens that they are overworked, that they can't always be there, and that they may even endorse citizens carrying a gun. We all know that police, objectively speaking, cannot "always be there," but these are alarming messages to hear from the very agents charged with "serving and protecting." Galvanized by these statements and within the broader context of socio-economic insecurity, gun carriers are not just supplementing the police but also forging a kind of citizenship centered around men's rejection of dependency on the police and their embrace of the duty to protect.

This first dynamic dovetails with a second dynamic—a long-standing association between masculinity and protection that has shaped policing in the United States since the country's inception.[43] Based on my findings, this association may be activated when the bases of alternative masculinities (breadwinning, for example) erode and where the problem of policing seems pressing, immediate, and unavoidable. In Michigan, the result is an enactment of the very model of citizenship promoted by the NRA: the citizen-protector. While the NRA provides the basic blueprint for how to become a different kind of citizen, as I showed in chapter 3, contexts like Michigan—both the state apparatus and the economy—provide the social context in which guns can become appealing tools of everyday protection. Guns, of course, are not the only or the most direct response to a broad-based context of socioeconomic decline, and so the objective of this chapter has been to demonstrate how guns—especially for men—become particularly appealing through their associations with independence, self-reliance, and civic duty. Not just an ideological platitude dreamed up in a lobbyist's office in Washington, DC, the citizen-protector is a social reality in Michigan.

By "social reality," I do not mean to imply that gun carriers are regularly brandishing their guns, threatening to shoot, or shooting. While these stories exist—there's Corey's story in chapter 1, Fred's story here, and Aaron's story in chapter 6—they are the exception, not the rule. For the most part, gun carry is symbolic: it is a way to "do something" in the face of state inefficacy and to assert oneself as a useful, relevant man willing to protect (even if that willingness is never tested). This was particularly true of the white, middle-class suburbanites I met—men like Tom, who likened belief in the police to belief in Santa Claus, or Connor, who eschewed "dependency" on police. Often experiencing lower crime rates and greater levels of police protection than their working-class and African American counterparts, white, middle-class suburbanites tended to embrace a symbolic politics that emphasized generalized insecurity. They acted within a culture of decline, but relatively speaking, they had some buffers—more secure jobs, safer neighborhoods, greater police presence, even geographic distance—to shield them from the raw ramifications of socioeconomic decline in Detroit, Flint, and elsewhere.

But African Americans, like Henry who said the police's job "is not to help you," and working-class white men, like Austin, who was instructed by police to shoot on sight, felt this insecurity most pointedly: they were directly confronted with the double threat of crime and economic insecurity, and they were most concerned not only with the problem of police inefficacy but also police harassment, as described in the next chapter. For these men, guns were not just a way to supplement the police but also a way to supplant them.

5

Policing Guns, Profiling People

IN MARCH 2012, A GROUP of African American men took the podium at a Detroit rally to demand justice for Trayvon Martin's killing. They were members of the Detroit 300, a community policing organization started in 2010 in response to a serial rapist on the loose in Detroit. As the rapes continued, radio personality, Pulitzer Prize winner, and activist Angelo Henderson called on "300 men" to take to the streets to protest Detroit's rampant problem of violent crime and the police's inability to do anything about it, and the group was formed.

On that day in March, Raphael Johnson, the group's leader at the time, demanded "that justice run its course, not just for George Zimmerman but for all the George Zimmermans throughout these United States of America, who think that all young Black people's life is valueless."[1] Johnson listed the young Black lives that had been deemed "valueless" in Detroit by police and criminals: Kade'jah Davis (who died in the crossfire of bullets over an argument about a cell phone),[2] Aiyana Jones (who was killed in a botched police raid),[3] Bianca Jones (who was allegedly kidnapped in a carjacking, but whose father was later found guilty of her murder).[4] One might expect the Detroit 300 to rigorously oppose laws that loosen restrictions on gun ownership and use, but instead the group encourages its members to understand and exercise their rights as law-abiding, gun-carrying citizens. Johnson concluded, "As long as grandmothers are being raped and babies are being killed, no man in this city should be sitting down on his backside. He should be standing behind us, out in the street, on the corner, in the alley, on the street—he should be getting up off his behind." This rally for Trayvon Martin had become a call to arms.

Although national debates about gun laws often presume that gun owners and carriers are white—an older white American man, like Wayne LaPierre, often figures as the face of pro-gun politics—these debates often overlook the very people with the most complex and contradictory relationships with guns and the politics of protection. Namely, these debates exclude people like the men gathered for the Detroit 300's Trayvon Martin rally and other people of color who are both most likely to be the victims of gun violence and most likely to be harassed by the police for their decisions to own and carry guns.

Young men of color are most affected by gun violence in America: gun-related homicide is the *leading cause of death among Black teens*, and gun injuries to Black teens outnumber those suffered by white teens by a ratio of 10 to 1.[5] According to the Bureau of Justice Statistics, this racial disparity is also visible in justifiable homicides: from 1976 to 2005, 43% of victims of justifiable homicides committed by civilians were African American, and most were in their twenties and thirties (this general pattern holds for justifiable homicides committed by police, as well). In urban contexts, guns add to a toxic mix of poverty, blocked upward mobility, and incarceration. One analysis of Chicago showed that people living close to areas where homicides had taken place over the last twelve years were more likely to be Black; they earned an average of $38,318 (compared to $61,175 in those households not near homicides) and were twice as likely to have not finished high school.[6]

My fieldwork shows that law-abiding men of color are also more likely to be harassed simply for choosing to carry a gun. They must navigate the widespread presumptions that they are criminals and that their guns are illegally possessed or carried. This finding reflects an expansion in intrusive, investigatory policing tactics: the post-2008 defunding of public law enforcement notwithstanding, the most dramatic transformations in public law enforcement over the past four decades involved massive police growth, not contraction, and the emergence of a new, proactive policing style aimed at implicitly and explicitly profiling suspected criminals based on a variety of factors—including but not limited to race. Even without formal arrest or incarceration, these practices undermine the dignity of those targeted by the police—particularly young men of color.[7] The young men of color who are disproportionately stopped by police learn that they are unworthy of fair treatment before the law. Reflecting racial profiling in American law enforcement, gun carriers of color told me they experienced unwanted police attention, and their guns heightened their existing vulnerability to police. This, of course, highlights the complex relationship between public law enforcement and communities of color: even as the Detroit Police Department works with the Detroit 300 and Chief James Craig endorses civilian self-defense, my research suggests that officers on the ground are still pursuing civilians who "profile" as criminals.

This chapter examines how gun carriers of color articulated a different kind of gun politics. For men of color, experiences of unwanted police attention sits within a long-standing, and broader, context of racist police practices and police militarization in the United States. This stands in contrast to the experiences of most white gun carriers: while, in theory, being licensed to carry a gun increases a gun carrier's vulnerability to police harassment, in practice, this is an empty threat. But some white gun carriers—working-class men or open carriers—do experience harassment, and interestingly, those who do tend to share similar attitudes toward the police as gun carriers of color. Perhaps an unlikely alliance against state abuse, these armed men also echoed the politics of the Black Panthers of the 1960s as they symbolically armed themselves against aggressive and/or illegitimate policing practices. Expressing deep doubts about the police's ability to protect them, they went further in their critique of police than other gun carriers, also seeing the police as a force against which they needed protection. They believed that guns—at least symbolically—could provide that protection.

Despite these unexpected similarities across lines of race, however, I found that the symbolic power and meaning of a gun had at least as much to do with the race and gender of its carrier as it did with the gun itself: while gun carriers of color were profiled as criminals, my research revealed that white gun carriers were more likely to be treated by the police as upstanding citizens (Corey, the gun carrier described in chapter 1 who was congratulated by a police officer after he committed justifiable homicide, is one example) or dismissed as overzealous political activists who were more irritating than threatening (such as the open carriers described in this chapter). I, too, found that my gun pigeonholed me, as a young, white woman, into a particular set of meanings: I was often mocked by bystanders for carrying my gun. Because guns meant different things when carried by different people, gun carriers approached the police with different levels of entitlement, kinds of fears, and varieties of tactics. Accounting for these differences, this chapter examines how some gun carriers subscribe to a distinct strain of gun politics that directly contests the desirability of public law enforcement's monopoly on policing in a variety of ways—whether through the simple, individual act of carrying a gun, within one-on-one interactions with police, or through involvement in armed community policing groups like the Detroit 300.

BMWG: Black Man with a Gun

Americans do not all experience the same police. True, the condemnation of police as absent, inadequate, and ineffective is widespread, and I did find that it crossed lines of race and class among gun carriers. But this narrative, taken alone, obscures critical aspects of American policing in the late twentieth and early twenty-first centuries, particularly the deep racial divide in how Americans experience, and understand, public law enforcement.

While the pursuit of criminal justice has long been used as a mechanism of racial control in the United States,[8] the roots of contemporary policing practices can be traced back to the late 1960s, rising amid the urban riots, assassinations, and social upheaval that marked that decade. The Detroit Riot of 1967, described in chapter 1, not only left a profound mark on the local racial politics of southeastern Michigan; it also served as one of the key events that inspired the 1968 Safe Streets Act,[9] which helped to inaugurate the American War on Crime.[10] As explained earlier in this book, the War on Crime represented a set of "tough on crime" discourses, strategies, and tactics. It was marked by the reallocation of public budgets from social welfare and toward criminal justice and militarized crime control techniques that situated crime as a central, organizing problem within American society. Expenditures on criminal justice—police, jails, prisons—skyrocketed after the passage of the Safe Streets Act in 1968 and for decades thereafter. The police borrowed tactics (such as SWAT teams), weaponry (such as assault rifles and armored vehicles), and even language from the military.[11]

Mobilized in response to spikes in urban violence and expanding illicit drug markets in the 1960s, '70s, and '80s, the War on Crime had a bifurcated impact on Americans. For some, the War on Crime heightened fears about crime and increased the appeal of so-called "tough on crime" policies. In this regard, there was a growing sense that no matter how much the state tried, the crime problem was intractable and overarching. The state could only fail, and so when police began calling attention to layoffs and response in the post-2008 recession, this message fell on listening ears, as described in chapter 4.

But this captures only one side of the War on Crime. To others, the War on Crime represented heightened, and unwanted, police attention, harassment, and abuse. These dynamics have been heavily targeted at men of color and have led to the disproportionate incarceration of people of color; the normalization of police abuse—harassment, physical assault, and even death—against people of color; and deep distrust of public law enforcement across the most disenfranchised groups of Americans, who, tragically, are most in need of police protection given their exposure to violent crime.[12]

In the wake of urban violence and an "out of control" drug epidemic in the 1970s and '80s,[13] law enforcement agencies across the country began designating specialized units to target poor urban communities known for gangs, drugs, and violence. In the aftermath of the Detroit Riot, for example, Detroit Police instituted the STRESS (Stop Robberies and Enjoy Safe Streets) program, aimed at aggressively stopping street crime. The squad became infamous when two of its white officers murdered a plainclothes African American officer because they found him "suspicious-looking."[14] George, an African American gun carrier from Detroit, told me that his group of friends were concerned about police abuse as far back as the 1970s, when the Detroit police increasingly embraced militarism as a police tactic in response to the Riot, the rise of drug markets, and heightened urban violence:

In our neighborhood, we had an all-white motorcycle gang [of civilians] that was literally getting away with sexual assaults. They were going to the bus stop on the main thoroughfare, almost like patrols. This was getting really rampant, and there was only one Black cop, all the rest of them were white. Me, being involved with different Black coalitions, we were like the prey for the police. They wanted to kill us. We never walked out alone. Couldn't afford to. A lot of my friends got beat down when caught by themselves. We were scared of assassination.

These experiences taught George, then a teenager, that he needed to protect himself not just against criminals but also against the police. As soon as could legally arm himself, he did.

Other gun carriers of color described more recent experiences of proactive profiling, reflecting a shift in policing practices since the 1970s.[15] In response to changing drug markets in the 1980s and '90s[16] and under a "fight crime" mandate, police in Detroit and elsewhere began proactively profiling men who "looked" like drug dealers—men of color who drove expensive cars, had pagers, and carried sheets of phone numbers with them, for example. This institutionalized practice was known as the "investigatory stop": unlike traffic-safety stops, where there is a clear-cut and major violation, during investigatory stops, motorists may be stopped for small violations (say, a broken license-plate light or going just a mile over the speed limit), marginally suspicious activities (e.g., parking in the shade) or for no stated reason at all.[17] Although African Americans are twice as likely to be stopped for investigatory stops, these stops are legal[18] so long as the officer can articulate a pretext *other* than the race of the driver to make the initial stop. Today's controversial stop-and-frisk policies, in which police shake down "suspicious-looking" men on foot for illegal drugs or weapons, are an extension of investigatory practices initially targeted at motorists. Meant to search for "drugs or guns," stop-and-frisk tactics are disproportionately used against racial minorities, but they rarely result in arrest.[19]

The increased reliance on investigatory stops was a result of law enforcement's "tough on crime" mandate, which legitimated aggressive police tactics. But it was also buttressed by the rise of community policing. In the 1990s, amid scandals such as the 1991 Rodney King Beating, public law enforcement increasingly came under pressure to adopt a more proactive, community-sensitive approach, which aimed at increasing the visibility of police, enhancing police-community ties, and diversifying law enforcement. Known as community policing, this proactive style of policing was also used to justify the investigatory stop, which has become a core policing practice targeted toward people of color. The rise of investigatory stops has created a stark divide in how Americans interact with, experience, and understand the police. As criminologists Charles Epp, Stephen Maynard-Moody, and Donald Haider-Markel write,

> Whites almost exclusively experience traffic-safety stops and gener-ally judge these stops to be basically fair. In addition to routine traffic stops, African Americans also experience investigatory stops and generally judge *these* stops to be fundamentally *unfair* . . . African Americans and Latinos have developed a shared knowledge of the investigatory stop: how to know when one has been stopped in such a way, how to endure the experience, and how to go on with life.[20]

In this way, racial profiling becomes embedded as part of just "doing police work," as evidenced by the tendency of police officers to pull over African American motorists, especially in predominantly white areas.[21] Racial minorities are much more likely to be stopped, arrested, and incarcerated as a result of traffic violations and marijuana use, yet there is scant evidence that racial minorities commit traffic violations or use marijuana at higher rates than whites.[22] It is true that some crimes are more likely to be committed by African Americans than whites, but police stops and arrests of African Americans far exceed this difference if crime was the only motivating factor.[23] This is why scholars, lawyers, activists, and everyday Americans use terms like "driving while Black" and "walking while Black"—to call attention to the criminalization of racial minorities. Phrased to parody crime designations (e.g., "driving under the influence"), these terms call attention to how people of color are criminalized for otherwise lawful activities.[24]

These kinds of experiences with police were reflected in many of my conversations with gun carriers of color. When I asked whether their interactions were different than white gun carriers', Black men repeatedly told me about harassment from the police,[25] and they often emphasized the chasm between their experiences with police and those of the broader population of gun carriers. In one online Michigan gun forum, a gun carrier became embroiled in a debate about racial profiling. Assuming that he was speaking to a mostly white audience, he described "driving while Black" (DWB):

> I don't know if some of you realize what DWB is like. And I don't mean black like Obama, I mean black . . . with slightly baggy clothes, tinted windows, rims, hoodies, and rap music. What upsets us is that we can get a ticket for playing "loud" music on Woodward [referencing the whiter suburbs of Royal Oak, Ferndale, Berkely, and Bloomfield Hills] at 5pm, but a Harley Motorcycle can ride through my residential neighborhood after 8 and roam freely while setting off every car alarm it rides by. I have personally been stopped and searched by cops at Hart Plaza because my cell phone case "looked" like a gun holster. My whole car was searched because they couldn't figure out what the two switches under my radio were for . . . as if I had some hidden Batman compartment concealing all of my weed.

This poster's "slightly baggy clothes, tinted windows, rims, hoodies, and rap music" marked him, to police, as suspicious and provided a pretext for a vehicle stop and an investigatory search. People of color who chose to carry firearms experienced profiling *both* as people of color and as gun carriers: Bobby, a Hispanic gun carrier who had been harassed by police for openly (but legally) carrying a firearm, directly compared the police's harassment of gun carriers to racial profiling: *They're [the police] taught . . . if someone has a gun, [then they are a threat] . . . I understand what they've seen, but at the same time, that's like saying every Arab I run into is a terrorist. You can't have that mentality, as natural as it is.* Both Phil, an African American in his twenties, and Gerald, an African American in his thirties, saw their decision to carry a gun as embedded in broader practices of racial profiling they'd experienced:

> In Detroit, you can just be talking outside, and the police'll come up on you with their pistols drawn and say "Guns or drugs? Let

me see your IDs!" They'll put you up against the wall and pat you down. I think me being young, people figure, "Oh, he has [an illegal] gun." . . . A lot of people don't know their rights in Detroit, and I figure that's how they [the police] get away with it . . . I guess they think I'm irresponsible or something. (Phil)

Police officers are just angry, for whatever reason. I had this one officer who felt the need to question me as far as my reasons for wanting to [legally] carry [a gun]. I didn't see why I needed to discuss that. I'm trying to be respectful, but why I'm carrying shouldn't be any of your concern. I've heard plenty of times that there is a young Black male stopped, and the police say, "There's a problem in the area, and we just pulled you over, and we're just going through your trunk." I had an officer ask me where the drugs were. "We got your guns, where the drugs at?" And then they claimed that "You fit that description." They play those games, they play those games. (Gerald)

Legally licensed to carry a gun, Phil and Gerald both expressed exasperation at the police's insistence that they were involved in some kind of criminal activity—if not gun-related, then drug-related. Phil says that he is regularly stopped by police, while Gerald ran through a laundry list of his encounters with Detroit police officers, from invasive questioning to illegal searches. While Phil concludes that the police must think he's "irresponsible or something," because "people don't know their rights," Gerald insists police "play those games" with "young Black male[s]" who "fit that description" of criminals.[26] For men of color who lawfully carry guns, police attention conveys a message: you are not welcome to exercise your rights.

Such experiences help make sense of why African Americans in southeastern Michigan are in fact *more* likely to have a concealed-pistol license (CPL) than whites. African Americans are much more likely to be victims of gun violence than whites, but they are also caught in what scholars call the overpolicing/underpolicing paradox. People of color are both *least* likely to experience adequate police protection and *most* likely to experience unwanted police attention, whether in the form of violent force, surveillance, or harassment.

Guns are mobilized in response to this paradox by practically addressing inadequate police protection and the threat of violent crime *and* symbolically protesting public law enforcement's profiling of armed Black men as criminals. In Detroit, I found a critical mass of African American men who had embraced gun rights. Some organized to "take back" their communities from criminals while also contesting a police force they saw as simultaneously inadequate and abusive. George, for example, became involved in the Detroit 300, the organization of African American men described previously who proactively promote gun rights as an anti-crime strategy in the city of Detroit.

Other gun carriers of color took a more individualistic approach by simply openly carrying a gun in public. Open carrying a firearm provided men of color with an opportunity to model a kind of citizenship that is usually off limits for them—what Jason, an African American gun carrier, euphemistically described as "something you can [only] do north of 8 Mile," the border between Detroit and its whiter, wealthier suburbs. Recall Jason's story from chapter 1: Jason often went for long walks in Detroit while openly carrying a gun and has had several interactions with the police as a result. Though he has never been in violation of the law, he attracted much unwanted police attention and harassment. Why did he continue to open carry? On the one hand, Jason's decision to openly carry a gun allows him to navigate "the code of the street," a term sociologist Elijah Anderson uses to describe the informal rules and norms governing interpersonal behavior, especially the use of violence, in areas with high crime and limited police protection. Jason is able to publicly communicate his willingness to defend himself through being visibly armed, complying with the code. On the other hand, his ability to openly carry *simultaneously* communicates that he is a law-abiding citizen—i.e., he's "decent," to use Anderson's terminology. Neither criminal nor cop, Jason models a different kind of Black masculinity. As he describes it (as also noted in chapter 1), "There's a Black man here in my presence, open-carrying, and he's confident. He's not a thug, there's no police, he's walking out of a door, and he's not trying to cover it." His gun becomes a "confident" proclamation of his lawfulness—especially when, for example, police publicly return his lawfully carried gun in front of a crowd of bystanders, as described in chapter 1.[27] He tells me that he often catches looks from younger men who wonder how he is able to openly carry a firearm despite not being a cop. Referencing the legal restriction that forbids felons from owning or carrying firearms, he tells me that he has an easy message for them: " 'You want to do this? Stay out of trouble. Keep a clean record, and you can do the same thing I'm doing.' " Distancing himself from the criminalized hypermasculinity often ascribed to urban men of color,[28] Jason uses his gun to model a kind of citizenship available to those who "keep a clean record," a kind of citizenship tied to law-abidingness and the civic duty to protect oneself and others.

With the act of legally carrying a gun, armed men of color like Jason disrupt the premise that underlies policing practices like stop-and-frisk, that any "guns or drugs" found on the bodies of profiled men are necessarily illegal. True, in places like New York City or Los Angeles, where laws heavily restrict civilians from lawfully carrying guns, a gun found on a private citizen in a public space is almost certainly illegally carried. But this premise falls flat in southeastern Michigan, where Black men are more likely to have a CPL than their white counterparts and where many Black men also openly carry. Despite the lawfulness of their action, gun carriers of color still reported unwanted attention, surveillance, and harassment from the police. The term "BMWG"[29]—Black Man with a Gun—isn't just a play on law enforcement terms here—it's a description that can elicit pride, awe, and suspicion.

The Fine Line of the Law

Most white gun carriers did not have these kinds of experiences with public law enforcement. While, for many gun carriers, to carry a gun is to consciously experience the authority of the police for the first time, for white, middle-class gun carriers, that authority generally remains an abstraction. Carrying a gun increases the possibility of breaking the law: as one gun carrier told me as he pointed to my hip, where my firearm was presumably concealed, "You are never so close to becoming a criminal as you are now." He meant that a single misstep—failing to disclose my concealed firearm to a police officer during a minor traffic stop, carelessly stepping into a pistol-free zone with my gun, brandishing my firearm without "reasonable" fear of death or grave bodily harm—could lead me into a quagmire of problems. Gun carriers varied in how closely they walked the "fine line" of the law, but they almost unanimously articulated a heightened awareness of their interactions with the police as part of carrying a gun.

Most gun carriers viewed disclosure requirements, although a nuisance, as a small price to pay for the ability to legally carry a gun. According to Michigan law, a concealed carrier must "immediately" disclose that she has a permit to carry a gun concealed anytime she is stopped by a police officer—whether for jaywalking, speeding, reckless driving, or any other infraction, firearms-related or not. The failure to disclose immediately—even waiting a few minutes while the officer explains the reason for the stop—may result in a fine of up to five hundred dollars or a six-month CPL suspension the first time and a fine of up to one thousand dollars and revocation of the CPL for the second offense. Billy, a white gun carrier, explains,

> In Michigan, when you get the CPL, it's attached to your driving record. So if you get pulled over, they already know before they walk up to your car—they already know before they walk up to your car that you have a CPL. But the law requires that I have to disclose. First thing out of my mouth, I have to tell them that I have a CPL.

Gun carriers acknowledged that the purpose behind the disclosure requirement is to enhance officer safety (although some saw it as purely symbolic, given that the police could run their name or license plate number through Michigan's Law Enforcement Information Network (LEIN) and ascertain their CPL status without disclosure). Yet this legal requirement meant that interactions with police officers—generally stressful encounters in and of themselves—were heightened by the fact that they possessed a CPL. Ethan, a white gun carrier, explained, *if you are driving, the police can see your license and see right away that you have a CCW [sic] and you are conceal carrying, and you have to tell them that, anyway.*[30] He pulled out his driver's license to show me that he had placed a big yellow sticker on the back that states that he could be carrying a gun. He had chosen to place the sticker on his ID as a way to ensure that he "discloses" immediately. But, he warned, *a police officer—once he sees that—can automatically ask you to take a breathalyzer. So this means you are already giving up rights.*

In addition to non-firearms-related stops (such as traffic stops), gun carriers also anticipated police encounters that would come in the aftermath of a self-defense shooting. If traffic stops represent the more routine, if incidental, ways in which the police become a conscious factor in gun carry, self-defense shootings are the rare, yet ultimate, situation for which gun carriers prepare themselves. Gun carriers often told me they worried that they would be "victimized twice"—first by the initial assailant and then by law enforcement and the court system. In anticipation of this experience, gun carriers mentioned that they would exercise their Fifth Amendment rights to remain silent should they actually use their guns in self-defense. Henry, an African American gun carrier, explains:

> If you are involved in something, I wouldn't want to say anything; get your lawyer there. Because anything you say can be used against you in a court of law . . . Nothing you say is going to help you, so you need to be quiet and tell your lawyer and do things to help yourself. If you give them fuel for the fire that's what they're going to use . . . You don't want what you're saying misinterpreted. And you might even say the wrong thing!

Here, the police are not just failed protectors but potential threats. They are the state agents empowered with fining people for gun violations, suspending their CPLs, confiscating their guns, and even rescinding their gun rights altogether (as happened to one gun carrier I describe in detail in chapter 6). And in my conversations, on online gun forums, in firearms classes, and at shooting ranges, gun carriers and firearms instructors shared real-life stories and imagined scenarios to show the police violating their rights. The issue was never far from the surface.

However, amid the hypothetical circumstances, the vow to "plead the Fifth," and the insistence that they strained to be better drivers just to avoid interactions with the police, relatively few gun carriers will ever experience unwanted police attention, surveillance, abuse, or harassment. For most white gun carriers, this sense of police violation was more of an abstract possibility than a concrete reality, as would be expected based on scholarship on racial policing.[31] White men and women are simply not subjected to the same scrutiny as racial minorities—even if they commit crime at the same, or greater, rates. Nevertheless, some white gun carriers *had* been subject to similar police harassment, and among those that had, I found similar attitudes toward the police as those of gun carriers of color.

Entitlement to Rights, Expectation of Mistreatment

After sipping coffee for close to two hours, Richard, a white gun carrier, asked me a question that caught me off guard. He asked me if I knew about the case of Malice Green, an African American man who was beaten to death in 1992 by Detroit police officers after a routine traffic stop. Green allegedly had crack cocaine in his hand. Over twenty years ago, the case had been a flashpoint for concerns about police brutality and racism, framed against the LAPD's then-recent beating of Rodney King and the ensuing rioting. But in 2010, when I interviewed Richard, I was taken aback by the question: what meaning could Green's death still hold for someone like Richard, a middle-aged white man who grew up in Detroit and now lived in a middle-class suburb?

To Richard, Green's death mattered because it revealed a different side of public law enforcement: not just inadequate and absent, but also abusive and aggressive. As he explained,

> Malice Green was beaten to death with a flashlight and hit twenty-six times in the head after he was already legally dead. The cops said that they thought he had something in his hand, and he wouldn't open it. So the two big cops beat him to death. What really makes me ill is that Malice Green was, I don't know, five-seven, 140 pounds. Of course, that doesn't occur in Bloomfield Hills [a white, wealthy suburb of Detroit] . . . A person who's on crack and does petty street crime robberies to get twenty dollars a day doesn't have an attorney. Even if they did, no one would care. Because they don't profile for somebody whose life is worth anything. The negative experiences with police, the Rodney Kings, the Malice Greens—police get away with those because nobody cares.

Richard's critique was biting: police preyed upon the most marginalized of society because no one bothers to stop them.

Richard suggests that gun carriers of color were not alone in seeing police as racially biased, intrusive, and even violent. Indeed, I found a small, but loud, group of white gun carriers who also emphasized police harassment. Some left-leaning, most right-leaning, these white gun carriers differed from others in that they had direct contact with the police that they characterized as negative, and their attitudes about the police often aligned more with gun carriers of color than with other white gun carriers.[32] They articulated a libertarian stance against the state, including the police, and echoing Gerald, they emphasized the "anger" with which police approached civilians. They often talked about the militarization of US police forces, including, at times, the police's aggressive response to drug offenses.[33] A few complained that marijuana possession should not be a crime in the first place. Some worried about mission creep from the War on Drugs and the War on Terror—one gun carrier told me that he thought that Michigan's border with Canada expanded the police power of border control officials, who had no obligation to honor Americans' constitutional rights.

While these white men saw themselves as targets and even "test cases" for court action against the police, they also generally recognized that these police abuses tended to target poorer communities of color, like Detroit, and have been justified by moral panics over urban violence and drug problems (as Richard described with respect to Malice Green). They drew parallels between racially motivated police practices (e.g., profiling) and their experiences of being "profiled" as gun carriers, and they referenced Bobby, Jason, and other gun carriers whose stories of unwanted police attention were shared on online gun forums. This overlap in racial politics usually did not extend beyond the immediate problem of racial profiling, and no doubt, racial profiling provided white gun carriers with a convenient script to make sense of, and validate, their own police stops. Nevertheless, this overlap created an unexpected commonality between gun carriers of color and some white gun carriers. Both believed that the police can be more harmful than helpful by violating rights.

Some white gun carriers experienced police abuse as a result of living in over-policed urban environments. For example, Richard was raised by a single mother in a "rough" area of Detroit. Over coffee, he rattled off a lengthy list of police abuses—from his own experiences to those of high-profile cases like that of Malice Green. He told me that police "don't approach people in a way that's respectful anymore. It's accusatory, it's inflammatory, it's violating your rights 90% of the time. You know, police are civilians, too. They're not at war with anybody. [laughs] Other than civilians." This notion that police are "at war" with civilians is not typically embraced by white men, especially white conservative men,[34] but Richard's experiences growing up in Detroit provided him with a different perspective than white gun carriers who spent their entire lives in middle-class suburbs.[35] As described in chapter 2, in the aftermath of a gang attack he survived in Detroit in the 1980s,[36] Richard flagged down a police car, assuming that the police would take him to the nearest hospital. Instead, the two officers dropped him off in a "more dangerous" area of Detroit, where Richard eventually caught a bus and found his way to medical attention and months of surgeries.[37] It was the last time he'd depend on the police for help. Vowing to "never be defenseless again," his gun is a gesture against what he sees as an oftentimes illegitimately abusive police force.

Open carriers, most of whom were working-class white men, also shared Richard's attitudes toward police and protection. While completely legal, openly carrying a gun often leads to police interactions—not just for men of color like Jason, but also for white men. These stops routinely transformed these men's views of the police, leading them to view police as violators of rights.

One of these men was Anthony, a white carrier in his late twenties. He became interested in open carrying a firearm because he believed it made a strong statement about his commitment to Second Amendment rights as a visual act of "free speech" that forcefully communicated his attitudes about self-defense. Like other open carriers, Anthony wanted to use open carry to "desensitize" the public to guns and "normalize" guns as everyday tools of protection in public space, and for this reason, he openly carried his gun as often as possible. Unconcerned with onlookers who might feel uncomfortable or even threatened by his openly carried gun, Aaron believed that the more people who saw guns on law-abiding people who were not law enforcement, the greater support gun rights would find among the public. In other words, Anthony saw himself on the front lines of the battle for the hearts and minds of Americans on the issue of guns, and in some sense he was.

As ardent gun rights advocates, open carriers nevertheless saw themselves as pitted against the leader of the gun lobby—the National Rifle Association (NRA). Several open carriers criticized the NRA for promoting concealed carry at the expense of open carry, especially in Florida and Texas. Until recently, the NRA had treated open carry as a fringe element of gun advocacy, refusing to publicly endorse the practice. One 2014 article on the NRA's website even called the open carry movement "weird" and "scary"—comments the organization later retracted.[38] Furthermore, Anthony was not the norm among the concealed carriers I met in Michigan: at the time of my research, I found that concealed carriers often viewed open carriers and their actions as offensive, arrogant, pushy, and even dangerous. Although most gun carriers I talked to thought that open carry should be legal and were reluctant to advocate for anything that curtailed gun rights, several qualified their support by saying, "But just because something is legal doesn't mean you should do it."

Anthony met other like-minded open carriers mainly through the Internet forums OpenCarry.org and Michigan Open Carry. On both sites, open carriers disseminated information about constitutional rights, including but not limited to gun rights. As Kevin, a multiracial truck driver and supporter of open carry, told me, "We're supposed to be standing up for our rights. This isn't even just Second Amendment rights we're talking about. We're talking Fourth Amendment. Fourteenth Amendment." In addition to providing space for debate, these Internet forums also include threads for posters to chronicle their experiences open carrying—whether they involve interactions with the police or not.

Offline, open carriers came together in "open carry picnics," sometimes in jurisdictions with a history of police harassment, to gather like-minded people and encourage gun-shy members to try open carrying. They organized armed marches to protest police harassment of open carriers—as happened in Birmingham, Michigan, in the summer of 2013 and in Romulus, Michigan, in the spring of 2014—and met with law enforcement and other government officials to discuss the policing of open carriers. And they held open carry seminars in gun stores and shooting ranges to educate people about the legalities of open carry and related topics—at one seminar I attended, Fourth Amendment rights,

Fifth Amendment rights, and even citizen's arrest laws were discussed. The majority of open carriers who attended these kinds of events were white men, and they tended to take place in suburban and rural areas of Michigan—although events have taken place in Detroit, including an annual picnic at Belle Isle that draws mostly African Americans.

Like many open carriers, Anthony attended open carry events, and he open carried wherever he legally could—at coffee shops,[39] on walks around his neighborhood, even once on public school property.[40] His actions led to police interactions. Sometimes, a concerned citizen would see Anthony and dial 911 to report a "man with a gun"; other times, police would notice and confront him directly. Though arguably minor in consequence (after all, Anthony was never formally arrested), these interactions sharpened Anthony's belief that public law enforcement officers often violate the rights of citizens. From one interaction, Anthony learned that police could threaten to "illegally" arrest him:

> I got stopped [by the police], and the city's attorney came back and said that the police didn't break any law. Cops can threaten to make an illegal arrest. But until they actually go through with it and lie on a police report, there's no crime. So the attorney is saying the cop can legally *threaten* to arrest you if you don't leave a public place. To me, it's a Fourth Amendment issue. You're searching and seizing. You're forcing me to leave. To me, that is no different than saying "You're in our custody."

Among open carriers, Anthony's experiences and understandings of the police were not uncommon. Most open carriers emphasized that they are "not anti-police" and chalked up their experiences to a "few bad apples" within public law enforcement, but their attitudes toward police fundamentally differed from other white gun carriers'. They saw police not simply as ineffective and inadequate but also as manipulative, inflammatory, and accusatory.

Part of their dismay and even disbelief at their own experiences of police harassment might be explained by their own expectations about how they should be treated—expectations that differentiated them from gun carriers of color. Although a couple of white open carriers reported physical abuse by police,[41] for the most part, white open carriers echoed

Anthony in that they entered into encounters with police with an *entitlement to rights* rather than an *expectation of mistreatment*. White gun carriers seemed to sincerely believe in the force of the law,[42] trusting that as law-abiding Americans under the full protection of the law, police should, and ultimately must, recognize their rights. Anthony, for example, responded to these experiences by telling me that he now *wanted* to get arrested for gun rights. He believed that by becoming the "test case," his actions could eventually lead to police reform.

This is a very different approach than that taken by the gun carriers of color I met. Henry, an African American, told me that he appreciated people like Anthony but that he preferred to "fly under the radar":

> I like the fact that some people have enough nerve and are willing to put their freedom [on the line] to a certain degree or even their physical well-being at risk in order to push this law that's on the books, and help everyone to be able to carry without getting harassed by the police. I like those people, but I'm not one of the ones who would want to be out there and push this. It would go bad for me, probably. I couldn't stand a lot of the pushing around: the police approaching me, and I know he's in violation of my rights and he wants to push me around and handcuff me and slam me on the ground. I don't know how I'd react to stuff like that. It might go sideways on me, and I might end up getting shot up. So, I keep my gun covered. I try to obey the law. I try not to bring any unnecessary stress to myself. I try to fly under the radar, where I'm not bringing too much undue attention to myself.

Here, Henry describes an imagined police encounter that is at risk not of turning *illegal* but of becoming *lethal*. He wasn't thinking about arrest or about his various rights being violated, as Anthony was: he was worried about "getting shot up." Henry's concerns resonate with widespread presumptions within overpoliced communities about expectations of police harassment, much like Gerald, Phil, and George.

The expectation of mistreatment comprises an important difference that distinguishes gun carriers of color from white gun carriers who critique the police as rights violators. Both groups react with indignation, but from different starting points. For white gun carriers, police harassment shatters an entitlement to rights, whereas for minority gun carriers, it confirms an expectation of mistreatment.[43]

What Does a Gun Say?

It's not just that men attached different meanings to guns; it's also the case that the public and the police saw openly carried guns differently based on the race and gender of the carrier.[44] I learned this firsthand. As part of my research, I too occasionally carried a gun openly. Always unsolicited, I was often approached by male strangers (never female strangers) while openly armed: one white, thirty-something man approached me with his business card (he was a photographer) to tell me he was "pro-gun" and thinks it's "hot" when women carry; at a coffee shop, a white man in his seventies who could barely walk with a cane managed to make it over to my table to tell me that he was happy to see that "women are finally doing this"; two white men in their forties who waited behind me in line for coffee snickered, "Do you know how to actually use that?" and "Does your boyfriend know you do this?"; a police officer from a unit well known to harass open carriers whistled at me as I walked by; one twenty-something African American man walked past me in a grocery store, smiled, and jokingly put his hands up, laughing, "I didn't do it!" This last instance stuck out as particularly revealing, because it captured so succinctly the complicated social life of guns and their bearers. It hit right at the intersection of race and gender. On the one hand, the man explicitly called out my (racial) privilege by putting me into the role of law enforcer and him into the position of suspected criminal. On the other hand, he did so in a jocular way, simultaneously emphasizing my demoted status as a woman. Not a citizen-protector, not a criminal, I was a joke.

All of these instances suggest that the symbolic valence of guns—especially when wielded openly—is not fixed. It is informed by a much broader constellation of racial and gendered meanings. What a gun "says" is, in part, determined by who is carrying it. A gun may transform a Black man into a criminal; a white man into a citizen-protector; a white woman into a joke (perhaps a "hot" joke). Regardless of the carrier's intention, a gun could carry fundamentally different meanings on different bodies; it could provoke radically different kinds of responses from police; and it could compel quite different political orientations. As gun carriers struggled to assert themselves as citizen-protectors or to critique the police, race and gender made this easier for some gun carriers than for others.

"Outlawing" the Police

This point applies not just to individuals who are carrying guns for self-protection, but also to those who more proactively use guns to protest police misconduct. Open carriers in Michigan and elsewhere often use public gatherings of armed men (and sometimes women) to protest police harassment of open carriers; support businesses that refuse to ban open carry; and generally promote public awareness about Second Amendment rights. To protest police, open carriers generally take one of two tactics: they organize a public march or picnic in a jurisdiction where an open carrier had allegedly been harassed, in order to "reclaim" the city, or they gather a group of open-carrying men to enter a police station to protest an unlawful ticket, city ordinance, or act of police harassment. The latter, obviously, is a much more confrontational tactic. Open carry picnics and marches are fairly commonplace (in warmer months, open carry picnics occurred throughout the state on a monthly, bimonthly, and even weekly basis), but I only heard of a handful of cases in which open carriers entered police stations. I was invited to one of these protest events, and what I observed further demonstrated how race and gender shape not just how carriers think about their guns but what their guns mean to others.

About halfway through my fieldwork, a white open carrier I had met was ticketed and fined for openly carrying a firearm in a place where (according to the police officer) he was not legally entitled to carry. After reviewing the law, he realized that there was no legal basis for the ticket. He called up a few of his friends, and soon a group of open carriers decided to descend on the police station, located in a white inner suburb that bordered Detroit, openly carrying guns in order to demand that the ticket be dismissed. Open carriers had already staged a handful of such events, which are—to the surprise of people unaware of the intricacies of gun laws—entirely legal in Michigan. I was asked to come and—if I wanted to—open carry into the police station. After hearing stories about police interactions exclusively from men who openly carried, I was curious how police would react to an open-carrying woman. So, I decided to join them.

There were about eight men, all of whom were white, and they ranged in age from their early twenties to their mid-fifties. Some were fathers; one was a military veteran. An unarmed white woman in her early twenties volunteered to videotape the incident, while the male gun carriers wore audio recorders. We walked into the police station as a group on a Sunday morning, and the gun carrier who originally had been ticketed approached the front desk to demand that his ticket be dismissed. The police officer behind the counter stood up immediately, telling us to leave; we were told that none of us, beyond the ticketed person, were entitled to be there. One of gun carriers responded that the station was public property, while another gun carrier pulled out his cell phone to dial an on-call lawyer. About a half dozen officers appeared from a basement staircase, and we were instructed to raise our hands: each of our guns would be examined to see if it were legally registered to our name. It felt almost mechanical, like police were merely executing procedure; there was nothing else they could legally do. The gun carriers protested, but all of them submitted, raising their arms for the police to remove their guns from their holsters. As the police disarmed the gun carriers, they traded insults: *Oh, you think you're a big man now?* one cop asked facetiously of an open carrier.

Perhaps it was not surprising to hear cops use gendered jabs; in other audio-recorded stops open carriers shared, I heard police turn to gendered insults as police confrontations escalated. In one stop, an exasperated officer exclaimed, "I don't know what your big thing is. Wanna be a big man out here, walk around with a gun? 'Oh, I'm cool!'" On the one hand, this reflected the gendered nature of public law enforcement. With the police functioning as a social institution that both enforces the law and promotes masculine values,[45] police stops allow officers to criminalize civilians by asserting their own authoritative brand of masculinity.[46] Police stops, seizures, and searches are often executed by symbolically or physically dominating civilians in ways that ritualistically reinforce "the masculine esteem" of officers[47]—whether or not those civilians are armed with guns. And if it's true that "possession of a [gun] is an essential part of being an American policemen . . ."

and "even more than the badge, it sets an officer apart from ordinary citizens,"[48] then civilians who carry guns legally—*especially* into a police station—are a direct threat to the masculine authority of state officials, particularly when they compel police into recognizing their right to be armed.

On the other hand, open carriers often imputed gendered meanings to their interactions with police. They themselves portrayed police confrontations as masculinity contests, and at times they even described their ability to stand up to the police as a redemption of their masculine identity—the home page of Michigan Open Carry explicitly justified open carry as a way to say "to the world, I'm my own man . . . I'm willing to stand up and speak truth to authority, the very authority that we have empowered."[49] In doing so, they asserted not just an entitlement to fair treatment under the law but also authority *over* the police, often emphasizing that police serve the public, not the other way around. And to this end, they prided themselves in becoming well-versed in the legalities of open carry in order to "outlaw" the police, a term Richard used in passing to describe gun carriers who know firearms law better than the police do and who rally this knowledge during police stops.[50]

Back in the police station, gun carriers also imputed gender into this interaction, with one of the open carriers joking afterward that the entire incident was *a big dick-swinging contest.*[51] In other words, what was at stake in this interaction was not simply the proper enforcement of the law nor the actual threat of violence, but also a gendered game, which helped to make sense of the bizarre mood in the police station that day. Despite both sides being heavily armed and ostensibly gathered on behalf of the just enforcement of the law, neither the open carriers nor the police seemed fearful for their safety so much as irritated by the others' presence. Indeed, the police seemed to regard the processing of the guns as a formality. The serial numbers were slowly run. The guns were handed back, one by one, and the police officers asked each gun carrier if he could reload outside as a courtesy. The gun carriers agreed. The original ticketee's name was called, his gun returned, and he was told that his ticket would be dismissed. The officer said simply, *I'm not sure why they gave this to you.*

The incident could have ended there, but then something truly unexpected happened: with just my gun left, one of the officers pulled me aside to tell me—to my disbelief—that my gun turned up as unregistered in the state's database. I was shocked and upset, and immediately imagined the mocking headlines: "Berkeley PhD Student Arrested for Illegal Possession of Firearm."

But there would be no headlines; I quickly produced my registration card (which I always carried, even though I was not bound to do so by law). When the police officer saw the slip and returned my gun, he thanked me for having the piece of paper, but said it didn't really matter—he *trusted me* and would have let me have my gun back even without my paperwork.

Without this paperwork, however, the police officer had no way of knowing whether I was the victim of an honest bureaucratic error[52] or guilty of carrying an unregistered handgun, a felony that carries a sentence of up to five years in prison or a $2,500 fine. Perhaps the realities of race and gender transformed the meaning of my "unregistered" gun from a felony to a clerical snafu. Had I acted aggressively or presented myself as more masculine, I may have received different treatment. But because I played into the role of a compliant young woman, I was read as neither literally threatening the safety of the officers nor symbolically threatening the masculine monopoly on policing. My gun might as well have been loaded with blanks. Moreover, had I not been a *white* woman—had I been Gerald or Phil, for example—I'm not sure the officer would have viewed me as a lawful citizen who deserved a break. In other words, if what happened in that police station was a gendered game, this was also a game that white Americans—so often given the benefit of the doubt during police stops as compared to people of color—were better equipped to instigate by virtue of the broader context of race, policing, and profiling in America.

Conclusion: Everyday Infringements

For 130 years the National Rifle Association of America has stood in opposition to all who step-by-step would reduce the Second Amendment right to keep and bear arms to a privilege granted by those who govern. NRA continues to fight against those who would dictate that American citizens should seek police permission to exercise their constitutional rights.

—National Rifle Association Institute for Legislative Action

For most gun carriers in Michigan, "seeking police permission" means exactly that: an increased vulnerability to police because of disclosure requirements. Nevertheless, their right to carry a firearm is usually acknowledged by public law enforcement, especially if they are carrying concealed, are attentive to their other law-abiding behaviors (such as speeding), and don't look "suspicious." For the relatively small portion of gun carriers who step outside the boundaries of recognizably "lawful" gun carry (whether because they choose to carry openly or because they "look" like potential criminals), "seeking police permission" is not an abstract problem that only minimally affects whether and how one carries a gun. Instead, police harassment is an everyday possibility, and some gun carriers—like Jason or Anthony—see this possibility as an opportunity for modeling and asserting a particular kind of armed citizenship to the police and to the public more broadly.

Perhaps Richard, Jason, Anthony, Phil, and the other gun carriers described in this chapter are merely examples of the "paranoid gun nut," driven by irrational fears about growing police power and government tyranny. Perhaps their words are best laid alongside sentiments voiced by people like Alex Jones, who declared on CNN that "1776 will commence again!" if the US government attempts to ban guns, because the Second Amendment, after all, is about protecting against government tyranny, oppression, and infringement. But decontextualizing gun carriers' politics and reducing it to rhetoric obscures the kinds of everyday infringements that shape how some gun carriers understand and experience their guns and their relation to the police.

Open carriers and gun carriers of color represent distinct strands of gun politics, drawn together by their experiences of police violation. Of course, gun-carrying men who have experienced police harassment share much with gun-carrying men who have not. They are similar in how they understand crime and how they embrace both the right to self-defense and the duty to protect. The difference is that those gun carriers who have experienced police harassment are not just interested in supplementing a weak police force, but in symbolically challenging that force and its monopoly on policing. As Richard said, "Law enforcement says, 'Call 911. You know, you're not a police officer!' The reality is, you are and you can be if you want to be—strictly legally speaking."

Gun carriers like Richard saw their decision to carry a firearm as a way to publicly perform gun rights and model a particular kind of citizenship in which the public no longer relies on, or needs, the police. For these gun carriers, guns are not just tools of protection; they're also political tools used to "talk back" to the state in ways that are deeply shaped by race and gender. This need to talk back, especially for gun carriers of color, is embedded in public law enforcement practices—the overpolicing of poor people of color, the militarization of the police, and a swelling reliance on investigatory stops targeted at "suspicious" individuals—that unfolded as part of the War on Crime.

Experiences of government infringement came in the form of their local police departments, not hypothetical "jack-booted thugs" (as Wayne LaPierre famously described federal agents in the 1990s). Certainly, the NRA mobilizes anti-government rhetoric by emphasizing police *inefficacy* and, abstractly, government abrogation of gun rights. But the NRA does not endorse a more radical model of citizenship that centers on proactively and concretely confronting police *violation*. The NRA has consistently supported concealed carry over open carry, and I have never seen NRA materials that promoted directly confronting the police over rights violations in the ways described in this chapter.

Born out of a gun-rich environment the NRA helped to create through its promotion of gun carry laws, these gun carriers comprise a new generation of pro-gun Americans. They might be the target of police harassment because of the color of their skin, or they might attract additional police scrutiny due to their decision to openly carry a gun. Either way, their interactions with law enforcement provide an experiential awareness of police as inadequate protectors *and* as aggressive violators. Among these men, guns become the tools not just to claim a right to self-defense or a duty to protect, but also to assert oneself as lawful and to force police to recognize their guns as lawfully carried. This willingness and ability to compel recognition from the police is racialized and gendered. Confronted with the masculine authority of the police, white gun carriers *chose*, at times, to engage public law enforcement, while gun carriers of color (and, sometimes, white gun carriers as well) were *compelled* to do so. Their displays of lawfulness functioned as a form of political protest that, depending on gun carriers' social positionality, could challenge ideas about who counts as a criminal and who is authorized to police.

While not all gun carriers engaged the police in the ways described in this chapter, the gun carriers in this chapter did reveal a widely shared belief among pro-gun Americans: namely, that legally armed Americans are fundamentally lawful, morally upstanding people. Whether emphasizing their right to self-defense, their duty to protect others, or an obligation to "stand up" to police, gun carriers defined themselves—and distinguished themselves from armed criminals—through their embrace of the law and the moral politics they associate with gun carry. Bearing guns as evidence of their status as rights-bearing citizens, gun carriers defined themselves by their stance before the law.

This analysis, however, overlooks a small but important subset of gun carriers: those whose decision to carry a gun ultimately leads them to break the law. A stark contrast to open carriers—who fastidiously follow the law in order to push it to its limits—this subset includes those gun carriers who commit crimes like aggravated assault, domestic violence, or brandishing. Some may break the law out of an opportunistic use of their gun, but, as I will show in the next chapter, they may also come to break the law because they believe—erroneously—that they are acting within their rights. These are not the gun carriers celebrated by the NRA or other pro-gun groups as model citizens. Nevertheless, they reveal something about the broader moral politics of guns: that gun carriers may ultimately break the law not *despite* this broader moral politics, but *because* of it.

6

Jumping the Gun

IT SHOULD HAVE BEEN A forgettable stop. Aaron just wanted to grab a couple of lottery tickets on his drive home, and with his kids in tow, he pulled into a gas station in a Detroit suburb. He carried a gun out of a duty to protect himself and his children. However, his split-second decision to play the lotto would ultimately lead him to pull a firearm on an unarmed woman that he believed was threatening his children. He entered that gas station as one of the "good guys with a gun"; he left as one of the "bad guys," arrested for felonious assault and eventually pleading guilty to a charge of brandishing. This chapter examines how Aaron moved from one category of gun owner (lawful, citizen-protector) to another (criminal).

Policy debates about guns often presume that these two categories—lawful gun owners and criminal gun users—are mutually exclusive. Again and again, we hear both sides of the gun debate claim that (to paraphrase) "lawful gun owners should not be punished for the actions of criminals"; "no one wants to take away anyone's legitimate rights to self-defense"; and that gun policy should focus on "keeping firearms out of the wrong hands." The presumption behind all of these statements is that there is a clear line between the good, honest, and morally upstanding gun carrier, who never strays from the law, and the bad, depraved, armed criminal, intent on subverting lax gun laws for nefarious ends.

But what about the good guy who makes a mistake? Or the good guy who goes bad? Widespread gun carry opens up the possibility for otherwise law-abiding people to become embroiled in crimes such as brandishing, felonious assault,[1] and negligent discharge—crimes that they may well not have committed had they not been armed. Every year, gun carriers in Michigan have their gun licenses revoked. According to the Michigan State Police, from 2003 to 2013, almost 4,700 residents lost their licenses, with more than 3,800 revocations due to felony or misdemeanor charges or convictions. For the roughly 600,000 concealed pistol licenses (CPLs) issued from 2003 to 2013, there were 1,667 incidents of gun carriers arrested for a crime while using or brandishing a firearm. In this time, gun carriers were charged with 2,861 counts of assault and related offenses,[2] resulting in 846 convictions.

Gun carriers, though, are not more likely to commit crime than the general population. As a general rule, a gun carrier is *much* less likely to be arrested than the general population. This should not be surprising: concealed carriers are, by law, a select group of people. They are screened for clean criminal records; they have had some exposure to laws surrounding firearms and are probably more knowledgeable about them than the general population; and they are motivated to comply with the law in order to maintain their gun rights.

Nevertheless, some gun carriers break the law. Rather than asking whether gun carriers are inherently more or less law-abiding than the general population, this chapter examines the conditions under which some gun carriers come to break the law. What kinds of situations are guns—and their carriers—ill-prepared to address? How do some gun carriers come to make poor choices and ultimately break the law? How do implicit assumptions about what constitutes a threat lead some gun carriers to misinterpret or overreact to a threat?

This chapter argues that the answer may not lie in opportunistic uses of the law as much as in a commitment to the ideals of citizenship captured by the citizen-protector model, on the one hand, and inadequate formal and informal training, on the other. Gun carriers embrace a moral politics to explain and justify their decisions to carry a gun, but this politics—and the formal and informal training practices that go along with it—is not always enough to navigate real-life threats. Whereas self-defense laws open up the possibility for gun carriers (now armed like police) to engage in problematic policing tactics usually associated with public law enforcement (for example, racial profiling), training does little to shape students in terms of how they understand and adjudicate between what is a threat and what is a stereotype.

The ideals, obligations, and duties associated with gun carry do not just provide men with a sense of relevance, dignity, and authority. For some, like Aaron, guns also help create the conditions to overestimate and overreact to threats. Even with the best of intentions, gun carriers are susceptible to life-changing mistakes and misuses shaped by presumptions; these may result in arrest, injury, or even death. Put differently, gun carriers' embracing of guns to protect self and others provides a moral script to justify one's decision to carry, but simply carrying a firearm can't prepare one for navigating real-life threats. As gun carry becomes part of everyday life, carriers may paradoxically participate in the very acts of violence—from brandishing to shooting—that they profess to arm themselves against.

To this end, this chapter largely focuses on one case: it starts with an in-depth description of the encounter in which Aaron believed he was protecting his children. I focus on the step-by-step unfolding of this incident to emphasize the many factors that shaped the encounter, the confusion and mental fog that Aaron experienced, the way in which Aaron drew on the training and moral politics of gun carry in making sense of the incident, and how his training and moral politics failed to protect him from committing a crime.

From Citizen-Protector to Criminal

I met Aaron, an African American father, at a diner shortly after the incident. In the interview, I learned that in virtually all ways but one, Aaron was a model gun carrier: he had hundreds of hours of range training and he'd been an NRA-certified range safety officer for years before acquiring his firearms instructor certification from the NRA in the hopes of starting his own firearms business. He described himself as fastidiously law-abiding and meticulously safety-conscious, waxing on about his collection of 1911s, the precautions he took in securing his stash of firearms, and his outrage at the "angry" and "violent" rhetoric espoused by gun control advocates. He was soft-spoken and physically unintimidating, a churchgoer who rescheduled our interview to make sure he could attend service with his family. He mentioned his kids repeatedly.

Indeed, Aaron seemed to be just the kind of model citizen-protector that the NRA promoted in its training courses and that gun carriers embraced as their identity: articulate about guns and gun safety; well-versed in the law; cool, calm, collected, and morally motivated. What makes Aaron's story important is that he seemed to defy all of the stereotypes of gun carriers as trigger-happy macho men. That is, until he pulled his firearm on an unarmed woman.

Aaron said he "rarely" goes out at night, but one evening he decided he wanted to stop at a gas station for lottery tickets. He pulled up behind another car:

> I pull up to a gas station, and she's at a pump. I pull a good four to five feet away from her, not blocking right in front of her. I didn't come in and cut her off when she's pulling out or something. I get out of the car, and walk up to the door [of the gas station], and I see her coming up to the door. [She's] one of those people you see having a bad day, you know, pissed at something or someone. So I just give her a wide berth, float on by, and uh, as I'm going inside the doorway there, I've noticed she's talking to me, you know? She's giving it to me. You know, for a lady who's old enough to be my mother, to say the least—and for the situation, she's just belligerent. Cussing, F this, and B-I-Ts, all that! She's saying, "You're going to block me in!"

At this point in the conversation, Aaron maintains that he is on the right side of common sense: he is cognizant of his surroundings and stays a good distance away from a woman who he describes as "belligerent" and "having a bad day." According to Aaron, the woman then moved from just having a "bad day" to threatening him:

> So she was driving [a] nice truck, beautiful truck, right? At first I'm just kind of letting her talk, and then she says, well I'll move this MF [motherfucker] myself! I'll tear this—you know, B [bitch] up! You know, all that type of stuff! So I'm like, maybe you don't see it—I don't see how you couldn't see it, but my kids are right there, my children are in the car. "You need to just back the F [fuck] up!"

I asked Aaron for clarification as to whether she actually said those words. He responded, "Oh, yeah! 'You need to just back the F [fuck] up!' The way I responded to her was, 'Ma'am, now if you had just simply asked me to move my car.' I am a respectable guy. Here's an elder, clear enough. Like I said, she was probably old enough to be my mom." He said he would have happily moved the car to avoid a fight and be a role model to his kids. But, he insisted that she *ask* him to do so. "I turned to her, I was like 'Ma'am, if you would have just asked me, I wouldn't have had a problem. Both of my kids are sitting right there, you know, so I'm—I got to be a role model. But she's not pausing to hear what I was saying. So, I turn and walk away." He went back inside to buy his lottery tickets, leaving his kids alone in the car.

This turned out to be the pivotal moment. Before he could buy his tickets, Aaron heard someone say, "Oh, she's in the truck!" When he turned his head to look at the truck, he saw that it was just inches—not feet—away from his car. He rushed out to the car, primed to react:

> I had it [the gun] in my front right pocket, I had it on my side, finger off the trigger, and I'm in a defensive stance. Even in her statement [to police] she said I was four to five feet, so I didn't run up on [her] window or nothing like that. "Ma'am, you need to stop—you need to back up. I am a CPL holder, and I am armed." Now, this lady, she was mad. She gives me that look like "Uh, no you didn't!" You know what I mean? And reaches over and grabs her phone. So when she does that, I don't know what she's coming up with.

CCTV video showed that Aaron had actually removed the gun from the holster and was holding it in his hand. At this point, whether Aaron realized it or not, he had irrevocably escalated the situation. Now, the woman was grabbing for something—Aaron at first can't tell if it is a firearm or a cell phone to dial 911. It turned out to be the latter. Aaron continues:

> So I move to my right so I can get a visual with what is coming up. Keep in mind I'm already paying attention. I'm at a gas station, and I'm facing [a major road]. Okay? So, when she comes around, I notice the phone, I'm standing by the store doorway by now . . . realize

I don't have my phone, starting to get the sweats a little bit, now the adrenaline is kicking in, right? So I had to recollect myself. What am I doing here? Am I here to fight with people? Or am I here to take care of my business and move on? So I'm like, "You go over here, get my [lottery tickets]" [talking to himself].

Aaron now admits that the heated encounter clouded his ability to process the situation. Whether justified or not, his body told him to fight or flee, and he attempted to "recollect himself" by "taking care of business and moving on." Yet again, he missed a chance to move his car and protect his children (the reason, after all, that he maintained that he was concerned about the woman in the first place). He went back into the store for his lottery tickets *after* threatening the woman with his gun. Even Aaron admits that this was a bizarre reaction:

So when I come back to the store, I'm thinking, okay, this is one of those things that we teach all the time about, you know, try to limit your mistakes. So I can't find my phone, so I'm thinking—tell the store clerk to call the police, since I don't have my phone. But as I go up there, I ordered the [lottery tickets]. Why? I don't know. Sometimes in training—we have people go up to the line, and they say you go left, and everybody goes left—five people in front of you go left, and if for whatever reason, you get up there, the adrenaline is flowing, and a lot of stuff is going on, and it's to the right. So why did I go left instead of right? Why did I order [lottery tickets] instead of have the clerk call [the police]—I don't know! But I did that.

Though aware of his mental disarray ("Why did I go left instead of right? Why did I order [lottery tickets] instead of have the clerk call [the police]—I don't know!"), Aaron nevertheless maintained that he had followed his training, and that he had acted in a way that deterred further violence. He notes that "it could have gone a lot worse," and, by and large, he seems to believe that his actions were lawful and morally justified:

How I handled her—I actually was pleased, you know, because like I said, that's what you want in any situation to do. To deter before it becomes violent. Even though she was making that threat, you know, I'm glad that I didn't jump the gun—with adrenaline, all that stuff—I'm glad that I was able to keep some type of composure. As far as training—I am just trying to limit mistakes. It could have gone a lot worse.

Aaron wanted to be a "role model" for his kids, but he soon found himself embarrassed in front of them. After the woman called the police, officers started to show up:

I got ten cops standing around me—you know what I mean? Everybody who is riding down the street is looking out their windows and stuff. Plus, both of my kids are staring—*staring*—at me. So, I told them [the police officers] what happened . . . So, he [one of the officers] said, "Sir, could you turn around?" And I'm like, "Am I being arrested?" And he's like, "Yes." I'm like, "What for?" He's like, "We'll tell you after we put the handcuffs on." [Laughs]. They handcuffed me, let me know it was for felonious assault and this, that, and the other. So, now my daughter is screaming, and I'm trying to calm her down. I can't talk to him [the police officer] no more because I'm trying to calm her down.

He was arrested in front of his children for assaulting an unarmed woman with a deadly weapon. Maintaining that he "kept some type of composure" and "limited mistakes," he now offered that his major blunder was talking to the police:

One funny thing about the situation, and I teach it all the time, and I never really understood how powerful and overwhelming that urge to talk is. You understand? I'm telling myself the whole time, you don't need to talk, point out evidence. This is a bad situation, but I haven't done anything, and whatever I did, I know it's well within my rights, and [the officer] asked if I would make a statement, so I'm thinking—well, I've always prepared myself for a shooting [rather than a brandishing] . . . It's a fine line that you have to walk.

In the end, Aaron pled guilty to a charge of brandishing, was stripped of his gun rights for several years, and lost his collection of 1911 handguns.

Of course, Aaron's narrative paints only his side of the story—I was unable to speak to the woman who figures so prominently in it. As such, Aaron's story reveals not so much what happened as how Aaron, an otherwise law-abiding gun carrier, made sense of a situation and justified his response. Indeed, Aaron's story suggests that it is possible for gun carriers to be "too prepared" for trouble. Had the woman been armed and actively threatening the children, Aaron's gun could have been a lifesaver. But she wasn't, and Aaron seemed to have a hard time processing the ambiguous threat that she posed—or did not. Gun carriers often recite the adage that "you shouldn't bring a knife to a gunfight," but Aaron committed the opposite error: he brought a gun to a verbal fight, misreading the situation and misusing his gun. He paid dearly for the incident; the woman could have paid far more dearly had he pulled the trigger.

Ready for a Gunfight

As noted above, at one point in our conversation, Aaron told me, "I've always prepared myself for a shooting." He said this as a way of admitting that the incident at the gas station had caught him off guard precisely *because* he had prepared himself for the worst. Finding himself in a situation that had not escalated to the point of requiring a gun, Aaron's go-to response was still a gun. The concept of "forward panic" helps to clarify this response. Forward panic is "a period of prolonged tension/ fear" followed by "a frenzied rush of destruction."[3] Neither a product of the violent disposition of individuals nor a rational calculation of the threat at stake, this excessive aggression is a product of violent situations characterized by "a buildup of tension, which is released into a fren- zied attack when the situation makes it easy to do so."[4] At some point, violence moves from a rational choice to an "unstoppable" force: "the various kinds of tension/fear that come out in a rush of violence have often been described as an adrenalin rush" and violence feels "for the time being . . . unstoppable."[5] Phrases like "I was out of control" or "I don't know what I was thinking" capture this rush of aggression.

Some version of forward panic seems to have been at work in Aaron's decision-making: tension built as the woman verbally accosted Aaron and then started driving her car into his. Had she simply rear-ended his car, he might not have brandished his firearm: he would have had to figure out whether she had made a mistake, and whether her actions constituted violence. But with the buildup, he had already decided that she was a potential threat. A "sudden trigger"[6]—in this case, Aaron turning around to see her car within inches of his children—led him to overreact.

Forward panic helps make sense of how Aaron's incident escalated, but it doesn't explain why it started in the first place. Why was Aaron reacting at all? Why not simply drive away? Was Aaron engaged in a version of profiling (he never identifies the race or class status of the woman, but he emphasizes her street vernacular)—which led him to overreact to the threat? And what do we make of Aaron's repeated emphasis on his children and his role as their protector and role model?

Perhaps there is an easy answer to all of these questions: Aaron thought he was in the clear—at least legally speaking—because of expanded laws surrounding self-defense. As described in chapter 1, the United States has gradually moved from a "duty to retreat" doctrine, inherited from the English common law on self-defense, to "no duty to retreat." "Duty to retreat" means that anyone who uses force in self-defense must first show that they had made every "reasonable" attempt to flee the attack; "no duty to retreat" removes this legal imperative. Where and whether one doctrine or another applies varies by state. For example, by the early 1900s all states had adopted—formally or in practice—the "Castle Doctrine," providing an "exception" to the "duty to retreat" when an attack occurs in one's home (that is, there is no duty to retreat if someone unlawfully enters another's property). As legal theorist P. Luevonda Ross notes, "When a person is in his home, he is not required to retreat further. This is logical because when in the home, a person has already retreated as far as he can from the perils of society. By limiting the exception to the necessity to retreat to the castle, the self-defense doctrine was easy to enforce without difficulty in distinction."[7]

Stand Your Ground laws expand the "no duty to retreat" doctrine "beyond the castle and into the streets."[8] Under these laws, now in force in more than two dozen states, a person has no duty to retreat in any place he or she has a legal right to be. The law "presumes that the layperson is justified in the use of deadly force and prohibits [law enforcement from making] an arrest"[9] unless clear evidence exists to attest that force was not justified. This applies if the shooter is the victim of an attack or is in imminent danger or if they are intervening in a felony that places the victim at risk of grave bodily harm or death. In the absence of a threat or attack, however, a shooter is not defending but rather committing a felony with an armed weapon—brandishing, assaulting, or even murdering.

There is no reason to think that Aaron was not well aware of these laws and legalities, and there is no reason to believe that he disregarded them or felt that they entitled him to threaten others with his gun. Even though the state of Michigan only requires an eight-hour course to obtain a concealed pistol, Aaron was very well trained: he regularly practiced shooting, worked as a range safety officer at a local range, and received his certification as an NRA instructor. When I interviewed him, he was in the process of starting his own firearms academy—a process that was stalled when his firearms were confiscated.

Rather than revealing Aaron as inherently lawful or criminal, incidents such as this one demonstrate the impractical rationality of law. Despite a number of rules and laws that govern how to act in self-defense scenarios, violent interactions are governed by moral politics and interactional dynamics that often render law an afterthought. In their study of social workers, police officers, and teachers, for example, policing scholars Stephen Maynard-Moody and Michael Musheno[10] find that even state agents—people we would expect would to be most adept at applying the letter of the law—must engage in pragmatic improvisation to "fit" the law to everyday life. Their analysis desmontrates how the complexity of social life exceeds the simplicity of the law. When people are faced with unfamiliar situations, they unwittingly rely on deeply ingrained predispositions, expectations, and patterns of practice—recall that Pierre Bourdieu calls this "habitus"—to navigate them. Habitus can include deep-seated, and even unintentional, assumptions about what a threat looks like and how one should react to it.

Gendered Acts: From Masculine Protectionism to Macho Posturing

Aaron passingly acknowledges that he was "within [his] rights," but he never refers to self-defense when reflecting on his arrest. He emphasizes the verbal altercation, but insists that his gun use is wrapped up in his desire to protect his children, in line with what Iris Marion Young calls "masculinist protection."[11] This is reflected in the moment in which he sees the threat peaking: he rushes out to protect his children as the woman backs up her vehicle toward his car. Strikingly, the woman is not typecast with maternal imagery (as gun carriers often used to describe women) but is presented as an older, single, truck-driving woman unconcerned with the children inside of Aaron's car.

Masculine protectionism is also reflected in how Aaron understands his own actions: he repeatedly portrayed himself as a conscientious "role model" to his children, an image that is abruptly shattered when he is handcuffed in front of them and his "daughter starts screaming." Indeed, Aaron's actions are incomprehensible without taking into account how they are informed by his identity as a father. His narrative of events situates him as a citizen-protector[12] motivated to protect not just himself but also others, and, in pulling his gun on an unarmed woman, Aaron acted out a duty to protect others—or, at least, that's how Aaron understood the event.

But Aaron overestimated a threat that never materialized. His emphasis on protecting probably made it more likely that he would overreact. Seamlessly crossing the line from the honorable violence of protection into the masculine bravado of brandishing, that night made visible the fragile boundaries of masculinist protection and exposed how the moral politics of guns coexists with, and even gives rise to, a culture of masculine excess characterized by macho posturing.

Aaron was the only gun carrier I met who actually crossed this line from lawful gun owner to criminal. But other gun carriers emphasized the perils of masculinity by complaining about *other* gun carriers and *their* macho posturing. Henry, an African American, said "the macho thing is just terrible" because wanting to "play the hero" often lands men in trouble. Instead of de-escalating potentially violent situations, he suggested, men tend to exacerbate them. Eddie, a white gun carrier, echoed this sentiment by drawing a gender binary between men's and women's reactions to threats: women, he said, are more likely to find an exit strategy, while men are likely to endanger themselves and others by rushing to "prove" themselves in a fight. Timothy, a white gun carrier who embraced a duty to protect, also warned: "Vigilantism will get you killed . . . those who want to run out there and play vigilante, they're going to meet their own demise."

Gun carriers often stressed the importance of avoiding violence. As one instructor said, *Avoid a lethal engagement and you avoid the emergency room, the morgue, the cemetery. You can call me a name, and you know what? You're right. I'll let you be right.* Yet, mixed messages circulate within gun culture about whether to be cool, calm, and resolute citizen-protectors or trigger-happy macho men. Sayings like "I'd rather be tried by twelve than carried by six" (that is, they'd rather be in the courtroom than the cemetery) suggest that there is virtue in overreacting to a threat. Certainly, gun carriers *prepare* for the worst, even if they maintain that they would walk away from most threats.

In contrast to Aaron's case, most examples of "manly" posturing do not escalate into a criminal encounter. Nevertheless, I witnessed my own share of gun carriers engaging in masculinity contests, which often centered on establishing who had the best (biggest?) gun, who knew the most about the mechanical minutia of firearms, and who had the best shot. Gun carriers passionately argued online about Serpa holsters, bulletproof vests, defensive flashlights, pepper spray, Glocks, and 1911s. These debates often revolved around establishing who was *the* authority on the issue at hand.

Other times, gun carriers called each other out for what their guns presumably said about their masculine identity. A subtle but revealing example: I was at a shooting range with Larry, a white gun carrier. As we were changing targets, someone else arrived with a Desert Eagle—an infamously large handgun—and began setting up a few lanes down from us. Not knowing the man, Larry immediately quipped: *I'm sorry, but I have a normal-sized penis,* implying that the other gun owner was compensating for "something" (a lack of masculine confidence) by using an impractically large handgun. While Larry betrayed his irritation at some male gun carriers, Henry, Eddie, and Timothy maintained that that attitude went beyond annoying to dangerous. They saw men like the Desert Eagle owner as "alpha males" (or "wannabe alpha males") more likely to start than avoid a fight.

As my fieldwork unfolded, I often wondered how I managed to find so many non-macho, clear-headed, and morally upstanding gun carriers. Gun carriers complained incessantly about the preponderance of "macho men" within gun culture, and even Aaron portrayed himself as cool and levelheaded despite his recent arrest. Where *were* all these fly-off-the-handle, tougher-than-thou gunslingers?

No doubt, Aaron's narrative can partly be explained by a likely desire to portray himself in the best light. But it still shows the multiple levels at which different masculinities operate within gun culture. Protectionist masculinity is a means by which gun carriers understand and justify the moral uprightness of arming themselves—as described in chapter 4. At the same time, men also engage in a variety of masculinity rituals aimed not so much at navigating the moral politics of guns but at jostling with other men. These masculinity contests resemble what sociologist Randall Collins[13] calls "boasting and blustering":

> It might seem obvious that boasting leads to violence because it is part of the culture of those who habitually fight. But this is ignoring the dirty little secret of violence—the barrier of tension/fear that makes fighting incompetent when it happens, and produces much more gesture than real fight . . . The culture of machismo, of the tough guys, the action scene, is mainly the activity of staging an impression of violence, rather than the violence itself . . . the world of boasting and bluster is a repetitive set of situations; much of the time they have their own equilibrium, staying within their own limits.

Here, Collins is parsing out the "impression of violence" from "violence itself." His point is that the social function of machismo is the *opposite* of what it appears to be. Rather than a way to instigate violence, verbal jostling may substitute for and even lower the chances of actual physical violence.

The displays of machismo on the shooting range (e.g., the Desert Eagle) or in heated debates (e.g., about which gun holster is the best or how eagerly someone would respond to a home invasion) are contained rituals that "stay within their own limits."[14] In my research, I never witnessed gun carriers at shooting ranges, at activist events, or during my interviews become visibly angry, raise their voices, or explicitly threaten someone else with violence.

"But," as Collins goes on to write, "sometimes [debating and jostling] spill over those limits."[15] And this is where Aaron's story is suggestive: Although blustering generally operates on a different plane than "violence itself," sometimes, when faced with confusing, complex, and possibly life-threatening situations that lie outside a familiar, ritualized space (e.g., the shooting range, or a pro-gun picnic), the lines between masculine bravado and masculinist protection are, in the moment, blurry. Add a keen compulsion to protect others who may be vulnerable, and some gun carriers may react in hyperaggressive ways that mark them as criminals, not citizen-protectors.

Racial and Classed Dangers: Institutionalized Blusters, Misrecognized Threats

Aaron's overreaction was not just the result of an overzealous embrace of protectionism. It was also the result of his interpretation of the threat he faced. Aaron may have been rushing to "play the hero," but he was not the only one in a fighting stance. After all, the woman was reportedly threatening Aaron to move his car, exclaiming: "Well, I'll move this MF [motherfucker] myself! I'll tear this B [bitch] up! . . . You need to just back the F [fuck] up!" Was this a legitimate threat or a boast and bluster of its own? As I said before, Aaron never explicitly describes the race or class status of the woman, nor does he mention her skin tone. Nevertheless, his description of her language, embodiment, and actions fit stereotypical images[16] of women of color who "act ghetto": loud, assertive, aggressive, bitchy. While I considered pressing him to explicitly identify the race of the woman, I chose to let this detail remain unknown; it could simplify the much more complex racialized and classed affect that Aaron had *already* placed front and center in the encounter. Indeed, the woman's skin tone did not matter as much as how she evoked a particular style of comportment and social status commonly associated with urban women of color—factors that are central to the social construction of race (and class) and that imbue physical characteristics such as skin tone with their social meaning, rather than the other way around.[17] And here is where the "racial and class dangers" lie: not necessarily in the threat that the specific woman herself poses, but the ways in which certain styles of behavior and presentation of self come to be read, in certain contexts, not as acts of boasting and blustering but as immediate danger.

As described previously, boasting and blustering are socially patterned and contextual: the same jostling by one armed man to another in a shooting range may be an imminent threat when waged on the street between a man and a woman. Put differently, the "social rituals that pretend to fight" and "conventionalized gesturing" are shaped by gender, race, and class, and they vary across social groups and social contexts. For example, middle-class conversations may include griping, whining, arguing, and even quarreling, but the repetitive, commonplace nature of this verbal jostling keeps violent conflict to a minimum.[18] Meanwhile, more assertive, more overt, and less polite forms of boasting and blustering lie outside the institutionalized boundaries of the "polite middle-class conversational ritual"[19]—and are better characterized by what some scholars have called the "street code"[20] or a "code of honor."[21] These terms help describe the institutionalized tolerance of violence and carry particular racial and class connotations. Scholars have used the term "street code" almost exclusively to refer to styles of behavior and talk prevalent in violent urban areas with high proportions of racial minorities. Meanwhile, "code of honor" and "culture of honor" have been used to describe the tolerance of violence among whites and racial minorities in the southern and western regions of the United States, as well as in urban areas.

Much of the scholarship on the "street code" and the "culture of honor" treats these styles and mannerisms as a means of *facilitating* violence. But what if these "codes" act not only as *facilitators* of violence but also—in some contexts—as its impediment? This is the question Collins entertains as he compares examples of "institutionalized bluster" across racial and class groups. To this end, he reads Elijah Anderson's[22] ethnography of a neighborhood in Philadelphia through the lens of ritualized violence, arguing that the "code of the street" is an example of "institutionalized bluster." The street code grows, Anderson suggests, in certain social contexts—where police protection is unreliable (at best) and aggressive (at worst), and where conditions of poverty place individuals at greater risk of violent confrontation—and is at least as much about *avoiding* violence as *engaging in* it. As Collins summarizes further, those who adhere to the street code embrace "a distinctive visual appearance through clothing style, grooming, and accessories";

use "a style of talk . . . [that is] generally loud and accompanied by exaggerated gestures"; and "present oneself as explicitly willing to use violence."[23] In this way, the street code functions as a "frontstage" presentation of self that "attempt[s] to avoid violence by boasting and bluster [and by] projecting an image of confidence in one's ability to fight well."[24] While those engaging in the street code run the risk of instigating violence (including by those—like Aaron—who may not recognize the street code as such), their goal may have been to scare off a would-be aggressor *before* a fight. This means that hardened criminals may well use the street code to opportunistically intimidate and threaten targeted victims, but the street code is *also* a strategy used by regular folks navigating contexts in which violence is an everyday risk. While the street code often entails a degree of masculine bravado, it can function as a strategy for survival for men and women alike, as Nikki Jones[25] shows in her study of African American girls and young women in Philadelphia.

What happens when the street code leaves the urban street and comes, for example, to the suburban sprawl? Aaron's story suggests one outcome: the misrecognition of institutionalized bluster. Of course, the purpose of the woman's expletives is unclear; perhaps she really was just having a "bad day." Maybe she was trying to threaten Aaron, but changed her mind once she saw his gun. Maybe she had grown accustomed—as part of "institutionalized bluster"—to being more verbally aggressive than most in the "polite" society north of 8 Mile Road. In other words, perhaps her verbal aggression was nothing more than the manifestation of a code of behavior that was part of navigating her everyday life—a habitus of its own.[26]

We can't know. This line of analysis is aimed at raising further questions, rather than supplying definitive answers as to how Aaron came to be arrested that day. This story suggests that the misrecognition of "institutionalized bluster" (even if the woman came close to hitting Aaron's car, ultimately she fell short) could serve as a pathway into violence: while she postured, Aaron turned to his gun.

This raises a separate, but related, issue: how stereotypical and widespread, even if implicit and even unconscious, ideas about *what a threat looks like* can ramp up the possibility of violence. For example, researchers have focused on how race unconsciously informs how

Americans "see" threats—regardless of the *conscious* attitudes we may hold. In one experimental study, social psychologist B. Keith Payne[27] identified what he called "weapons bias": an ambiguous object was more likely to be identified as a gun when held by a darker-skinned person. The bias was particularly pronounced when study participants were asked to make split-second decisions about the object, and biases had absolutely nothing to do with people's conscious beliefs about race. People who held anti-racist beliefs were no less likely to exhibit this bias than those who expressed racist beliefs: across the board, participants in the study were more likely to "see" a gun in the hands of a Black man than a white man.

Already stereotyped as an angry woman having a bad day, could some version of a weapons bias—that the woman hassling Aaron profiled as someone likely to carry and use a gun—explain why Aaron believed she was reaching for a gun, rather than a cell phone? At the same time, when she saw Aaron, a Black man coming toward her with a gun, did she see a murderer rather than a protective father? It's hard to say. Yet, what his account highlights is how easily a threat can be misrecognized and mistaken—not just because of Aaron's own desire to protect his children but also because of presumptions about what constitutes a threat.

What Do You Bring to a Gunfight?

Guns are not the only thing that gun carriers bring to a gunfight: they may bring a sense of moral duty and responsibility; they may bring masculine bravado and macho posturing; they may bring particular presumptions about what a threat looks like; they may bring training that gives them the tools to defend themselves in an all-out violent confrontation but that provides less guidance on how to de-escalate threats or to recognize harmless acts of boasting and blustering. Aaron's story suggests how much these other factors can matter in addition to the gun itself. Given these other factors, could Aaron have prepared himself differently—not for a gunfight, but for a nonviolent resolution that didn't result in his arrest and ultimate conviction?

Aaron may have had countless hours of formal and informal training under his belt, but based on my observations of training and discussions

with gun carriers, he probably did not have extensive practice distin-
guishing the murky regions between "not a threat," "potential threat,"
and "active threat," nor about how presumptions of what a threat looks
like could shape a gun carrier's response. When I talked to gun carriers,
this critical juncture was mostly overlooked: the overriding assumption
was that, as long as you were alert and cognizant of your surroundings
(and willing to take decisive action if necessary), you would be able to
ascertain threats and protect against them. This was illustrated by gun
carriers' emphasis on tactical, over cognitive, ability. For example, Billy,
a white gun carrier, told me about his training regimen:

> I don't think I'll ever be prepared to the fullest, because in whatever
> encounter it happens, it's going to be in seconds. And you don't know
> what's going to happen, so the best thing to do is to be prepared for
> the worst. The best thing—aside from the rules, point in a safe direc-
> tion, keep your finger off the trigger, blah blah blah. Yeah, getting
> that gun out of the holster, that's 90% of it. Get that gun out of the
> holster. So you do it this way, you see people do this—pull it up
> and out, straight up and out. It's the fastest. You can—if you begin
> right here . . . But it only takes an individual to charge 1.5 seconds
> to go from [twenty-one feet] to you. 1.5 seconds is the time it takes.
> Or thereabouts. So the faster you can pull it out—and it's all muscle
> memory. You know?

Like Aaron, Billy prepares for a gunfight. Billy is sure that the threat he
experiences will be quick and require split-second, decisive action. His
biggest issue he sees is "get[ting] that gun out of the holster." What's
missing isn't whether Billy can draw quickly and shoot straight, but his
ability to figure out if he *should*. The presumption is that the easy part
is ascertaining the threat; the hard part is dealing with it.

The firearms training I observed likewise tended to overlook this
critical component of ascertaining threat. Instructors might go through
an array of self-defense scenarios to talk through whether lethal force
is warranted—as noted in chapter 2—but often, these scenarios were
abstract. There was rarely any mention of the kinds of cues—such as
race—that people may rely on (even consciously) to ascertain threats.
There was certainly no mention of racial stereotypes of criminals in

NRA materials, only individualistic and color-blind renderings of "bad criminals" and "good guys." There is no mention, for example, of the weapons bias.[28] However, the avoidance of race and other stereotypes about criminals may actually increase the likelihood that individuals make split-second judgments based on subconscious prejudicial beliefs rather than reasonable evaluations of a threat. As a result, students may well leave the class feeling free to use whatever cues they find "reasonable" to ascertain a threat.

To be clear: my argument focuses more on the standardized elements of the NRA course rather than the idiosyncratic elements that individual instructors may integrate into their courses. Individual instructors may choose to explicitly include these conversations, but that's their personal choice. My conversations with gun instructors suggest that at least a few are concerned about racial stereotypes and the dangers of "overtraining," and they told me they addressed these issues as they "came up" in class. One instructor even said that he actively screens students for racist attitudes by meeting with them before allowing them to register for his class.

That said, I never witnessed such conversations in the classes I attended, and a handful of proactive, concerned instructors cannot compensate for the systematic inadequacies of the firearms training required to obtain a CPL in Michigan. Required firearms training courses could be a venue for people to evaluate their beliefs and think about how those beliefs shape what and whom they see as a threat. But that introspection and honesty is impossible without talking explicitly about ideas, stereotypes, and prejudices regarding what a criminal threat does *and* does not "look like." Like the cultural sensitivity training that many police departments undergo around issues like racial profiling, firearms courses could serve as a forum for frank discussion about how racial stereotypes, perhaps aggravated by the misrecognition of "institutionalized bluster" in the form of clothing, talk, or empty threats of violence, can easily escalate into real violence through forward panic. Ideally, courses could require students to participate in simulated self-defense scenarios (not all of which would require the use of lethal force) in which they must ascertain and physically respond to threats quickly and decisively. Afterward, focused discussion might evaluate how a student did, or did not, come to view a particular person or situation as an imminent threat. Such simulations would help to rework embodied responses to a threat, and they might help to expose the implicit markers and cues that students hold and use to evaluate a threat.

In this regard, the presumptions that gun carriers may carry with them may be wide-ranging, and they may lead gun carriers to overestimate *or* underestimate a threat. Students should leave training with a better understanding of both *how threats unfold* and *what threats look like*, as well as the full totality of what they—in addition to a gun—might bring to a fight. They should not find this out in the moment, as Aaron did, only after they've committed an act of avoidable violence.

Conclusion: The Last Resort of the Law

Self-defense laws are, at best, a makeshift way of adjudicating situations that—as Collins' analysis shows—can spiral out of control, situations where concepts like "reasonableness" and "proportional force" become effectively (if not legally) irrelevant. Meanwhile, training (at least, required training) generally does not adequately address the social parameters of self-defense scenarios—especially how social identities and differences may escalate fights. The assumption is that students will just "know." These formal (the law) and semiformal (legally required training) mechanisms open up gaps for error, misunderstanding, and misuse of firearms.

Whether gun laws are misused, then, depends not on the letter of the law but also the social world in which the law is enacted. In other words, misuse rests on whether well-intentioned individuals who use guns are able to ascertain threats "reasonably." Subconscious beliefs and the centripetal pull of fight dynamics can compel people to react with violence and can lead gun carriers to take actions that ultimately propel them to act more like citizen-vigilantes than the calm, cool, and collected citizen-protectors that they aspire to be. This means that, on their own, well-written laws will never be enough to ensure that armed individuals will not put themselves or innocent people in danger. And by the time a gun carrier steps into a courtroom, the damage is already done: someone has already been threatened, injured, or killed.

The law, at this point, can serve to adjudicate whether the gun carrier acted lawfully and reasonably, or criminally and unreasonably, but it cannot reverse the actions already undertaken, ostensibly to defend and protect.

Further, the law can make matters worse by serving as a shield to excuse otherwise criminal behavior as "reasonable." This emphasis on "reasonableness" comprised the legal defense of George Zimmerman and Michael Dunn when each stood trial. Their attorneys argued that these men were not guilty of manslaughter or murder because Zimmerman and Dunn believed that they were acting in self-defense. Zimmerman shot and killed the unarmed Trayvon Martin in a gated community in Sanford, Florida, after Zimmerman reported Martin to the police, then followed Martin because he looked "suspicious," even as a 911 dispatcher instructed him to desist. Dunn shot and killed Jordan Davis while Davis was parked outside a convenience store. Bothered by loud music coming from Davis's car, Dunn first demanded that Davis turn the music down, then concluded that the car's occupants were "threatening" and shot through the car, killing Davis.

Ultimately, the difference in these cases' outcomes (Zimmerman was acquitted of all charges; Dunn was convicted of attempted murder) hinged on the reasonableness of the beliefs of the defendants. Dunn's insistence that he was acting in self-defense was easily discredited: he was slow to notify police and seemed unconcerned with whether the shots he fired into Davis' car had injured or killed anyone. Dunn was using gun laws to get away with murder; we can see from his testimony and evidence that, at some level, even he knew this.

Zimmerman, however, represents a very different case: rather than disregard police, Zimmerman was in regular contact with them. He had a track record of involvement in community safety and neighborhood watch initiatives. He had taken criminal justice classes and even considered a career in law enforcement. Zimmerman may have gotten away with a racially charged murder, but there's not much evidence that, as an individual, Zimmerman saw himself as anything but a citizen-protector, making a life-and-death decision in the context of defending himself and his neighborhood.

If Dunn is an example of how a criminal takes advantage of lenient gun laws, Zimmerman represents something more complex—the liminal zone between the "bad guy" and the "good guy." The terrifying possibility is not that George Zimmerman is a "bad guy" who used gun laws to commit a racially motivated murder out of hatred and malice. It's that he—not unlike police officers who insist they do not hold racist views even while engaging in the practice of racial profiling—may have sincerely believed that he was doing the "right" thing, with "good" intentions. In either case, it's the same result: a dead seventeen-year-old African American boy who paid for "profiling" as a criminal with his life.

Unpacking Aaron's case, I've examined how gun carriers may come to find themselves in this liminal zone and how gender, class, and race, alongside the situational dynamics of violence, may lead some gun carriers to overestimate and overreact to threats. I've suggested that formal and informal training does not provide adequate tools and may, in fact, exacerbate gun carriers' propensity to overestimate and overreact to threats, if only by leading them to believe that they will *know*, on some deep level and in a moment, what kind of situation they're caught up in and how to react appropriately. Examining the blurred the lines between "bad guys" and "good guys," I've highlighted the inadequacy of debating gun laws and policies on the basis of whether these policies can keep guns out of the hands of "bad guys." Instead, we must begin by having a different, broader conversation that centers on the moral politics of guns and their implications.

Conclusion

We Hope for Better Things; It Shall Rise from the Ashes

AFTER COREY SHOT THE NINETEEN-YEAR-OLD African American in his store, he was taken to the Flint police station and then released without arrest. The police ruled the case a justifiable homicide. Faced with a gun at point-blank range, Corey was trapped in a zero-sum game: only one person would have come out alive. Staring down the barrel of a gun, Corey shot to survive. The details were unpleasant and unsavory, but Corey's logic seemed unassailable. He had acted in a clear-cut case of self-defense, and otherwise might have paid with his life.

However, Corey's life was not in danger from the gun he saw pointed at him. In the immediate aftermath of the shooting, the police chose to withhold a critical detail from Corey, the public, and the family of the deceased, perhaps in an attempt to avoid a controversy or even to protect Corey. Over a year later, the police released this detail: the gun that was used in the attempted robbery was *fake*.

The Politics of Protection

I open and close this book with Corey, a man from Flint who shot and killed someone attempting to rob his store. Victimized before, Corey had purchased the revolver he used not long before the attempted robbery. What would have happened had Corey not purchased his gun or not brought it to the store that day? Would he have survived—or would the assailant or the assailant's partner have pulled a real gun? Could Corey have known the gun was fake? *Should* he have known? And if the assailant's purpose was to intimidate Corey, does it even matter that the gun was fake?

Corey's case raises many questions, but it offers few answers. There are complicated and tragic politics of protection that arise when guns become everyday tools of protection against a backdrop of socioeconomic decline, and Corey's situation calls attention to the kinds of life-and-death confrontations that arise among an armed populace. Corey is one of the many gun carriers I met whose stories defy the simplistic narratives usually privileged in national debates between pro- and anti-gun advocates. There's Jason, the African American man who used his openly carried gun to model good citizenship to young men in Detroit. There's Austin, the white man who was explicitly encouraged by a Flint police officer to shoot home invaders on sight. There's Aaron, an African American father who pulled a gun on an unarmed woman under the belief that he was protecting his children. And then there's Timothy, a white father who talked much of his obligation to protect others but struggled with the idea of intervening in a crime if it meant endangering his child.

Examining these stories and others, this book uses gun carry as a window into the complexities of American gun culture and the dramatic changes it has undergone over the past several decades. The millions of Americans who are now licensed to carry guns do not just find gun politics ideologically appealing; they also see guns as a concrete part of their lives.

Understanding the everyday politics of guns is critical for making sense of the millions of Americans who remain committed to a pro-gun stance. In the several years since the stories that animate this book took place, a number of flashpoint events have transpired—there was the 2012 massacre in Newtown, Connecticut, which resulted in the death of almost two dozen kindergarteners and first graders; a Florida jury's 2013 ruling that the killing of Trayvon Martin, an unarmed teenager, was not murder but justifiable homicide; and the bloody months of May and June 2014, which included Elliot Rodger's stabbing and shooting spree near the University of California at Santa Barbara and

Jerad and Amanda Miller's armed confrontation with Las Vegas police that left three officers dead. In the wake of these incidents, gun control advocates felt hopeful that the tragedies would result in renewed public support for gun control and, eventually, legislative changes, but none of these events has fundamentally altered American public opinion (let alone public policy) on guns.

The country is about evenly split between those who want to maintain existing gun laws and those who want stricter laws. A Pew poll conducted in February 2013 shows that 50% of Americans favor gun control; 46% prioritize gun rights.[1] Divisions become particularly stark when broken down by political affiliation and political ideology: Those who identified as Democrats in an October 2013 Gallup poll overwhelmingly supported stricter gun laws (77%), as did self-identified liberals (72%). In contrast, self-identified Republicans (23%) and conservatives (33%) strongly opposed stricter laws.[2]

These divisions also play out in terms of race and gender: nonwhites and women are more likely to support stricter gun laws; whites and men are more likely to oppose them. In the poll administered by the Pew Research Center just after the Newtown shooting,[3] women were about a third less likely than men to prioritize gun rights over gun control; African Americans were half as likely as whites. One of the biggest indicators of support for gun rights is whether one owns guns, and gun ownership is skewed by race, gender, and political ideology: men are more than three times more likely than women to personally own a gun; whites are twice as likely to own a gun as African Americans (this includes long guns and handguns; recall that handgun ownership appears to be roughly equal across race as noted in chapter 5); those who identify as or lean Republican are roughly 38% more likely to own a gun than those who identify as or lean Democrat.[4] Roughly half of gun owners identified as Independents.[5]

These data points indicate deep divisions over the issue of guns in America, yet they tell only part of the story. They fail to disentangle the multiple meanings Americans attribute to guns and the many reasons why and contexts in which we turn to guns. Alongside these divisions, there are also factors that pull Americans' opinions on guns together. A central factor is protection. According to the same February 2013 Pew data, Americans who own guns do so increasingly for the sake of protection (even as survey data suggest that the number of gun-owning American households has declined since the 1970s).[6] Compared with 1999, when 26% of Americans reported that they owned guns for protection, today 48% own guns for protection,[7] and Gallup data put this figure closer to 60%.[8] According to aggregated polling data collected in 2000 and 2005, protection cuts across party lines much more so than target shooting or hunting: 69% of gun-owning Democrats cite protection, compared to 65% and 64% of gun-owning Republicans and Independents.[9]

Indicative of this embrace of protection, Americans overwhelmingly oppose a handgun ban: in a 2013 Gallup poll, a "record-high 74%" of Americans opposed such a ban.[10] By 2014's end, Americans supported guns for protection more vigorously than ever. New data from Gallup and Pew, released as this book goes to press, suggest that Americans—including African Americans and women—believe in the majority that gun ownership makes people safer rather than less safe. This is a dramatic reversal from previous polling conducted just years prior.[11]

Strange Bedfellows, Usual Suspects

What does examining gun-toting men in Michigan—a subset of the millions of Americans who own and carry guns—tell us about nation-wide figures?

This book reveals how guns bring together strange bedfellows—men of diverse socioeconomic backgrounds—who nevertheless converge on the practice of gun carry. Gun carry is popular across broad swaths of men in southeastern Michigan. Differently situated in contexts of decline, the men I met during my research turned to guns to embrace and assert their roles as protectors of their families and their communities. Acknowledging that public law enforcement often cannot, or is unwilling to, provide adequate protection, the gun carriers I met embraced guns as a way to step up to a problem that they saw as aggravated by an ever-present threat of crime, a crumbling economy, and an unraveling community.

With guns, carriers (mostly men) saw themselves as good men, respectable husbands, and responsible fathers not just because they can provide for their families but because, they maintained, they can provide protection. This is not to say that men had to choose to be *either* providers *or* protectors, or that these men rejected their identities as breadwinners: rather, guns provide another "tool" in the gendered toolbox to assert their masculine identities. In this way, privileged and marginalized gun carriers nevertheless participate in the production of a certain version of masculinity that frames gender relations around men's ability to protect. For more class- and race-marginalized gun carriers, this was a response to more immediate experiences of economic insecurity, a greater exposure to crime, and more exposure to police harassment, while race- and class-privileged gun carriers experienced economic decline, crime, and police inefficacy more as abstract anxiety than immediate threat. Nevertheless, their overlapping gender politics, grounded in contexts of American socioeconomic decline, provided an unexpected alliance of different kinds of gun carriers through their mutual embrace of what I've called the citizen-protector.

At the same time, this politics of guns buttresses a simplified narrative about socioeconomic decline, reducing a complex constellation of social transformations to a more digestible problem of crime and police inefficacy. This means that the unexpectedly inclusionary project of gun carry is predicated on an exclusionary politics centered on a fear of crime and a fear of the "usual suspects": people (often economically marginalized, urban men of color) who are stereotyped and feared as hyperaggressive criminals. Drawing on distinct narratives of race, class, and masculinity, gun carriers articulated criminality in a variety of key ways, but a language of exclusion was often at work, implicitly or explicitly, as the men talked about protecting "their" families and "their" communities.

The reproduction of social inequality through the politics of crime and justice is not new. Such projects litter American history: in the 1880s, Southern whites used property crime laws to pummel recently freed slaves into the convict leasing system; in the 1930s, law enforcement in the North responded to the Great Migration of Southern Blacks by arresting and incarcerating them; and in the 1960s and beyond, politicians rallied around the War on Crime to zealously prosecute Blacks for drug convictions, despite the fact that whites used drugs as much or more than Blacks.

Intersecting with these projects in expected and unexpected ways, today's gun politics represents an unprecedented democratization of the right to self-defense, which in turn has been taken up by men, and to a lesser extent women, of diverse backgrounds. Americans in the vast majority of states are now able to obtain a license to carry a gun into public space on a non-discretionary basis. Further, the right to use guns defensively has expanded into public space. The "no duty to retreat" doctrine, which held that an individual did not have an obligation to retreat during an attack in his[12] home, has expanded to cover any public space that an individual is legally occupying. Florida was the first to pass this so-called "Stand Your Ground" legislation, and around two dozen states have followed suit. Rather than a radical departure, Stand Your Ground laws represent the deepening of gun carry culture: if the pervasiveness of gun carry reflects Americans' ability to imagine themselves as victims, then the support for Stand Your Ground laws reflects their ability to imagine themselves as citizen-protectors.

But if gun carry culture suggests a democratization and deepening of the right to self-defense across surprisingly diverse groups, it is young men of color who disproportionately pay its costs. This paradox is borne out in data on justifiable homicides. On the one hand, some African Americans have benefited from self-defense laws: from 2000 to 2010 in Michigan, ninety-nine African Americans, as compared to twenty-three whites, committed justifiable homicide in self-defense. On the other hand, African Americans are also strikingly overrepresented among those killed: 108 out of 117 of those killed in justifiable homicides in Michigan were Black.[13] Data suggest that, with respect to justifiable homicide, this is not just the result of African Americans' greater involvement in certain kinds of crime. John Roman's recent analysis of justifiable-homicide data reveals an interaction between the race of the shooter and the race of the person shot: white-on-black shootings are most likely to be ruled justified, and black-on-white least likely. Moreover, in white-on-black shootings, race, gender, and age interact such that the killings of young, Black men are particularly likely to be ruled justifiable, especially in states with Stand Your Ground laws.[14]

Despite the increased visibility of these issues in the wake of the George Zimmerman verdict, there has been little public willpower to unpack them in their uncomfortable complexity. And it is indicative of this lack of public willpower, combined with the ambiguous relationship between race and guns, that some African Americans have responded to bleak race relations in the United States with guns. If, in the 1960s, Huey Newton (himself a child of the Great Migration) wielded a shotgun and quoted constitutional law to Oakland police officers (just before the California State Legislature voted to disarm Blacks), in 2012 Stic.man, a member of the hip-hop group Dead Prez, wielded words to respond to the George Zimmerman verdict:

> *Now let's put it all in perspective*
> *Before the outrage burns out misdirected*
> *What can we do so our community's protected?*
> *I believe that should be our main objective*
> *While we full of rage and we wanna make a difference*
> *Let's do more than protest*
> *Let's make a commitment, to be proactive*
> *Not just emotional reactin'.*
> *Move like Gs, never passive*
> *Organize safe teams, martial art classes*
> *Get to the gun range and make your aim accurate*
> *Self-defense is a must by any tactic*
> *Security protocol, make it a daily practice.*

The Practical Politics of Guns

This book has examined people for whom guns provide a measure to address problems of social insecurity and disorder. Taking a bottom-up perspective, it unpacks the everyday contexts of decline that make guns "practical" as a point of departure for understanding the broader politics of guns. Embracing guns as tools of self-defense and as symbols of self-reliance, gun rights proponents define themselves against gun control advocates they see as hypocritical and even weak-spirited for promoting gun bans while relying on police or private security—particularly politicians with extensive security details. The NRA actively cultivates these attitudes: one advertisement put together by the organization after the Sandy Hook shootings asks, "Are the President's kids more important than yours? . . . Mr. Obama demands the wealthy pay their fair share of taxes, but he's just another elitist hypocrite when it comes to a fair share of security. Protection for their kids, and gun-free zones for ours."

What does this caricature of gun control advocates—and it is a caricature—tell us about those who embrace guns?

On the one hand, this lamentation is explained by studies that emphasize gun politics as conservative backlash politics: the indictment of gun control advocates as arrogant elitists can be read as an articulation of the anti-statist, backlash politics that have long rallied Americans into opposition to the federal government, starting with Barry Goldwater's ill-fated presidential campaign of 1964. The NRA's post–Sandy Hook advertisement and the broader stance of anti-elitism it represents sits well with analyses such as Melzer's, which emphasizes how the NRA uses culture war rhetoric to galvanize pro-gun, conservative America.[15] By situating President Obama as Public Enemy No. 1 in the culture war, the gun lobby channels anti-Obama sentiment into a pro-gun agenda.

However, backlash politics cannot explain the anti-elitist ethos of gun politics alone. It certainly sheds light on the top-down dynamics through which organizations like the NRA mobilize pro-gun sentiment, but not the bottom-up dynamics that make certain politics and policies appealing. The NRA is a central figure in the story of contemporary gun politics in America, as scholars such as Melzer have persuasively shown.[16] But analyses of the NRA must be understood alongside another story centered on the everyday concerns of those who feel left behind, stranded, or threatened by the changing socioeconomic (and political) landscape in the United States. These concerns are also expressed through guns and are not confined to the white, conservative men who, nevertheless, dominate pro-gun America.

The gun carriers I interviewed in Michigan were aware that they were part of the "flyover states"—a part of America rendered irrelevant to political decision-making and often ridiculed in national media. Many are desperate to leave—if they can. Michigan, after all, actually *lost* population from 2000 to 2010 because of the exodus of people from the state. For those who stayed behind, guns offer one form of security. Not everyone chooses to carry a gun, but the number of people who do has expanded significantly since concealed carry legislation was passed in Michigan in 2001.

The act of carrying a gun transforms gun politics from an ideological debate to a concrete part of life—a weight on the hip and on the mind. The exercise of gun rights is not a way to *talk* about solutions to problems of social insecurity, but to *practice* a solution by embracing a particular variant of good citizenship (the citizen-protector) that sets gun carriers apart from others. As I have argued, this moral politics is particularly appealing to men looking to distinguish themselves from criminal, violent, or just lazy men. To gun carriers, the gun represents an affirmation of one's commitment to life, and to carry a gun is to bring together a powerful mix of practical and moral politics into everyday life.

Rethinking Policing, Citizenship, and Masculinity

As criminologists who study the contemporary American carceral system remind us,[17] the work of the criminal justice system is not confined to the prison cell, the courtroom, or the back of a police car. Private and public security apparatuses have seen massive, and innovative, growth over the past several decades. Nevertheless, scholars often approach this broad carceral apparatus as if its main effect has been to control (disproportionately racially and economically marginalized) Americans. The shocking statistics often cited—that one in one hundred Americans are behind bars, and that there are more African Americans implicated in the criminal justice system now than the number of enslaved African Americans at any time during slavery—demonstrate the enormity of this neoliberal system of social control.

Yet an exclusive emphasis on Americans (particularly young Black men) as aggressively policed, prosecuted, and punished obscures how everyday Americans participate in this system not as state or market actors, but as political actors—as citizen-protectors. Empowered to engage in the coercive work of policing, these Americans see themselves as both stepping in for the state and, in some cases, standing up to the state. And the statistics here are startling, too: there are close to five licensed gun carriers for every incarcerated American, and from 2008 to 2012, there were more than five justifiable homicides committed by private citizens using guns for every one state-administered execution in the United States.[18] During the same period, private citizens committed just over half as many justifiable homicides with guns as public law enforcement.[19]

Gun carry can tell us something new and important about the contemporary carceral apparatus in the United States. It is a critical, but largely overlooked, way in which policing has seeped beyond the formal boundaries of the state over the past several decades, and it also calls our attention to how policing has transformed—at least symbolically—from a state function to a generalized civic duty, shaped by broader gender ideologies surrounding the obligations of men as protectors. Taken together, this study therefore makes three scholarly contributions.

First, it forces us to rethink what we mean by "third-party policing," "private policing," and other terms that capture the seepage of policing duties outside formal public law enforcement.[20] Rather than emphasizing how police are adopting new strategies of social control,[21] this study shows how new actors are participating in a much more traditional notion of policing: the use of force for the enactment of social order. I want to be careful in summarizing this argument, as gun carriers are not in the habit of enforcing laws or even of intervening in crimes (even if they are legally sanctioned to do so in some cases). Nevertheless, gun carry further pushes the question of how, and in what contexts, third-party policing and private policing buttress or erode state monopolies on control and forces us to think in terms of parallel sovereignties, competing police powers, and forms of coercion marked by their dispersion and diffusion among many actors rather than their centralization among a few.

Scholars have long sought to disrupt the notion that public law enforcement monopolizes policing.[22] However, they've often done so by emphasizing the role of market actors. Today, private, market entities engage in policing in a variety of ways: firms such as the Digital Recognition Network track and compile license plate numbers into databases available to public law enforcement;[23] private crime labs, such as the Target Corporation's crime lab,[24] supplement backlogged, publicly funded labs used by public law enforcement; home security firms, such as ADT and Brinks Home Security, act as liaisons between victimized citizens and public law enforcement; private security guards, which outnumber public law enforcement,[25] proactively police private property; and security commodity companies like TASER, which vows to "Protect Life, Protect Truth, and Protect Family,"[26] provide products ranging from cameras to stun guns to law enforcement and civilians alike. And then, of course, there is the six-billion-dollar (and growing) gun industry.[27]

While gun carriers are private actors buttressed by the gun industry, they belong in a slightly different analytical category than market actors—they are not the citizen-consumer often envisioned in studies of neoliberal citizenship.[28] Poised between the state and the market, gun carriers are political actors insofar as they are mobilized by a particular notion of policing and insofar as this becomes tethered to a partic- ular understanding of "good citizenship." Enabled by the state and the market, this new kind of citizenship extends the punitive state beyond the market and onto the bodies of everyday Americans. Here, policing is not simply a state capacity, nor is it a commodity; with gun carry, policing becomes a political culture.

Secondly, thus, this study asks us to rethink how policing serves as a basis for political culture, rather than a dispassionate function of the state. Cultural sociologists emphasize culture as a set of discourses and practices aimed at navigating unfamiliar problems embedded in social institutions that, in turn, shape the very "solution" to the problem to be solved. The everyday efficaciousness of guns as tools—not in the sense that gun carriers mean when they say that guns are "just a tool, like a hammer," but as tools in a "cultural toolkit"[29]—does much in explaining the basic attractiveness of guns beyond their ideological appeal. Policing requires a physical relationship with a weapon of force, whether merely carried or actually used. The millions of Americans who carry a gun rework the unsavory nature of police work;[30] in the case of the men I studied in Michigan, they remake it as an attractive ideal of citizenship by celebrating their commitment to innocent life by embracing the willingness to protect it, with lethal force, if necessary. Gun carry shows that, when not monopolized by the state or even by market actors, policing can function as an everyday, moralized capacity that allows individuals to navigate one set of social problems (say, social insecurity, fear of crime, victimization, etc.), which may give rise to a different set of social problems (the possibility of life-threatening mistakes, misunderstandings, and misuses of guns).

American history, together with the enshrinement of gun rights in the Second Amendment of the US Constitution and countless state constitutions, provides a necessary baseline for imagining the contemporary gun carrier as a Good Samaritan participating in the maintenance of social order through the generalized practice of gun carry. Without the exceptional significance of guns in shaping American history at critical junctures, we'd be unlikely to have the vigorous gun culture we see today. Civilian guns provided Americans with the tools to achieve independence from the British; they were crucial to the systems of race oppression and class privilege in the antebellum and Jim Crow South and, to a lesser extent, the Midwest; and they were requisite tools of Manifest Destiny in the settlement of the West.

However, chalking up the proliferation and prevalence of gun carry to history effaces the contemporary, everyday pulls on a variety of different kinds of Americans to take up guns. It is not cultural inertia that motivates Americans to go through the time-consuming and expensive process of obtaining a concealed carry license and to navigate the unpleasant reality that they, like the criminals against whom they presumably defend themselves, can kill.[31] Rather, the guns in this study are taken up and carried by people attempting to navigate circumstances not of their own choosing.[32] Against the backdrop of decline, gun carry is both an apology for and a critique of contemporary policing; it is an attempt to recuperate social order while also rejecting the state's monopoly of it, a strategy that arguably enhances the social status of men by charging them with the social utility of protecting not only themselves but also others. The NRA presses policing as a problem, and it promotes guns as a solution to this problem by emphasizing, as Kevin O'Neill[33] argues, the masculine heroism of those men who do use guns to protect themselves from violent threats. This solution would be far less appealing without a social context of decline that reinforces the NRA's message.

Finally, as a result of this reframing of policing as civic duty, gendered notions of duty and obligation lie at the heart of gun carry. Scholarship on masculinity and guns tends to focus on the feelings and fantasies of domination, authority, and control that men may accrue from the guns they own and carry. While this scholarship hits a critical nerve within the gendered politics of guns (see, for example, the botched self-defense encounter described in chapter 6), it misses the broader socioeconomic context in which guns become appealing and, with it, the multiple roles that guns can serve for their owners and carriers. On the whole, I found that gun politics is deeply gendered not because it is dominated by men who celebrate violent masculinity, but because it provides a way for men to embrace protectionist masculinity. Armed men draw on the same kind of moral authority usually associated with public law enforcement, where violence is embraced to fulfill a duty to protect.

This is a subtle, but crucial, distinction for understanding how guns become normalized and celebrated and the broader work that guns do for men negotiating their positions in a climate of socioeconomic decline. The men I met in Michigan could no longer assume easy access to the kinds of jobs and economic security available to their parents, and many of them had experienced economic insecurity firsthand, with periods of unemployment, moving from job to job, or even relying on their wives for income. If they could not be sure of being *providers*, guns made them sure of their role as *protectors*. Justified by a sense of duty and moral obligation, guns provide the tools to forge new kinds of care work, centered neither on the traditionally feminized caregiving responsibilities of housework and direct childcare nor on the traditionally masculine responsibilities of provision—but on protection.

This gender analysis sheds light on why states similar to Michigan—historically blue or purple states with strong manufacturing bases—are seeing increasing support for gun carry among residents. Fifty years ago, being a pro-union Democrat and sole breadwinner defined masculinity in these areas. Today, protecting one's family is viewed as an increasingly appealing way to achieve masculinity. Because gun carriers extend, even if just symbolically, the masculine duty to protect their families to their communities more generally, the social implication of the turn toward guns involves a much broader reconfiguration of gendered rights and citizenship.

Missing the Target

How, then, do we move forward in today's deadlocked gun debate? It is customary for academic books on guns to end with a ringing endorsement of gun control (or, more rarely, gun rights) policies. Instead,

I want to spend the remaining pages talking about how we might imagine a different, more productive national debate about the social life of guns in the United States. Specifically, I'd prefer to entertain the question of making guns less socially relevant, rather than illegal.

To be as clear as possible to those who strongly identify as either gun control or gun rights advocates: I close this book, and the years of research it entailed, finding myself more dissatisfied with the current state of the gun debate than when I started. I am all the more certain that the polarized positions so often prioritized within popular debates on guns only make sense in the abstract. When faced with messy, real-life examples—like the Detroit 300, the group of African American men who arm themselves in protest of lost Black lives like Trayvon Martin's, or Corey, the white man with a history of victimization who eventually used a gun to defend himself from an assailant armed with a toy gun—the clarity offered by the two sides of the gun debate is no longer so persuasive to me. Thus, my simple goal as an author has been to write a book that documents what gun carry culture looks like on the ground. In other words, I've tried to do the impossible: write an illuminating but apolitical book about guns. Whether I have succeeded is ultimately up to the reader.

At the very least, I feel it is my obligation as a scholar to emphasize that staking a claim on one side of this hackneyed debate—emotionally satisfying as it may be—is unlikely to move us forward in terms of addressing the all-too-real problem of American gun violence, which both sides maintain motivates their position. While both gun rights and gun control activists clamor to make statements about the moral uprightness of their position, perhaps the truly radical stance is to endorse neither, and to envision a different debate.

Gun-rights proponents often maintain that "an armed society is a polite society." The gun debate, I argue, has been focused too much on whether we should be an armed society and far too little on the social determinants that have driven the United States—a country with roughly three hundred million guns already in civilian hands—to become the armed society that it is today and the moral politics that result. Questions surrounding the legality of gun ownership and Second Amendment rights have been largely settled for the foreseeable future by US Supreme Court decisions. Guns—handguns, shotguns, rifles—are legal in the United States, and there is little chance of the Second Amendment being "repealed." Of course, there is an important conversation to be had about mechanisms to keep guns out of the hands of people who will use them to commit crimes, and given the broad-based support for universal background checks,[34] both sides of the gun debate should be motivated to have that conversation. What I question is what else we need to talk about as dramatic changes in gun laws and the spread of gun carry as an everyday moral politics changes how we live—and die—together. Rather than debating whether the United States should be an armed society (we already are), we need a clear-headed conversation about the kind of "polite society" we have become with guns.

With the exception of public interest in Stand Your Ground laws after Trayvon Martin's death, there has been little public interest outside pro-gun circles in the extent to which legally carried guns have become a part of everyday life for millions of Americans. Meanwhile, gun *control* advocates too often debate gun policy as if it is still the 1990s, when the Brady Campaign successfully pushed through a series of federal gun control laws that implemented a more stringent background-check system and banned certain guns as "assault weapons." This approach, however, fails to fully appreciate that today's gun politics are not just about abstract Second Amendment rights.

Gun carry, at least in Metro Detroit, is also about responding to conditions of decline. It's about redefining the use of deadly force as a necessary and even admirable act in certain cases, which also means criminalizing certain lives and rendering them disposable. It's about placing the capacity to to protect life—even if that means taking life—at the center of a new form of citizenship. And ultimately it's about acknowledging the uncomfortable idea that violence, or the threat thereof, guarantees peace even in modern society. Gun carriers act like police because they are negotiating a core contradiction of police work: that the peace is premised on force.

In rethinking the terms of the gun debate, we must remember that not only does the United States have an exceptional gun culture compared with other Western nations, but it is also an exceptionally unequal society. It is a country where public law enforcement, personal safety, crime rates, income, access to healthcare, access to education, and a variety of other resources are distributed in such a way that individuals have very different relations to violence, guns, and crime, as well as to social mobility, the American Dream, and Mayberry America. Against this backdrop, justifiable homicide by private citizens (and police) is one of many contemporary examples of the racial disparities in life and death that have already marred American history for hundreds of years—and the increased reliance on firearms as everyday tools of self-defense threatens to further desensitize us to this loss of life. At the same time, I think it is naïve and dangerous to believe that gun control policies necessarily help residents of high-crime, gun-rich places like Detroit, where police response time are too long and where gun laws can be so easily used to further criminalize minorities.

In closing, I will say this: we should not feel rushed to embrace gun policies that leave untouched the deep and uneven problems of decline that aggravate fear, exacerbate inequality, and drive many Americans to guns in the first place. There is no clear-cut answer to the question of guns, because guns are embedded in different, and starkly unequal, realities of policing, protection, and insecurity. This book shows that guns appeal not only to Americans who hold tightly onto the American Dream's ideology of rugged individualism but also to those Americans who live in an American nightmare that requires self-reliance and survival skills more than ideological preferences.

Guns solve problems for the people who bear them. Nevertheless, engaged voters, activists, politicians, policymakers, and lobbyists—whether promoting gun rights or promoting gun control interests—play a critical role in shaping the contexts in which guns become appealing tools and with what ramifications. As the motto of Detroit says, *Speramus Meliora; Resurget Cineribus*: "We hope for better things; it shall rise from the ashes." To what extent those "better things" ultimately involve guns is a question of how we—from everyday Americans to national policymakers—choose to rebuild broken dreams.

NOTES

Chapter 1

1. Corey—and several others I met during my research—gave me permission to use their real names. However, all names—including Corey's—are psuedonyms.
2. Pew (2013a).
3. While this study focuses on the self-defense politics of guns, this is not to imply that policing and personal protection comprise the only reasons that Americans own guns: American gun owners are also hunters, collectors, and target shooters. Moreover, while this study looks at Americans who own guns *legally*, there is a wealth of literature on Americans who own and use illegal guns for personal protection and other reasons; see Harcourt (2006b).
4. According to Pew (2013a), 74% of gun owners in the United States are men, while 26% are women. Meanwhile, although there is no national database of concealed carry license holders, state-level statistics suggest men's overrepresentation among gun carriers.
5. When asked by Pew Research in February 2013 about their reasons for owning a gun, 48% of gun owners cited personal protection, compared to 26% in August 1999 (Pew, 2013a).
6. Unfortunately, the data obtained from the Michigan State Police do not include race/gender breakdown, but because of the disproportionate representation of men among concealed-pistol license holders, it is likely that this consistency across race holds for African American men and white men.
7. Although some states recognized the "No Duty to Retreat" doctrine within the home earlier, the US Supreme Court adopted the doctrine in Beard v. United States (1985) and Brown v. United States (1921).

8. On average, 228 justifiable homicides were committed with firearms each year from 2008 to 2012, with a peak of 258 in 2012 (FBI, 2012b).

9. Violence Policy Center (2013).

10. Leshner et al. (2013).

11. Hemenway (2004).

12. Hemenway (2004).

13. Zimring (2011).

14. Statistics Canada (2006).

15. Vernick, Hodge, and Webster (2007).

16. Saad (2013).

17. Kellermann et al. (1993); Kellermann et al. (1998). For critiques, see Kleck (2001).

18. Tark and Kleck (2014); Kleck and McElrath (1991).

19. Leshner et al. (2013: 41).

20. I use this phrasing to highlight the false binary that is often drawn between rational and irrational fears. See Lupton and Tulloch (1999).

21. This is suggestive of Lipsitz's (2011: 29) notion of the "white spatial imaginary": a way of viewing and valuing space that sublimates problems of privilege and inequality into a moral defense of " 'pure' and homogenous spaces, controlled environments, and predictable patterns of design and behavior."

22. Sugrue (2005).

23. Coontz (1993); Heath (2012).

24. Simon (2004: 339).

25. Cohen (2002 [1972]); Hall et al. (2013 [1978]).

26. Garland (2000; 2002); Simon (2004).

27. Simon (2007; 2010).

28. Simon (2004).

29. Marx and Archer (1979: 38).

30. McDowall and Loftin (1983); Smith and Uchida (1988).

31. Peters and Wessel (2014).

32. Pew (2013b).

33. Contreras (2013); Rios (2011).

34. Gallaher (2003).

35. Putnam (2001).

36. See, for example, the passage of exclusionary homophobic measures in small towns like Timbertown, a declining Oregon town that Stein (2002; 2005) studied, or the Tea Party's outcry against "freeloaders"—racial minorities, immigrants, and young people—who are "bankrupting" the United States (Skocpol and Williamson, 2012).

37. Klinenberg (2001), in his aptly titled response to Putnam, "Bowling Alone, Policing Together," emphasizes that Americans are replacing earlier forms of civic engagement with community crime-control initiatives, an argument I consider in more detail later. This book takes this one step further and suggests that we should analyze the appeal of guns as tools of policing

and protection as a means of addressing American decline in three key areas—economy, crime, and community.

38. Nisbett and Cohen (1996); see also Down (2002).

39. These include LeDuff's (2013) *Detroit: An American Autopsy*, Binelli's (2012) *Detroit City Is the Place to Be: The Afterlife of an American Metropolis*, and the film *Detropia* (2012).

40. This is not to downplay the historic and present-day significance of race in co-constitutively shaping Michigan's decline: starting with the Great Migration in the 1920s to the white flight of the 1950s, '60s, and '70s, Detroit has exhibited some of the most dramatic manifestations of America's troublesome race politics. Today, racial prejudice and institutionalized racism shape crime and insecurity in a myriad of ways, including people's perceptions of crime, criminal justice responses, and the extent to which criminal justice institutions (such as police) are viewed as legitimate, just, and fair. As previously noted, earlier studies on the relationship between race and crime provide much insight into the masculine appeal of guns; however, they do not clarify how class matters for pro-gun men or how class intersects with race in this regard.

41. This figure does not include the NRA-certified firearms instructors I interviewed who did not earn a living from that alone. Overall, I interviewed twenty firearms instructors and met several more through participant observation. As many respondents were certified instructors but not all were actively involved in instruction, let alone had their own firearms schools, I primarily designate instructor status as relevant to my analysis in chapter 3 on NRA training.

42. At the time of writing, California continues to operate under a "may-issue" system, whereby county sheriffs issue concealed carry permits to civilians at their discretion. While some counties in California operate as de facto "shall-issue" counties (i.e., the sheriffs approve all requests for concealed licenses, provided licensees have no criminal history and fulfill a handful of other stipulated requirements), most sheriffs in urban California counties, such as Alameda County and San Francisco County, strictly regulate the issuance of concealed carry permits and rarely grant them to civilians.

43. In addition to attending a half dozen such classes, which lasted eight hours on average and included both classroom and range time, I also underwent training to become an instructor, receiving National Rifle Certification in 2010 for Basic Pistol and Personal Protection in the Home, two of the classes that would-be carriers can take to fulfill their training requirements.

44. Brown (1991).

45. Bernhard Goetz shot four African American teenage boys in 1984. He was acquitted of attempted murder but convicted of possession of an illegal weapon. Known as the "Subway Vigilante," Goetz was a symbol of a citizen frustrated with high crime rates who garnered broad public support. According to Brown (1991: 134), "a nationwide poll taken two months after

the event showed that 57% (including 39% of nonwhites) approved of Goetz's action and that, true to the spirit of no duty to retreat, 78% would, following Goetz's presumed example, use deadly force in self-defense."

46. Stand Your Ground laws not only allow individuals to defend themselves but also *intervene* in some felonies in order to defend others, as described in further detail in chapter 4.

47. Horwitz and Anderson (2009).

48. O'Neill (2007).

49. Lott (1998). For critiques, see Ayres and Donohue (2003); Duggan (2001).

50. See, for example, Melzer's (2009) *Gun Crusaders: The Culture War*, Winkler's (2013) *Gunfight*, Feldman's (2008) *Ricochet: Confessions of a Gun Lobbyist*, and Brown and Abel's (2003) *Outgunned: Up Against the NRA*.

51. Lamont (2002).

52. Rios (2011).

53. Scott (1987).

54. West and Zimmerman (1987).

55. Anderson (1999: 38).

56. This subset of gun carriers are not the only Americans who have organized to defend white, middle-class social order: in small-town America (Stein, 2002) and along the United States–Mexico border (Shapira, 2013), a variety of political projects—including anti-gay marriage mobilization and anti-immigrant politics—have been mobilized to this end.

57. See Berlet and Lyons (2000) and Burbick (2006) as examples.

58. Black (1983).

Chapter 2

1. While this increase over time is partly explained by pent-up demand for such licenses, the continued steady increase more than a decade later is suggestive that socioeconomic decline, which has also deepened since 2001, enhances the appeal of guns.

2. Steinmetz (2009); see also Loïc Wacquant's (2011: 103–106) analysis of the "hyperghetto."

3. In this regard, Frankie and the other gun carriers I interviewed resonate with the white rural Kentucky men who joined the US Patriot movement out of economic despair and restructuring, as studied by critical geographer Carolyn Gallaher (2002), and the "angry white men" alienated by underemployment and stagnating wages, as analyzed by gender scholar Michael Kimmel (2013).

4. Although I emphasize socioeconomic decline and precariousness, the men in this study do not constitute the precariat in the extreme sense of "advanced marginality" described by Loïc Wacquant (2008), not least by virtue of the fact that they can own and carry guns (felons cannot own or carry guns, and the process of obtaining a gun and a concealed-pistol license can cost more than five hundred dollars; see chapter 3). Nevertheless, the gun carriers

I interviewed still articulated a generalized sense of social precariousness informed by socioeconomic decline and crime.

5. Recall that whites and African Americans are licensed at equal rates in Michigan. In Oakland, Wayne, and Macomb Counties, African Americans outnumber whites in per capita concealed carry licenses.
6. Melzer (2009).
7. Sugrue (2005).
8. Coates (2011). Note that Boustan and Margo (2013) find that white flight to the suburbs, which was already under way in 1950, also played a role in facilitating African American homeownership in Detroit.
9. Fine (2000); Steinmetz (2009).
10. Hartmann (1976).
11. Fine (2000).
12. Anderson (1999); Tonry (1995).
13. This resonates with Putnam's diagnosis in *Bowling Alone* (2001) regarding the unraveling of civic engagement and community within American society.
14. Ashburn (1962).
15. Right-to-work states prohibit unions from negotiating with companies to demand that union membership be a condition of employment, severely weakening union power.
16. Ross (2011).
17. NPR (2009).
18. Platzer and Harrison (2009).
19. Helper, Kruger, and Wial (2012).
20. Bureau of Labor Statistics (2013); Hanenal (2013).
21. Wilson (2013).
22. Wilson (2013).
23. Farley, Danziger, and Holzer (2000: 1, 2).
24. Chambers (2014).
25. Block (2013).
26. Based on data from the US Census and Michigan Department of Technology, Management and Budget; see Abbey-Lamberts (2013).
27. Simon (2010).
28. Peck and Tickell (2002).
29. Gable and Hall (2013).
30. Gable and Hall (2013).
31. Hajal (2012a).
32. Martin (1993).
33. Sugrue (2005).
34. Martin (1993: 47).
35. Katzman (1973: 162).
36. Sugrue (2005).
37. Boyle (2005, 39).
38. Georgakas, Surkin, and Marable (1998).

39. Sugrue (2005).
40. Kenyon (2004).
41. Fine (2007).
42. Fine (2007: 161).
43. Austin (2006: 83).
44. In the aftermath, there was a distinct disparity between whites' and Blacks' perceptions of the Riot's causes and characteristics. While 69% of Detroit Blacks in one survey said that the Riot occurred because people were "being treated badly," only 28% of whites agreed. Moreover, 31% of whites said that "criminals" had started the Riot; 11% of Blacks thought so. Strikingly, 37% of surveyed Detroit whites said that stronger law enforcement was needed as a preventative measure against future riots; within a few months after the Riot, this proportion among whites grew to 51% (Fine, 2007: 391). In contrast to the alleged criminality of rioters and the Riot itself, a few months after the Riot, 56% of Blacks preferred "rebellion or revolution" to the term "riot" to describe Detroit's civil unrest (Fine, 2007: 351), suggesting that "pride and a sense of cohesion" (Warren, 1975: 17) emerged among Blacks through this highly politicized form of looting and rioting (Austin, 2006: 171).
45. Madriz (1997); see also Stabile (2006).
46. Austin (2006).
47. Georgakas, Surkin, and Marable (1998).
48. Simon (2007).
49. Pew Center on the States (2009).
50. Kenyon (2004: 15, 36).
51. This suburban imaginary evokes what Lipsitz (2011: 29) calls a "white spatial imaginary"; see Chapter 1, Footnote 21.
52. Hagerdorn (1998: 393).
53. Mieczkowski (1986); see also Taylor (1990).
54. Chicago Tribune (1988).
55. Cooper (1987: 29).
56. Wacquant (2008; 2009; 2012).
57. Harcourt (2010).
58. Soss, Fording, and Schram (2011).
59. Cohen (2002 [1972]).
60. Richard was the only gun carrier I met who regularly carried three firearms. It was not, however, unusual for gun carriers to carry two guns: a larger "carry" gun alongside a smaller "backup" gun.
61. David Garland (2002), for example, examines how rising crime rates were transformed into a politically charged project. Focusing on the 1980s and 1990s, he identifies an emergent narrative of crime—what he calls the "criminology of the other"—that stipulates the offender as "the threatening outcast, the fearsome stranger, the excluded and the embittered," a narrative that "functions to demonize the criminal, to act out popular fears and resentments, and to promote support for state punishment" (2002: 137). He

connects this formulation of crime and "tough on crime" politics to the rise of the New Right and the mass media. Although right-wing politicians *were* frontrunners in this regard, politicians across the spectrum used the fear of rising crime to secure electoral success and pass "law and order" policies—mandatory minimum sentences, zero tolerance policies, Three Strikes laws—that would rapidly expand the incarceration apparatus in the United States in the decades to come.

62. This led Fisher (1976: 398–399) to conclude that "although not the single causal factor, firearm availability contributes significantly to the magnitude of the homicide rate." Indeed, this period of rampant gun violence led many scholars to examine the relationship between firearms and violent death and crime (Newton and Zimring, 1970), with some developing complex models that take into account not only firearms accessibility but also race, gun control, and other factors to explain the sudden surge in gun-related violence. For example, in an argument that bears some elective affinity to "culture of poverty" reasoning, Seitz (1972) suggests that the impact of race is so great that while gun control laws may reduce homicides committed by whites, they would be unlikely to impact homicides committed by nonwhites, unable to counter a culture of illegal firearms use. This idea has not been contradicted by contemporary accounts of inner-city violence (Anderson, 1999). Despite the longevity of this debate, scholars such as Jens Ludwig (2000) maintain that the evidence between gun prevalence and crime remains "ambiguous" and "inconclusive."

63. Time Magazine (1984).

64. Hajal (2012b).

65. Damron (2013).

66. See the FBI Uniform Crime Report online database at http://ucrdatatool. gov/Search/Crime/Crime.cfm, accessed April 16, 2014.

67. See the FBI Uniform Crime Report online database at http://ucrdatatool. gov/Search/Crime/Crime.cfm, accessed April 16, 2014.

68. See the FBI Uniform Crime Report online database at http://ucrdatatool. gov/Search/Crime/Crime.cfm>, accessed April 16, 2014.

69. Simon (2010).

70. Madriz (1997); Tonry (2011).

71. The pervasiveness of Black stereotypes across racial groups is demonstrated in an experimental study by Sagar and Schofield (1980) in which white and Black sixth-grade students were asked to evaluate examples of ambiguous aggression. All students were more likely to view actions as mean and threatening when performed by a Black rather than a white student.

72. Madriz (1997).

73. Rose (2002).

74. Feeley and Simon (1992).

75. To use sociological terminology, race becomes what Pierre Bourdieu (1989) calls a "principle of social vision and division" or what Eduardo Bonilla-Silva

(2012: 173) calls an everyday "grammar" that "structures cognition, vision, and even feelings."

76. Hartigan (1998).
77. Rosenfeld and Messner (2013).
78. Ames (2006).
79. Comaroff and Comaroff (2004: 822).

Chapter 3

1. Italicized text indicates material from field notes.
2. Special Weapons and Tactical Team.
3. International Defensive Pistol Association.
4. See footnote 56.
5. Berkvist (2008).
6. The "New Right" refers to a highly effective movement of think tanks, politicians, alternative-media outlets, churches, and grass-roots organizations that culminated in Ronald Reagan's presidential election in 1980 and has swayed politics to the right ever since (Hardisty, 2000; Berlet and Lyons, 2000; Diamond, 1995). While some popular writers have dismissed the New Right as a cacophony of disgruntled, but privileged, Americans and working-class simpletons (see Thomas Frank's 2005 *What's the Matter with Kansas?*), scholars have shown that the New Right's political success has resulted from a sophisticated coordination across multiple strands of American conservatism—religious conservatism, libertarianism, social traditionalism, neoconservatism, and others (Blee and Creasap, 2010). While American conservatism was mainly a small, intellectual movement from the 1930s to the 1950s, it is now a complex, broad-based, and powerful political ideology characterized by a general suspicion of the American government and strong support for punitive and traditionalist approaches to social problems (Himmelstein, 1990; Micklethwait and Wooldridge, 2005; Lakoff, 2002). Because of the broad-based appeal of US conservatism, scholars have shifted from analyzing conservative beliefs as irrational paranoia (as per the scholarship of the 1960s and 1970s; see Hofstadter (1964) and Bell (2001)) to unpacking the moral universe and cultural worldviews (Lakoff, 2002) in which conservative politics becomes rational, upstanding, and virtuous (for a particularly excellent example, see Luker (1985)).
7. The NRA profits from certifying instructors as well as selling course materials to instructors for use in their classes. In order for the NRA course to comply with concealed-pistol license requirements, each student must receive an original course packet from the NRA and an original NRA certificate of completion, both of which must be purchased by the NRA-certified instructor from the NRA.
8. I would like to thank Josh Page for his guidance in formulating this term.
9. Davidson (1998); Melzer (2009); Sugarman (1992); O'Neill (2007).
10. Davidson (1998: 27).

11. Waldman (2014: 88).
12. Davidson (1998: 29).
13. Davidson (1998: 31).
14. Waldman (2014: 91).
15. Davidson (1998: 30).
16. Carter (2012: 323)
17. Winkler (2013).
18. Some argue that the 1986 Firearms Owners Protection Act was also a defeat for the gun lobby because it banned new manufacturing and importation of fully automatic firearms for civilian use. However, given that this legislation included provisions that protected gun rights as well, I do not consider the 1986 Act an outright legislative defeat for the gun lobby.
19. Waldman (2014: 94).
20. Shaiko and Wallace (1998).
21. At the time of this writing, these include Alabama, Arkansas, Colorado, Florida, Georgia, Idaho, Illinois, Indiana, Iowa, Kansas, Kentucky, Louisiana, Maine, Michigan, Minnesota, Mississippi, Missouri, Montana, Nebraska, Nevada, New Hampshire, New Mexico, North Carolina, North Dakota, Ohio, Oklahoma, Oregon, Pennsylvania, South Carolina, South Dakota, Tennessee, Texas, Utah, Virginia, Washington, West Virginia, Wisconsin, and the additional three states (Alaska, Arizona, and Wyoming) with "Constitutional" carry systems that still issue permits on a shall-issue basis for out-of-state carry (see footnote 22). Note that two additional states (Connecticut and Delaware) do not have shall-issue laws but issue permits on a de facto shall-issue basis, while Vermont allows anyone able to legally own a gun to carry it and has no state system for issuing carry permits.
22. In addition, some states operate under a "no permit" or "Constitutional" carry system. Under Constitutional carry, no permit is required to carry a firearm concealed; any person who is legally able to own a gun is also legally able to carry it. Alaska, Arizona, Wyoming, and Vermont allow carry without a concealed carry permit, but Alaska, Arizona, and Wyoming still issue permits on a shall-issue basis for residents wishing to conceal carry in other states where a permit is required.
23. A number of political, social, and demographic factors shape when and which states adopt shall-issue laws. For example, Grossman and Lee (2008) found that less urban states and states that bordered other states that had already adopted shall-issue legislation were more likely to also adopt shall-issue legislation, and this adoption was accelerated by increases in crime. In addition, political process is a key factor: in Michigan, the passage of this law was largely the result of the combined lobbying efforts of the NRA and the Michigan Coalition for Responsible Gun Owners (MCRGO), a statewide organization that formed in the late 1990s.

24. At the time of my research, the Personal Protection Outside the Home course was not approved for basic CPL instruction in Michigan. Therefore, instructors used—and many still continue to use—the Personal Protection Inside the Home course to license people to carry guns outside of the home.

25. Based on my observations in Michigan, gun carriers typically spend about $100 to $200 on required firearms instruction, $300 to $1,000 on a firearm, ammunition, and related accessories, and $105 on state processing of the CPL, resulting in an initial investment of about $500 to $1,300.

26. Armstrong (2002).

27. Foucault (1982; 1990); Mahmood (2004).

28. To use Goold, Loader, and Thumala's (2010: 38) terminology, shall-issue laws, by requiring training to obtain a concealed-pistol permit, provide the NRA with "ideological and cultural soil in which to grow."

29. Bittner (1970).

30. This is what scholars call "substantive" or "cultural" citizenship; see Glenn (2011); Ong (1996); Miller (2006).

31. O'Malley (1992).

32. This is evocative of O'Malley's (1992) analysis of *homo prudens* as a *crime*-preventing "responsibilized" subject: a self-regulating, self-governing subject that emerges through the individualization of responsibility for crime prevention (Garland, 1996).

33. Nevertheless, the moral ambiguities discussed here are not limited to guns but may shape other security commodities as well; see Loader, Goold, and Thumala's (2014) analysis of the moral economy of security consumption.

34. Bourdieu (1980 [1990]).

35. To use Van Wolputte's (2004) turn of phrase.

36. In the sections that follow, I rely on NRA training materials distributed to students as well as interviews and participant observation. I forefront excerpts from the NRA training materials in order to highlight the moral impulse that grounds these courses. The training materials demonstrate that this moral politics is not idiosyncratic to my sample but rather a core aspect of contemporary gun politics when it comes to concealed carry. Direct quotations from NRA materials are taken from the NRA's *Personal Protection Inside the Home* (2000) handbook, used in most of the classes I attended in Michigan.

37. It is important to note, however, that the NRA is not the only pro-gun organization within Michigan and that there are many opportunities for enthusiastic gun carriers in Michigan to become involved in gun culture beyond the NRA, including non-NRA state-level organizations such as the Michigan Coalition for Responsible Gun Ownership, the Shooters' Alliance for Firearms Rights and Michigan Open Carry; print material like *Concealed Carry Magazine*; and online blogs and forums such as MIGunOwners.Org

and OpenCarry.Org. The NRA is not the only game in town, but it is one of the most powerful organizations helping to set the rules.

38. A number of firearms instructors opposed required training on political grounds. Nevertheless, they agreed that any responsible gun owner should take the initiative to train far beyond the training required by Michigan law to obtain a carry permit.

39. Paraphrased from NRA materials and instructors' questions.

40. NRA (2000: 25).

41. This is also reminiscent of O'Malley's (1992) discussion of "responsibilization."

42. NRA (2000: 26).

43. See chapter 4.

44. Bittner (1970: 44).

45. O'Neill (2007).

46. It also glosses over the difficult task of ascertaining who is, and who is not, a criminal, which I examine in more detail in chapter 6.

47. NRA (2000: 26).

48. NRA (2000: 140).

49. NRA (2000: 139).

50. NRA (2000: 27).

51. NRA (2000: 26-27).

52. As I discuss in more detail in chapter 6, NRA course materials do not challenge students' perceptions of *what* constitutes a threat; they only provide suggestions on *how* to remain vigilant.

53. NRA (2000: 131, 147).

54. Weber (2002).

55. In hunting subcultures, for example, this knack communicates subculture membership. Likewise, "such cardinal sins as moving 'off-peg,' loading early or shooting low birds," as Hillyard and Burridge (2012: 402) describe with respect to game hunting in England, signal a shooter's novice status.

56. Some gun carriers take simulated gunfights even further by participating in close-combat "simunition" exercises beyond the basic NRA courses: individuals are ensconced in protective clothing, armed with guns loaded with "non-lethal" ammunition, and act out scenarios that require them to quickly ascertain and react to threats. The firm Simunition specializes in conversion kits, ammunition, and other accessories for these exercises.

57. NRA (2000: 107).

58. Bourdieu (1980[1990]); see earlier in chapter 3 for definition.

59. Legal scholars Patricia Ewick and Susan Silbey (1998) developed the term "legal consciousness" to capture how law comes to matter in everyday life. Guns—when embedded into everyday life through concealed carry laws—can be understood as vehicles of a particular version of legal consciousness whereby gun carriers see themselves as empowered as not only lawful but also morally upstanding citizens.

60. The citizen-protector thus provides a slightly different reading of gun culture compared to the self-reliant, independent American figured in the studies of Kahan and Braman (2003) and Down (2002) and the "cultural warriors" in studies like Melzer (2009) and Burbick (2006).

61. NRA (2000: 217).

Chapter 4

1. Legal gun use *in general* is not consistent across race. According to the 2010 General Social Survey, 36.5% of whites own guns, versus 15.5% of African Americans, with an average of 8.7% ownership across other racial and ethnic groups. Breaking this number down for handguns, the difference shrinks dramatically: according to a national survey of private gun ownership released in 1997, about 16.5% of whites and 13.1% of African Americans own handguns (Cook and Ludwig, 1997). These numbers have probably changed somewhat over the past fifteen years, but they suggest that the racial difference in gun ownership may not hold as strongly with respect to gun ownership for self-defense. This also echoes findings by McClain (1983), who found in the early 1980s that African Americans are more likely to own guns for protection than recreation as compared to whites. Controlling for protection versus recreation appears, therefore, to significantly reduce the racial disparity of gun ownership.

2. These figures become more compelling when comparing racial disparities (or lack thereof) in concealed licenses in the three most populous counties in Michigan: as noted in the introduction, African Americans in all three counties are more likely to have a permit to carry a gun concealed than whites, suggesting that portrayals of gun rights as an all-white affair are quite inaccurate.

3. Over the past several decades, American law enforcement unions have deployed and galvanized fear of crime in order to promote their organizational agendas (DeLord, Burpo, Shannon, and Spearing, 2008; Page, 2011a and 2011b). For example, police unions in Memphis, Tennessee (Miles, 2013); Stockton, California (Massey, 2012); Bay City, Michigan (Murphy, 2010), and other cities have protested police layoffs by proclaiming that, in the case of Jersey City, "police layoffs and demotions mean more crime, shootings, murders" (Hayes, 2010).

4. Larson (2012).

5. Community Oriented Policing Services (2011); Reaves (2012).

6. By and large, the reductions in social welfare state functions remain significantly larger than cuts to the penal functions of the state. In other words, the carceral state remains resilient relative to the welfare state even as both undergo contraction; see Wacquant (2012). For example, while ten thousand to fifteen thousand police officers lost their jobs since 2008 (see below), more than three hundred thousand teachers have been laid off, according to a report entitled "Teacher Jobs at Risk" (Executive Office of the President, 2011).

7. Community Oriented Policing Services (2011: 3).
8. Barnes (August 2013).
9. Barnes (August 2013).
10. Italicized text indicates material from field notes.
11. Community Oriented Policing Services (2011).
12. Carr (2005).
13. Feeney (2014).
14. Stevens (1999).
15. Porter (2013).
16. Garland (1996; 2000; 2002).
17. Micklethwait and Wooldridge (2005).
18. See also the discussion of "responsibilization" in chapter 3.
19. Haas, de Keijser, and Bruinsma (2014); McDowall and Loftin (1983); Smith and Uchida (1988).
20. Haas, de Keijser, and Bruinsma (2014).
21. Fraser and Gordon (1994); Soss, Fording, and Schram (2011).
22. Micklethwait and Wooldridge (2005). Recall also from chapter 1 that the vast majority of interviewees were right-leaning conservatives and libertarians, although left-leaning libertarians also embraced an anti-statist stance toward the police. As I describe in more detail in chapter 5, some gun carriers blended anti-statist, pro-gun stances with more radical, rather than conservative, politics, and these sentiments are also inflected by gun carriers' racialized relations to the police; see also footnote 23.
23. One exception to this is the Detroit 300, a group of African American men who target serial criminals who victimize women, children, and the elderly. Members of the organization have performed citizen's arrests, delivering suspects to law enforcement officials for subsequent criminal prosecution. While the Detroit 300 has been recognized by city officials and even works with law enforcement officials in Detroit once the group has apprehended suspects, I am not aware of incidents in which Detroit 300 worked in tandem with law enforcement to actuate the arrest of a specific suspect. See chapter 5.
24. Young (2003).
25. Young (2003: 4).
26. Brown (1995); Dubber (2005); Spierenburg (1998).
27. Jeffords (1989); Kellner (2008).
28. While the race of the (male) hostage-taker varied somewhat in the targets I saw during my fieldwork, the hostage herself was almost always a female and almost always white, embodying what Esther Madriz (1997) calls an "ideal victim." Relatedly, my own race and gender probably played a role in gun carriers' willingness to take a protective stance toward me; not only did I not threaten gun carriers with my presence, but my social status allowed them to enact familiar scripts regarding the role of men in protecting women. I explore my gender and racial positionality further in chapter 5.

29. See Madriz (1997) on "ideal victims."
30. Messner (2007).
31. Messner (2007: 466); see also Stroud (2012).
32. Burbick (2006); Connell (2005); Melzer (2009).
33. Kahan and Braman (2003); Braman and Kahan (2006); Lakoff (2002); Down (2002).
34. Lakoff (2002) develops two metaphors for understanding the underlying differences between conservative and liberal ideology—the "strict father" model and the "nurturant parent" model. The "strict father" model tends to emphasize individualism, harsh discipline, and power structures organized around a dominant figure—the "father." Most people embrace a blend of Lakoff's two models.
35. Jones (2013).
36. This contrasts with some previous accounts of pro-gun men; Burbick (2006), for example, argues that pro-gun men tend to understand women as anti-gun "gun grabbers."
37. Throughout her 2008 bid for US vice president and thereafter, Palin described herself as a "mama grizzly" to emphasize her maternal toughness: "You don't want to mess with moms who are rising up . . . if you thought pit bulls were tough, you don't want to mess with mama grizzlies" (*The Telegraph,* 2010).
38. These data are drawn from eleven interviews conducted with women gun carriers in Michigan as a part of my larger project that focuses on gun-carrying men. While the bulk of this book focuses on men, I introduce these data here in order to emphasize the gendered nuance of guns, particularly with respect to the duty to protect others.
39. Resonant with analyses of contemporary policing as organized in terms of "security bubbles" and "nodes of governance" (Shearing and Wood, 2003), this movement of the Castle Doctrine into the public sphere extends the right to privacy (as per Don Mitchell's [2003] model of SUV citizenship), in addition to further expanding men's duty to protect. Gun carriers frequently cited the "twenty-one-foot rule." This rule stipulates that an approaching threat within "twenty-one feet" should be treated as "imminent," and therefore, it is appropriate to deploy lethal force in response. Thus, gun carriers have a very precise measurement of their "security bubble"—twenty-one feet.
40. Young (2003).
41. Klinenberg (2001).
42. Klinenberg (2001: 80).
43. Dubber (2005).

Chapter 5

1. WCHB (2012).
2. Angel (2012).
3. Pilkington (2014).
4. Battaglia (2012).

5. Children's Defense Fund (2012).
6. Bostock, Carter, and Quealy (2013); see also Sampson (2012).
7. Rios (2011); Epp, Maynard-Moody, and Haider-Markel (2014).
8. Behrens, Uggen, and Manza (2003); Manza and Uggen (2006); Western (2006); Tonry (2011); Muller (2012).
9. The Safe Streets Act of 1968 empowered law enforcement by increasing funding to agencies and earmarking research support for criminal justice studies. It also loosened guidelines for wiretapping and tightened gun control restrictions.
10. Simon (2007).
11. Kraska and Cubellis (1997); Kraska and Kappeler (1997); Kraska (2007); Balko (2013).
12. Epp, Maynard-Moody, and Haider-Markel (2014); Harcourt (2006a).
13. Kraska (1996: 414).
14. Georgakas, Surkin, and Marable (1998).
15. Epp, Maynard-Moody, and Haider-Markel (2014).
16. See Contreras (2013) for a social history of the American crack market.
17. Epp, Maynard-Moody, and Haider-Markel (2014).
18. *Whren et al. v. United States*, 517 U.S. 806 (1996).
19. Under their official "stop-and-frisk" policy, the NYPD has stopped five million New Yorkers since 2002, the vast majority of whom were innocent. As the New York City Bar Association (2013) notes, 85% of those stopped have been Black or Latino, a disparity that cannot be accounted for by neighborhood crime rates or demographics. Only 6% of these stops have resulted in arrest, and only 2% have resulted in a weapon recovery. While the NYPD is unique in having an overt policy of "stop-and-frisk," less overt versions of these policies are widespread across US law enforcement agencies.
20. Epp, Maynard-Moody, and Haider-Markel (2014: 15, 8).
21. Meehan and Ponder (2002).
22. Provine (2007).
23. Epp, Maynard-Moody, and Haider-Markel (2014); Gelman, Fagan, and Kiss (2007).
24. Webb and Marshall (1995); Sampson and Bartusch (1998); Harris (1999); Weisburd, Greenspan, and Hamilton (2000); Rose (2002); Brunson (2007); Morrison (2007); Gau and Brunson (2010).
25. On the whole, gun carriers of color were much more concerned about racism from police than the overt racism they experienced from other gun carriers. Despite probing for stories, I was unable to collect more than four specific stories—three from white gun carriers—about the problem of racism among gun carriers.
26. A recent analysis of hip-hop lyrics shows that, while rappers are often characterized as promoting criminality and aggression against police, lyrics about police are more likely to express sentiments that police unfairly and harshly target racial minorities. See Steinmetz and Henderson (2012).

27. This reverses the all too common roadside rituals in which "Blacks and other minorities are the ones who are held by the side of the road while police officers rummage through their cars"; according to Epp, Maynard-Moody, and Haider-Markel (2014: 24), such incidents become the means by which "police stops shape the meaning of race in an ongoing way."

28. Rios (2011).

29. "BMWG" and "MWG" are common slang on online gun forums for "Black man with a gun" and "man with a gun," respectively. One national gun advocate, Kenneth Blanchard, advertises his pro-gun books and media under the moniker "Black Man with a Gun."

30. Italicized text indicates material from field notes.

31. Morrison (2007).

32. Epp, Maynard-Moody, and Haider-Markel (2014: 157) summarize the impact of different experiences with the police on evaluations of the police by drawing attention to the role of police stops in producing a profound racial divide: "No one likes to be pulled over, but police stops teach different lessons to African Americans and whites. They teach African Americans that police stops are unpredictable, arbitrary, and a tool of surveillance. They teach whites that police stops are predictable consequences of unsafe driving, and, remarkably, that even well-deserved stops may lead to being let off with a warning if the driver is respectful and polite to the officers." They relate these findings to Soss's (1999) study on the divergent impacts of welfare participation. Delineating people who participated in programs experienced as predictable and rule-bound versus those experienced as arbitrary and unfair, Soss finds that people's direct interaction with local government shapes their political behavior and broader attitudes about the state.

33. There is a growing "libertarian/conservative consensus" about the need to reform the criminal justice system, currently exemplified by the Right on Crime Initiative.

34. Although confidence in the police appears to be decreasing and police defunding appears to be on the rise, gun carriers generally still come from demographic groups most likely to exhibit relatively high levels of confidence in the police—that is, white conservative men. Both within and beyond the United States, confidence in the police is significantly correlated with political conservatism (Stack and Cao, 1998). According to a 2005 Gallup poll (Jones, 2005) on confidence in the police, conservatives are also much more likely than liberals to be confident in the police (58% versus 40%) and to own guns. However, gun owners are about as confident in the police as respondents on the whole—about 52% versus 53%. This suggests that conservative gun owners may differ, to some degree, from their non-gun-owning conservative counterparts in having less confidence in the police to control crime, a difference that may also be partly explained by the observation that not all gun owners are conservative.

35. This resonates with Webb and Marshall's (1995) and Gau and Brunson's (2010) findings that other factors, such as class, may also be important in

structuring who has negative police encounters and, therefore, negative attitudes toward the police.

36. See chapter 2.

37. Dropping civilians off in unknown or unsafe areas appears to be associated with other police abuses, like racial profiling, in large urban areas; this was described by the African American men in Brunson's (2007) study on experiences of police harassment in St. Louis.

38. Williams (2014).

39. This was before Starbucks effectively banned open carry in its stores in 2013; see Schultz (2013).

40. According to the Gun-Free School Zones Act of 1990, no one may carry a gun into a designated school zone without a license to carry. According to Michigan's shall-issue law, a CPL holder is licensed to carry concealed *except* in designated "pistol-free zones," including school zones. However, the shall-issue law *does not* prohibit open carrying in school zones. Therefore, CPL holders may *openly* carry guns into school zones, because, as licensed gun carriers, they are compliant with the Gun-Free School Zones Act. Open carry does not require a carry license outside of pistol-free zones.

41. During my fieldwork, I became aware of two cases of alleged police assault against white open carriers, both of which were under investigation while I was conducting fieldwork. One involved officers allegedly physically beating an open carrier; the other involved an open carrier being pushed to the ground while the officers had their guns drawn.

42. This expectation of law as objective and reasonable resonates with Ewick and Silbey's (1998) notion of "before the law" legal consciousness.

43. This disjuncture resonates with the different frames that white versus African American motorists use to make sense of police stops more generally (Epp, Maynard-Moody, and Haider-Markel, 2014: 47–48).

44. This question—What does a gun say?—was provocatively posed in a *New York Times* op-ed by Patrick Blanchfield (2014) on the topic of open carry. Here, I address this question by calling attention to the racial and gender nuance of guns and their carriers.

45. Herbert (2001).

46. Cooper (2009).

47. Herbert (2001); Cooper (2009).

48. Bayley (1976: 165).

49. None of the eleven female gun carriers I interviewed made similar statements about "standing up" to police, nor have I come across such statements from women in published pro-gun sources.

50. Richard's double entendre in using the term "outlaw", I think, was intentional: he meant both that the gun carrier should be *more* knowledgeable about the law than the police officer *and* that the gun carrier should expose the illegitimate or unlawful use of police power by public law enforcement.

51. By highlighting this incident, my goal is not to imply that this very deliberate act of police confrontation is similar to the uninvited instances of

police harassment that people of color face. Based on my conversations with non-open carriers, this incident likely appears to the bulk of gun-carrying Americans, let alone Americans in general, as an overreaction by the open carriers to a minor instance of misunderstanding on the part of the police.

52. After following up with the Oakland County clerk, I found out that my registration paperwork had not been properly processed, due to a clerical error. Stuck on the back of another card, my registration card was physically in the possession of the clerk, but it had not been entered into the Michigan State Police database of registered guns.

Chapter 6

1. Brandishing refers to the threatening display of a weapon (see Michigan Penal Code Act 328 of 1931, Section 750.234e); felonious assault refers to the overt display of a deadly weapon with the intent to injure the victim or to cause fear of an immediate attack (Michigan Penal Code Act 328 of 1931, Section 750.82). Whereas brandishing may involve simply exposing the weapon (e.g., by menacingly lifting a shirt), felonious assault may involve, for example, pointing a gun at a victim, even if the gun is not fired. Note that as of this writing, "brandishing" is not explicitly defined by Michigan law.

2. For these figures, I aggregated all charges and convictions reported to the Michigan State Police that fall under Michigan Penal Code Act 328 of 1931, Section 750.8X, in the CCW Annual Reports from 2003 through 2013.

3. Collins (2009: 88).

4. Collins (2009: 89).

5. Collins (2009: 92, 94).

6. Collins (2009: 113).

7. Ross (2007: 2).

8. Ross (2007: 2).

9. Ross (2007: 2).

10. Maynard-Moody and Musheno (2003).

11. See chapter 4; Young (2003).

12. See chapter 4.

13. Collins (2009: 338–339).

14. Collins (2009: 339).

15. Collins (2009: 339).

16. Sociologist Patricia Hill Collins (2008) calls these "controlling images."

17. For example, sociologists Andrew Penner and Aliya Saperstein (2013) have interrogated how social status changes racial classification. They use longitudinal data in which interviewers were asked to classify the racial status of interviewees and then examined a subset of cases for which racial classification changes over time for the same interviewee. They find that women classified as white were later classified as racial minorities after receiving public assistance, while men ascribed as white were later classified as racial minorities after acquiring a criminal justice record. Poor people were more likely to

be classified as nonwhite as well. The analysis provides strong evidence that social status—rather than skin tone—is critical in racial classification.

18. Collins (2009: 342–344).
19. Collins (2009: 345).
20. Fagan and Wilkinson (1998); Anderson (1999).
21. Horowitz (1983); Nisbett and Cohen (1996).
22. Anderson (1999).
23. Collins (2009: 350, 352).
24. Collins (2009: 351).
25. Jones (2009).
26. Jones (2009).
27. Payne (2006); see also Correll et al. (2002).
28. Payne (2006).

Conclusion

1. With a margin of error of 2.9%, these numbers suggests that Americans are effectively split evenly between favoring gun control versus gun rights. See Pew (2013a).
2. Saad (2013).
3. Pew (2012).
4. Pew (2013a).
5. Pew (2013a).
6. The number of gun-owning American households is the subject of much debate; see Pew (2013a). The two major surveys that have collected longitudinal data since the 1970s conflict: the General Social Survey (GSS) shows gun ownership dropping from a high of over 50% of all households to roughly a third, while Gallup shows a much more erratic pattern, with the same percentage of households—43%—reporting guns in 2012 as in 1972. While gun ownership today is lower than the peak measured by both surveys, the surveys conflict in terms of whether a large, long-term decline in gun ownership has occurred. This is further complicated by recent spikes in FBI background checks for firearms sales.
7. The figures for hunting versus protection have reversed: in 1999, 49% of gun owners said they owned guns for hunting; 26% cited protection as the main reason. In 2013, these figures were 32% and 48%, respectively. Interestingly, in the February 2013 Pew survey, only 2% of gun owners in that survey said that they owned guns primarily because of their beliefs about the Second Amendment—a drop from 4% since 1999.
8. Swift (2013). This survey item allowed multiple responses. Here, the percentage of people who cited Second Amendment beliefs was 5%.
9. Carroll (2005). Fifty-three percent of gun-owning Democrats cited target shooting, compared to 71% of gun-owning Republicans and 72% of gun-owning Independents. These figures were 53%, 64%, and 58% for hunting, respectively.

10. Saad (2013).
11. McCarthy (2014); Pew (2014). Note also that in 1991 a majority of Democrats, Easterners, women, and Americans living in households without a gun supported a handgun ban. By 2011 *there was no subgroup of Americans based on gender, region, political affiliation, or household gun ownership that supported a ban on handguns in the majority* (Jones, 2011). While restricting *sale* of firearms enjoyed greater popularity (with many groups supporting such restrictions in the majority in 2011), these numbers still showed a dramatic drop from 1991 levels.
12. I am using masculine pronouns here deliberately: these laws have historically protected men's right to violence within the household (Gillespie, 1989).
13. Barnes (2013).
14. Roman (2013).
15. Melzer (2009).
16. Melzer (2009).
17. Bayley and Shearing (1996); Beckett and Murakawa (2012); Desmond and Valdez (2013); Gilliom (2001); Shearing and Marks (2011); Simon (2007).
18. Death Penalty Information Center (2014); Federal Bureau of Investigation (2012b).
19. Federal Bureau of Investigation (2012a; 2012b).
20. Desmond and Valdez (2013); Beckett and Herbert (2011); Loader and Walker (2001); Monahan (2010).
21. Beckett and Herbert (2011).
22. Shearing and Stenning (1983); Bayley and Shearing (1996); Zedner (2006).
23. Faturechi (2014).
24. Target (2013).
25. Goldstein (2007).
26. TASER (2014).
27. Sanburn (2012).
28. Miller (2006).
29. Swidler (1986).
30. Bittner (1970).
31. Collins (2009).
32. Gamson (1992).
33. O'Neill (2007).
34. According to a February 2013 Pew poll, 74% of households that included at least one NRA member supported "the idea of making private gun sales and sales at gun shows subject to [background] checks"; 83% of non-NRA households agreed. See Drake (2014).

BIBLIOGRAPHY

Abbey-Lamberts, Kate. March 29, 2013. "Michigan Unemployment Drops to 8.8, Detroit Unemployment Still 19 Percent." *The Huffington Post*. <http://www.huffingtonpost.com/2012/03/29/michigan-unemployment-february-detroit-unemployment_n_1388455.html>. Accessed April 25, 2014.

Ames, Mark. (2006). *Going Postal: Rage, Murder, and Rebellion from Reagan's Workplaces to Clinton's Columbine and Beyond*. Brooklyn, NY: Soft Skull Press.

Angel, Cecil. February 10, 2012. "Kade'jah Davis, 12, Mourned by Hundreds in Detroit Funeral: 'It's Sad She Had to Go Like This.'" Detroit, MI: *The Detroit Free Press*. <http://www.freep.com/article/20120210/NEWS01/120210047/Kade-jah-Davis-girl-12-funeral>. Accessed July 1, 2014.

Anderson, Elijah. (1999). *Code of the Street*. New York, NY: W. W. Norton & Company.

Armstrong, Elizabeth A. (2002). *Forging Gay Identities: Organizing Sexuality in San Francisco, 1950–1994*. Chicago, IL: University of Chicago Press.

Ashburn, Anderson. (1962). "Detroit Automation." *The ANNALS of the American Academy of Political and Social Science, 340*(1), 21–28.

Austin, Curtis. (2006). *Up Against the Wall: Violence in the Making and Unmaking of the Black Panther Party*. Fayetteville, AR: University of Arkansas Press.

Ayres, Ian, and John Donohue. (2003). "The Latest Misfires in Support of the 'More Guns, Less Crime' Hypothesis." *Stanford Law Review, 55*(4), 1371–1398.

Balko, Radley. (2013). *Rise of the Warrior Cop: The Militarization of America's Police Forces*. Philadelphia, PA: Public Affairs.

Battaglia, Tammy Stables. October 12, 2012. "D'Andre Lane Found Guilty of Murder in Death of Daughter Bianca Jones." Detroit, MI: *The Detroit Free Press*.

<http://www.freep.com/article/20121012/NEWS01/121012043/D-Andre-L ane-Bianca-Jones-verdict>. Accessed July 1, 2014.

Bayley, David H. (1976). *Forces of Order*. Berkeley, CA: University of California Press.

Bayley, David H., and Clifford D. Shearing. (1996). "The Future of Policing." *Law & Society Review, 30*(3), 585–606.

Barnes, John. May 24, 2013. "Justified to Kill: An MLive Special Report on Self-Defense Homicides in Michigan." Grand Rapids, MI: *MLive.com.* <http:// www.mlive.com/news/index.ssf/2012/06/justified_to_kill_an_mlive_spe. html>. Accessed May 21, 2014.

Barnes, John. August 25, 2013. "Fewer Cops, Less Crime: MLive Investigation Finds Michigan Safer Even as Police Numbers Decline." Grand Rapids, MI: *MLive.com.* <http://www.mlive.com/news/index.ssf/2013/08/less_cops_ less_crime_mlive_inv.html>. Accessed January 3, 2014.

Beard v. United States, 158 U.S. 550 (1895).

Beckett, Katherine, and Steve Herbert. (2011). *Banished: The New Social Control in Urban America*. New York, NY: Oxford University Press.

Beckett, Katherine, and Naomi Murakawa. (2012). "Mapping the Shadow Carceral State: Toward an Institutionally Capacious Approach to Punishment." *Theoretical Criminology, 16*(2), 221–244.

Behrens, Angela, Christopher Uggen, and Jeff Manza. (2003). "Ballot Manipulation and the 'Menace of Negro Domination': Racial Threat and Felon Disenfranchisement in the United States, 1850–2002." *American Journal of Sociology, 109*(3), 559–605.

Bell, Daniel (Ed.). (2001). *The Radical Right*. Piscataway, NJ: Transaction Publishers.

Berlet, Chip, and Matthew Nemiroff Lyons. (2000). *Right-Wing Populism in America: Too Close for Comfort*. New York, NY: Guilford Press.

Bernstein, Mary. (1997). "Celebration and Suppression: The Strategic Uses of Identity by the Lesbian and Gay Movement." *American Journal of Sociology, 103*(3), 531–565.

Berkvist, Robert. April 6, 2008. "Charlton Heston, Epic Film Star and Voice of NRA, Dies at 84. New York, NY: *New York Times.* <http://www.nytimes. com/2008/04/06/movies/06heston.html?_r=2&bl&ex=1207713600&en=55b5 ab5e7044b201&ei=5087%0A&oref=slogin&>. Accessed April 30, 2014.

Binelli, Mark. (2012). *Detroit City Is the Place to Be: The Afterlife of an American Metropolis*. New York, NY: Metropolitan Books.

Bittner, Egon. (1970). *The Functions of Police in Modern Society*. Washington, DC: National Institute of Mental Health.

Black, Donald. (1983). "Crime as Social Control." *American Sociological Review, 48*(1), 34–45.

Blanchfield, Patrick. May 4, 2014. "What Do Guns Say?" New York, NY: *New York Times.* <http://opinionator.blogs.nytimes.com/2014/05/04/what-do-guns-

say/?_php=true&_type=blogs&_php=true&_type=blogs&hp& rref=opinion&_r=1&>. Accessed May 8, 2014.

Blee, Kathleen M., and Kimberly A. Creasap. (2010). "Conservative and Right-Wing Movements." *Annual Review of Sociology, 36,* 269–286.

Block, Dustin. November 16, 2013. "Detroit Ranks Last Among Top 50 US Cities in Median Home Value, Survey Finds." Grand Rapids, MI: *mLive.com.* <http://www.mlive.com/business/detroit/index.ssf/2013/11/database_detroit_ ranks_last_am.html>. Accessed April 25, 2014.

Bloom, Joshua, and Waldo E. Martin Jr. (2013). *Black Against Empire: The History and Politics of the Black Panther Party.* Berkeley, CA: University of California Press.

Bonilla-Silva, Eduardo. (2012). "The Invisible Weight of Whiteness: The Racial Grammar of Everyday Life in Contemporary America." *Ethnic and Racial Studies, 35*(2), 173–94.

Bostock, Mike, Shan Carter, and Kevin Quealy. January 3, 2013. "A Chicago Divided by Killings." New York, NY: *The New York Times.* <http://www. nytimes.com/interactive/2013/01/02/us/chicago-killings.html?ref=us&_r=0>. Accessed August 4, 2014.

Bourdieu, Pierre. (1980 [1990]). *The Logic of Practice.* Palo Alto, CA: Stanford University Press.

Bourdieu, Pierre. (1989). "Social Space and Symbolic Power." *Sociological Theory, 71*(2), 18–26.

Boustan, Leah, and Robert Margo. (2013). "A Silver Lining to White Flight? White Suburbanization and African-American Homeownership, 1940–1980." *Journal of Urban Economics, 78,* 71–80.

Boyle, Kevin. (2005). *Arc of Justice: A Saga of Race, Civil Rights, and Murder in the Jazz Age.* New York, NY: Holt Publishers.

Braman, Donald, and Dan M. Kahan. (2006). "Overcoming the Fear of Guns, the Fear of Gun Control, and the Fear of Cultural Politics: Constructing a Better Gun Debate." *Emory Law Journal, 55*(4), 569–607.

Brown, Richard Maxwell. (1991). *No Duty to Retreat: Violence and Values in American History and Society.* New York, NY: Oxford University Press.

Brown, Wendy. (1995). *States of Injury.* Princeton, NJ: Princeton University Press.

Brown, Peter Harry, and Daniel G. Abel. (2003). *Outgunned: Up Against the NRA.* New York, NY: The Free Press.

Brown v. United States, 256 U.S. 335 (1921).

Brunson, Rod. (2007). "Police Don't Like Black People: African American Young Men's Accumulated Police Experiences." *Criminology & Public Policy, 6*(1), 71–102.

Burbick, Joan. (2006). *Gun Show Nation: Gun Culture and American Democracy.* New York, NY: W.W. Norton & Company.

Bureau of Labor Statistics. (2013). Union Membership in Michigan 2012. *Bureau of Labor Statistics, June 3.* <http://www.bls.gov/ro5/unionmi.htm> Accessed September 20, 2013.

Carr, Patrick J. (2005). *Clean Streets: Controlling Crime, Maintaining Order, and Building a Community*. New York, NY: New York University Press.

Carroll, Joseph. November 22, 2005. "Gun Ownership and Use in America." Washington, DC: Gallup. <http://www.gallup.com/poll/20098/Gun-Owner ship-Use-America.aspx>. Accessed May 20, 2014.

Carter, Gregg Lee (Ed.). (2012). *Guns in American Society: An Encyclopedia of History, Politics, Culture and the Law*. Santa Barbara, CA: ABC-CLIO, Inc.

Chambers, Jennifer. February 27, 2014. "Michigan's Four-Year High School Graduation Rate Rises to Nearly 77%." Detroit, MI: *The Detroit News*. <http://www.detroitnews.com/article/20140227/SCHOOLS/302270090>. Accessed April 25, 2014.

Children's Defense Fund. (2012). *Protect Children, Not Guns*. Washington, DC: Children's Defense Fund.

Coates, Ta-Nehisi. March 9, 2011. "Detroit Was Like *Cheers*: Everyone Knew Your Name." New York, NY: *The Atlantic Monthly*. <http://www.the-atlantic.com/national/archive/2011/03/detroit-was-like-cheers-everyone-k new-your-name/72226/>. Accessed April 25, 2014.

Collins, Patricia Hill. (2008). *Black Feminist Thought: Knowledge, Consciousness, and the Politics of Empowerment*. New York, NY: Routledge Classics.

Collins, Randall. (2009). *Violence: A Micro-Sociological Theory*. Princeton, NJ: Princeton University Press.

Comaroff, Jean, and John Comaroff. (2004). "Criminal Obsessions, After Foucault: Postcoloniality, Policing, and the Metaphysics of Disorder." *Critical Inquiry*, *30*, 800–824.

Connell, Raewyn. (2005). *Masculinities*. Berkeley, CA: University of California Press.

Contreras, Randol. (2013). *The Stick-Up Kids*. Berkeley, CA: University of California Press.

Coontz, Stephanie. (1993). *The Way We Never Were*. New York, NY: Basic Books.

Correll, Joshua, Bernadette Park, Charles Judd, and Bernard Wittenbrink. (2002). "The Police Officer's Dilemma: Using Ethnicity to Disambiguate Potentially Threatening Individuals." *Journal of Personality and Social Psychology*, *83*(6): 1314–1329.

Cook, Philip J., and Jens Ludwig. (1997). "Guns in America: National Survey on Private Ownership and Use of Firearms." *Research in Brief*. Washington, DC: National Institute of Justice.

Cohen, Stanley. (2002 [1972]). *Folk Devils and Moral Panics*. New York, NY: Routledge Press.

Cooper, Barry Michael. December 1, 1987. "Kids Killing Kids: New Jack City Eats Its Young." *The Village Voice*, 23–29.

Cooper, Frank. (2009). "'Who's the Man?' Masculinities Studies, Terry Stops, and Police Training." *Columbia Journal of Gender and Law*, *18*, 671–742.

Community Oriented Policing Services. (2011). *The Impact of the Economic Downturn on American Police Agencies*. Washington, DC: US Department of Justice.

Damron, Gina. January 4, 2013. "2012 Was Detroit's Most Violent in Nearly 20 Years; Shootings, Bloodshed Have 'Become the Norm.'" Detroit, MI: *The Detroit Free Press*. <http://www.freep.com/apps/pbcs.dll/article?AID=/201301040300/NEWS01/301040139>. Accessed April 25, 2014.

Danziger, Sheldon H., and Reynolds Farley. (2010). "Troubling Times: The Declining Economic Status of Michigan Relative to the Rest of the United States, High School Graduates Relative to College Graduates and Men Relative to Women." Ann Arbor, MI: University of Michigan School of Social Work & Nokomis Foundation.

Davidson, Osha Gray. (1998). *Under Fire: The NRA and the Battle for Gun Control*. Iowa City, IA: University of Iowa Press.

Death Penalty Information Center. (2014). "Executions by Year." Washington, DC: Death Penalty Information Center. <http://www.deathpenaltyinfo.org/executions-year>. Accessed July 6, 2014.

DeLord, Ron, Jon Burpo, Michael Shannon, and Jim Spearing. (2008). *Police Union Power, Politics and Confrontation in the 21st Century*. Springfield, IL: Charles C. Thomas Publisher.

Desmond, Matthew, and Nicol Valdez. (2013). "Unpolicing the Urban Poor: Consequences of Third-Party Policing for Inner-City Women." *American Sociological Review*, *78*(1), 117–141.

Chicago Tribune. December 11, 1988. "Detroit's Crack Mobs Spread Out, Drug Entrepreneurs Invade Other Areas." Chicago, IL: *Chicago Tribune*.

Diamond, Sarah. (1995). *Roads to Dominion: Right-Wing Movements and Political Power in the United States*. New York, NY: Guilford Press.

Down, Douglas. (2002). "Representing Gun Owners: Frame Identification as Social Responsibility in News Media Discourse." *Written Communication*, *19*(1), 44–75.

Drake, Bruce. Apr 24, 2014. "5 Facts about the NRA and Guns in America." Washington, DC: Pew Charitable Trusts. <http://www.pewresearch.org/fact-tank/2014/04/24/5-facts-about-the-nra-and-guns-in-america/>. Accessed May 21, 2014.

Dubber, Markus Dirk. (2005). *The Police Power: Patriarchy and the Foundations of American Government*. New York, NY: Columbia University Press.

Duggan, Mark. (2001). "More Guns, More Crime." *Journal of Political Economy*, *109*(5), 1086–1114.

Epp, Charles, Steven Maynard-Moody, and Donald Haider-Markel. (2014). *Pulled Over: How Police Stops Define Race and Citizenship*. Chicago, IL: University of Chicago Press.

Ewick, Patricia, and Susan S. Silbey. (1998). *The Common Place of Law: Stories from Everyday Life*. Chicago, IL: University of Chicago Press.

Ewing, Heidi, and Rachel Grade (Writers). (2012). *Detropia*. In L. Films (Producer).

Executive Office of the President. (2011). "Teacher Jobs at Risk." Washington, DC: The White House.

Fagan, Jeffrey and Deanna Wilkinson. (1998). "Guns, Youth Violence, and Social Identity in Inner Cities." *Crime and Justice, 24*, 105–188.

Farley, Reynolds, Sheldon Danziger, and Harry J. Holzer. (2000). *Detroit Divided*. New York, NY: Russell Sage Foundation.

Faturechi, Robert. May 16, 2014. "Use of License Plate Photo Database Is Raising Privacy Concerns." Los Angeles, CA: *The Los Angeles Times*. <http://touch.latimes.com/#section/-1/article/p2p-80228893/>. Accessed May 21, 2014.

Federal Bureau of Investigation. (2012a). "Expanded Homicide Data Table 14: Justifiable Homicide by Weapon, Law Enforcement, 2008–2012." Washington, DC: The Department of Justice. <http://www.fbi.gov/about-us/cjis/ucr/crime-in-the-u.s/2012/crime-in-the-u.s.-2012/offenses-known-to-law-enforcement/expanded-homicide/expanded_homicide_data_table_14_justifi-able_homicide_by_weapon_law_enforcement_2008-2012.xls>. Accessed July 6, 2014.

Federal Bureau of Investigation. (2012b). "Expanded Homicide Data Table 15: Justifiable Homicide by Weapon, Private Citizen, 2008–2012." Washington, DC: The Department of Justice. <http://www.fbi.gov/about-us/cjis/ucr/crime-in-the-u.s/2012/crime-in-the-u.s.-2012/offenses-known-to-law-enforcement/expanded-homicide/expanded_homicide_data_table_15_justifiable_homicide_by_weapon_private_citizen_2008-2012.xls>. Accessed July 6, 2014.

Feeley, Malcolm M., and Jonathan Simon. (1992). "The New Penology: Notes on the Emerging Strategy of Corrections and Its Implications." *Criminology*, *30*(4), 449–474.

Feeney, Matthew. January 3, 2014. "Legal Gun Owners Can Deter Crime, Says Detroit Police Chief." *Reason Magazine*. <http://reason.com/blog/2014/01/03/legal-gun-owners-can-deter-crime-says-d>. Accessed April 25, 2014.

Feldman, Richard. (2008). *Ricochet: Confessions of a Gun Lobbyist*. Hoboken, NJ: John Wiley & Sons, Inc.

Fine, Lisa M. (2000). "Rights of Men, Rites of Passage: Hunting and Masculinity at Reo Motors of Lansing, Michigan, 1945–1975." *Journal of Social History*, *33*(4), 805–823.

Fine, Sidney. (2007). *Violence in the Model City*. Lansing, MI: Michigan State University Press.

Fisher, Joseph C. (1976). "Homicide In Detroit: The Role of Firearms." *Criminology*, *14*(3), 387–400.

Foucault, Michel. (1982). "The Subject and Power." In J. Faubion (Ed.), *Michel Foucault: Power (The Essential Works of Foucault 1954–1984)*. London, UK: Penguin.

Foucault Michel. (1990). *History of Sexuality, Volume 2: The Use of Pleasure*. New York, NY: Vintage Books.

Frank, Thomas. (2005). *What's the Matter with Kansas? How Conservatives Won the Heart of America*. New York, NY: Holt Paperbacks.

Fraser, Nancy, and Linda Gordon. (1994). "A Genealogy of Dependency: Tracing a Keyword of the U.S. Welfare State." *Signs: Journal of Women in Culture and Society*, *19*(2), 309–336.

Gable, Mary, and Douglas Hall. May 16, 2013. "Ongoing Joblessness in Michigan." Washington, DC: Economic Policy Institute. <http://www.epi.org/publication/ongoing-joblessness-michigan-unemployment/>. Accessed September 20, 2013.

Gallaher, Carolyn. (2003). *On the Fault Line: Race, Class, and the American Patriot Movement*. New York, NY: Rowman & Littlefield Publishers.

Gamson, William A. (1992). *Talking Politics*. New York, NY: Cambridge University Press.

Garland, David. (1996). "The Limits of the Sovereign State: Strategies of Crime Control in Contemporary Society." *British Journal of Criminology, 36*(4), 445–471.

Garland, David. (2000). "The Culture of High Crime Societies." *British Journal of Criminology, 40*(3), 347–375.

Garland, David. (2002). *The Culture of Control: Crime and Social Order in Contemporary Society*. Chicago, IL: University of Chicago Press.

Garriott, William. (2011). *Policing Methamphetamine: Narcopolitics in Rural America*. New York, NY: New York University Press.

Gau, Jacinta, and Rod Brunson. (2010). "Procedural Justice and Order Maintenance Policing: A Study of Inner-City Young Men's Perceptions of Police Legitimacy." *Justice Quarterly, 27*(2), 255–279.

Gelman, Andrew, Jeffrey Fagan, and Alex Kiss. (2007). "An Analysis of the New York City Police Department's 'Stop & Frisk' Policy in the Context of Claims of Racial Bias." *Journal of the American Statistical Association, 102*(479), 813–823.

Georgakas, Dan, Marvin Surkin, and Manning Marable. (1998). *Detroit, I Do Mind Dying: A Study in Urban Revolution*. Cambridge, MA: South End Press.

Gillespie, Cynthia. (1989). *Justifiable Homicide: Battered Women, Self-defense and the Law*. Columbus, OH: Ohio State University Press.

Gilliom, John. (2001). *Overseers of the Poor: Surveillance, Resistance, and the Limits of Privacy*. Chicago, IL: University of Chicago Press.

Glenn, Evelyn Nakano. (2011). "Constructing Citizenship: Exclusion, Subordination, and Resistance." *American Sociological Review, 76*(1), 1024.

Goldstein, Amy. January 2, 2007. "The Private Arm of the Law." Washington, DC: *The Washington Post*. <http://www.washingtonpost.com/wp-dyn/content/article/2007/01/01/AR2007010100665.html>. Accessed May 21, 2014.

Goold, Benjamin, Ian Loader, and Angelica Thumala. (2010). "Consuming Security?: Tools for a Sociology of Security Consumption." *Theoretical Criminology, 14*(1), 3–30.

Goss, Kristin. January 4, 2013. "Why We Need to Talk About Guns." New York, NY: Newsweek Magazine. <http://www.newsweek.com/why-we-need-talk-about-guns-63103>. Accessed July 11, 2014.

Goss, Kristin A. (2008). *Disarmed: The Missing Movement for Gun Control in America*. Princeton, NJ: Princeton University Press.

Grossman, Richard, and Stephen A. Lee. (2008). "May Issue versus Shall Issue: Explaining the Pattern of Concealed-Carry Handgun Laws, 1960–2001." *Contemporary Economic Policy, 26*(2), 198–206.

Haas, Nicole, Jan de Keijser, and Gerben Bruinsma. (2014). "Public Support for Vigilantism, Confidence in the Police, and Police Responsiveness." *Policing and Society, 24*(2), 224–241.

Hagerdorn, John. (1998). "Gang Violence in the Postindustrial Era." *Crime and Justice, 24*, 365–419.

Hall, Stuart, Chas Critcher, Tony Jefferson, John Clarke, and Brian Roberts. (2013 [1978]). *Policing the Crisis: Mugging, the State and Law and Order.* New York, NY: Palgrave Macmillan.

Hanenal, Sam. January 13, 2013. "Unions Suffer Sharp Decline in Membership, Nationally and in Michigan." Grand Rapids, MI: *mLive.com.* <http://www.mlive.com/business/index.ssf/2013/01/unions_suffer_sharp_decline_in.html>. Accessed September 20, 2013.

Hajal, Khalil Al. September 21, 2012a. "Detroit has half the median income, three times the poverty rate of the nation, new Census numbers show." Grand Rapids, MI: *mLive.com.* <http://www.mlive.com/news/detroit/index.ssf/2012/09/detroit_has_half_the_median_in.html>. Accessed April 16, 2014.

Hajal, Khalil Al. July 12, 2012b. "Flint No. 1., Detroit Second Among Nation's Most Violent Cities. Grand Rapids, MI: *mLive.com.* <http://www.mlive.com/news/flint/index.ssf/2012/06/flint_no_1_detroit_second_amon.html>. Accessed April 16, 2014.

Harcourt, Bernard E. (2010). "Neoliberal Penality: A Brief Genealogy." *Theoretical Criminology, 14*(1), 74–92.

Harcourt, Bernard E. (2006a). *Against Prediction: Profiling, Policing and Punishing in an Actuarial Age.* Chicago, IL: University of Chicago Press.

Harcourt, Bernard E. (2006b). *Language of the Gun: Youth, Crime, and Public Policy.* Chicago, IL: University of Chicago Press.

Hartmann, Heidi. (1976). "Capitalism, Patriarchy, and Job Segregation by Sex." *Signs: Journal of Women in Culture and Society, 1*(3),137–169.

Hardisty, Jean. (2000). *Mobilizing Resentment: Conservative Resurgence from the John Birch Society to the Promise Keepers.* New York, NY: Beacon Press.

Harvey, David. (2005). *A Brief History of Neoliberalism.* Oxford, UK: Oxford University Press.

Harris, David A. (1999). "The Stories, The Statistics, and the Law: Why 'Driving While Black' Matters." *Minnesota Law Review, 94*, 265–326.

Hartigan, John. (1999). *Racial Situations: Class Predicaments of Whiteness in Detroit.* Princeton, NJ: Princeton University Press.

Hartmann, Heidi. (1979). "The Unhappy Marriage of Marxism and Feminism: Towards a more Progressive Union." *Capital and Class, 3*(2), 1–33.

Hayes, Melissa. December 13, 2010. "Billboards Urge Healy to Back Off Police Layoffs." Jersey City, NJ: *The Jersey Journal.* <http://www.nj.com/hudson/index.ssf/2010/12/billboards_urge_healy_to_back.html>. Accessed May 4, 2014.

Heath, Melanie. (2012). *One Marriage Under God*. New York, NY: New York University Press.

Helper, Susan, Timothy Krueger, and Howard Wial. (2012). *Locating American Manufacturing: Trends in the Geography of Production*. Washington, DC: The Brookings Institute.

Hemenway, David. (2004). *Private Guns, Public Health*. Ann Arbor, MI: University of Michigan Press.

Herbert, Steve. (2001). "'Hard Charger' or 'Station Queen'? Policing and the Masculinist State." *Gender, Place & Culture: A Journal of Feminist Geography*, *8*(1), 55–71.

Hillyard, Sam, and Joseph Burridge. (2012). "Shotguns and Firearms in the UK: A Call for a Distinctively Sociological Contribution to the Debate." *Sociology of Sport Journal*, *46*(3), 395–410.

Himmelstein, Jerome L. (1990). *To the Right: The Transformation of American Conservatism*. Berkeley, CA: University of California Press.

Hofstadter, Richard. (1964). "The Paranoid Style in American Politics." *Harper's Magazine*, November, 77–86.

Horowitz, Ruth. (1983). *Honor and the American Dream: Culture and Identity in a Chicago Community*. Rutgers, NJ: Rutgers University Press.

Horwitz, Joshua, and Casey Anderson. (2009). *Guns, Democracy and the Insurrectionist Idea*. Ann Arbor, MI: University of Michigan Press.

Jeffords, Susan. (1989). *The Remasculinization of America: Gender and the Vietnam War*. Bloomington, IN: Indiana University Press.

Jones, Jeffrey M. (2005). "Confidence in Local Police Drops to 10-Year Low." Washington, DC: Gallup. <http://www.gallup.com/poll/19783/confidence-local-police-drops-10year-low.aspx>. Accessed May 7, 2014.

Jones, Jeffrey. October 26, 2011. "Record-low 26% in US Favor Handgun Ban." Washington, DC: Gallup. <http://www.gallup.com/poll/150341/Record-Low-Favor-Handgun-Ban.aspx>. Accessed May 20, 2014.

Jones, Jeffrey. February 1, 2013. "Men, Married, Southerners Most Likely to Be Gun Owners." Washington, DC: Gallup. <http://www.gallup.com/poll/160223/men-married-southerners-likely-gun-owners.aspx>. Accessed May 2, 2014.

Jones, Nikki. (2009). *Between Good and Ghetto: African American Girls and Inner-City Violence*. New Brunswick, NJ: Rutgers University Press.

Kahan, Dan M., and Donald Braman. (2003). "More Statistics, Less Persuasion: A Cultural Theory of Gun-Risk Perceptions." *University of Pennsylvannia Law Review*, *15*(4), 1291–1327.

Katzman, David. (1973). *Before the Ghetto: Black Detroit in the Nineteenth Century*. Champaign-Urbana, IL: University of Illinois Press.

Kellermann, Arthur, Frederick Rivara, Norman Rushforth, Joyce Banton, Donald Reay, Jerry Francisco, Ana Locci, Janice Prodzinski, Bela Hackman, and Grant Somes. (1993). "Gun Ownership as a Risk Factor for Homicide in the Home." *New England Journal of Medicine* *329*(15), 1084–1091.

Kellermann, Arthur, Grant Somes, Frederick Rivara, Roberta Lee, and Joyce Banton. (1998). "Injuries and Deaths Due to Firearms in the Home." *Journal of Trauma*, 45(2), 263–267.

Kellner, Douglas. (2008). *Guys and Guns Amok: Domestic Terrorism and School Shootings from the Oklahoma City Bombing to the Virginia Tech Massacre.* New York, NY: Paradigm.

Kenyon, Amy Maria. (2004). *Dreaming Suburbia: Detroit and the Production of Postwar Space and Culture.* Detroit, MI: Wayne State University Press.

Kimmel, Michael. (2013). *Angry White Men: American Masculinity at the End of an Era.* New York, NY: Nation Books.

Kleck, Gary. (2001). "Can Owning a Gun Really Triple the Owner's Chances of Being Murdered?" *Homicide Studies*, 5(1), 64–77.

Kleck, Gary, and Karen McElrath. (1991). "The Effects of Weaponry on Human Violence." *Social Forces*, 69(3), 669–92.

Klinenberg, Eric. (2001). "Bowling Alone, Policing Together." *Social Justice*, 28(3), 75–80.

Kraska, Peter. (1996). "Enjoying Militarism: Political/Personal Dilemmas in Studying U.S. Police Paramilitary Units." *Justice Quarterly*, 13(3), 405–429.

Kraska, Peter and Louis Cubellis. (1997). "Militarizing Mayberry and Beyond: Making Sense of American Paramilitary Policing." *Justice Quarterly*, 14(4), 607–629.

Kraska, Peter and Victor Kappeler. (1997). "Militarizing American Police: The Rise and Normalization of Paramilitary Units." *Social Problems*, 44(1), 1–44.

Kraska, Peter. (2007). "Militarization and Policing: Its Relevance to 21st Century Police." *Policing*, 1(4), 501–513.

Lakoff, George. (2002). *Moral Politics: How Liberals and Conservatives Think.* Chicago, IL: University of Chicago Press.

Lamont, Michelle. (2002). *The Dignity of Working Men.* Cambridge, MA: Harvard University Press.

Larson, Kathryn. October 6, 2012. "Enter at Your Own Risk: Police Union Says 'War-Like' Detroit is Unsafe for Visitors." Detroit, MI: *CBS Local.* <http://detroit.cbslocal.com/2012/10/06/enter-at-your-own-risk-police-union-says-war-like-detroit-is-unsafe-for-visitors/>. Accessed May 2, 2014.

LeDuff, Charlie. (2013). *Detroit: An American Autopsy.* New York, NY: Penguin Books.

Leshner, Alan I., Bruce M. Altevogt, Arlene F. Lee, Margaret A. McCoy, and Patrick W. Kelley, (Eds.); Committee on Priorities for a Public Health Research Agenda to Reduce the Threat of Firearm-Related Violence; Executive Office, Institute of Medicine (EO); Institute of Medicine (IOM); Committee on Law and Justice; Division of Behavioral and Social Sciences and Education (DBASSE); National Research Council. (2013). *Firearm-Related Violence.* Washington, DC: The National Academies Press.

Linebaugh, Kate. July 19, 2013. "Rising from the Ashes: The Origins of Detroit's Motto." New York, NY: *The Wall Street Journal.* <http://blogs.wsj.com/corporate-intelligence/2013/07/19/rising-from-the-ashes-the-origins-of-detroits-motto/>. Accessed May 19, 2014.

Lipsitz, George. (2011). *How Racism Takes Place*. Temple, PA: Temple University Press.

Loader, Ian, and Neil Walker. (2001). "Policing as a Public Good: Reconstituting the Connections between Policing and the State." *Theoretical Criminology*, *5*(1), 9–35.

Loader, Ian, Benjamin Goold, and Angelica Thumala. (2014). "The Moral Economy of Security." *Theoretical Criminology*, *18*(4), 469–488.

Lott, John. (1998). *More Guns, Less Crime: Understanding Crime and Gun Control Laws*. Chicago, IL: University of Chicago Press.

Ludwig, Jens. (2000). "Gun Self-Defense and Deterrence." *Crime and Justice*, *27*, 363–417.

Luker, Kristin. (1985). *Abortion and the Politics of Motherhood*. Berkeley, CA: University of California Press.

Lupton, Deborah, and John Tulloch. (1999). "Theorizing Fear of Crime: Beyond the Rational/Irrational Opposition." *British Journal of Sociology*, *50*(3), 507–523.

Madriz, Esther. (1997). *Nothing Bad Happens to Good Girls: Fear of Crime in Women's Lives*. Berkeley, CA: University of California Press.

Mahmood, Saba. (2004). *The Politics of Piety: The Islamic Revival and the Feminist Subject*. Princeton, NJ: Princeton University Press.

Manza, Jeff, and Christopher Uggen. (2006). *Locked Out: Felon Disenfranchisement and American Democracy*. New York, NY: Oxford University Press.

Martin, Elizabeth Anne. (1993). *Detroit and the Great Migration: 1816–1929*. Ann Arbor, MI: University of Michigan Press.

Marx, Gary, and Dane Archer. (1976). "Community Self-Defense: Citizen Involvement in Law Enforcement is an American Tradition." *Society*, *13*(3), 38–43.

Massey, Skippy. March 2, 2012. "Weekly Round-up for March 2, 2012: Don't Go the Way of Stockton." Humboldt, CA: *Humboldt Sentinel*. <http://humboldt-sentinel.com/2012/03/02/weekly-roundup-for-march-2-2012/>. Accessed May 4, 2014.

Maynard-Moody, Steven, and Michael Musheno. (2003). *Cops, Teaachers, Counselors: Stories from the Front Lines of Public Service*. Ann Arbor, MI: University of Michigan Press.

McCarthy, Justin. November 7, 2014. "More than Six in 10 Americans say Guns Make Homes Safer." Washington, DC: Gallup. <http://www.gallup.com/poll/179213/six-americans-say-guns-homes-safer.aspx>. Accessed January 3, 2015.

McClain, Paula. (1983). "Firearms Ownership, Gun Control Attitudes, and Neighborhood Environment." *Law & Policy Quarterly*, *5*(3), 299–323.

McDowall, David, and Colin Loftin. (1983). "Collective Security and the Demand for Legal Handguns." *American Journal of Sociology*, *88*(6), 1146–1161.

Meehan, Albert, and Michael Ponder. (2002). "Race & Place: The Ecology of Racial Profiling African American Drivers." *Justice Quarterly*, *19*(3), 399–430.

Melzer, Scott. (2009). *Gun Crusaders: The NRA's Culture War*. New York, NY: New York University Press.

Messner, Michael. (2007). "The Masculinity of the Governator: Muscle and Compassion in American Politics." *Gender & Society*, *21*(4), 461–480.

Micklethwait, John, and Adrian Wooldridge. (2005). *The Right Nation: Conservative Power in America.* New York, NY: Penguin Books.

Mieczkowski, Thomas. (1986). "Geeking Up and Throwing Down: Heroin Street Life in Detroit." *Criminology, 24*(4), 645–666.

Miles, Jason. April 23, 2013. "MPA Billboards Warn to Enter Memphis 'At Your Own Risk.'" Memphis, TN: *WMC-TV.* <http://www.wmctv.com/story/22047563/police-union-billboards-spark-criticism>. Accessed May 4, 2014.

Miller, Toby. (2006). *Cultural Citizenship: Cosmopolitanism, Consumerism, and Television in a Neoliberal Age.* Philadelphia, PA: Temple University Press.

Mitchell, Don. (2003). "The SUV Model of Citizenship: Floating Bubbles, Buffer Zones, and the Rise of the 'Purely Atomic' Individual." *Political Geography, 24*(1), 77–100.

Monahan, Torin. (2010). *Surveillance in the Time of Insecurity.* Boston, MA: Rutgers University Press.

Morrison, Steven R. (2007). "Will to Power, Will to Reality, and Racial Profiling: How the White Male Dominant Power Structure Creates Itself as Law Abiding Citizen Through the Creation of Black as Criminal." *Northwestern Journal of Law & Social Policy, 2*(1), 63–104.

Muller, Chris. (2012). "Northward Migration and the Rise of Racial Disparity in American Incarceration, 1880–1950." *American Journal of Sociology, 118*(2), 281–326.

Murphy, Shannon. July 29, 2010. "Billboard Battle: Do the Bay City Police Union Billboards Questioning Safety Go Too Far?" Grand Rapids, MI: *mLive.com.* <http://www.mlive.com/news/bay-city/index.ssf/2010/07/billboard_battle_do_the_bay_ci.html>. Accessed May 4, 2014.

Myler, Kofi. July 23, 2013. "Detroit's Population from 1840 to 2012 Shows High Points, Decades of Decline." Detroit, MI: *Detroit Free Press* <http://www.freep.com/interactive/article/20130723/NEWS01/130721003/detroit-city-population>. Accessed April 16, 2014.

National Public Radio (NPR). March 17, 2009. "Michigan Gov.: Job Loss 'Our Own Katrina.'" Washington, DC: NPR. <http://www.npr.org/templates/story/story.php?storyId=101990867>. Accessed September 20, 2013.

Nisbett, Richard E., and Dov Cohen. (1996). *Culture of Honor: The Psychology of Violence in the South.* Boulder, CO: Westview Press.

New York City Bar Association. (2013). *Report on the NYPD's Stop-and-Frisk Policy.* New York, NY: New York City Bar Association. < http://www2.nycbar.org/pdf/report/uploads/20072495-StopFriskReport.pdf>. Accessed May 8, 2014.

Newton, George D., and Frank E. Zimring. (1970). *Firearms and Violence in American Life.* Washington, DC: US Department of Commerce, Bureau of the Census Vital Statistics.

NRA. (2000). *NRA Guide to the Basics of Personal Protection in the Home.* Fairfax, VA: National Rifle Association of America.

O'Malley, Pat. (1992). "Risk, Power and Crime Prevention." *Economy and Society, 21*(3), 252–275.

O'Malley, Pat. (2000). "Uncertain Subjects: Risks, Liberalism and Contract." *Economy and Society, 29*(4), 460–484.

O'Neill, Kevin Lewis. (2007). "Armed Citizens and the Stories They Tell: The National Rifle Association's Achievement of Terror and Masculinity." *Men and Masculinities, 9*(4), 457–475.

Ong, Aihwa. (1996). "Cultural Citizenship as Subject-Making." *Current Anthropology, 37*(5), 737–762.

Page, Joshua. (2011a). "Prison Officer Unions and the Perpetuation of the Penal Status Quo." *Criminology and Public Policy, 10*(3), 735–770.

Page, Joshua. (2011b). *The Toughest Beat: Politics, Punishment and the Prison Officers Union in California*. New York, NY: Oxford University Press.

Payne, B. Keith. (2006). "Weapons Bias: Split Second Decisions and Unintended Stereotyping." *Current Directions in Psychological Science, 15*(6), 287–291.

Peck, Jamie, and Adam Tickell. (2002). "Neoliberalizing Space." *Antipode, 34*(3), 380–404.

Penner, Andrew, and Aliya Saperstein. (2013). "Engendering Racial Perceptions: An Intersectional Analysis of How Social Status Shapes Race." *Gender & Society, 27*(3), 319–344.

Peters, Mark, and David Wessel. February 6, 2014. "More Men in Prime Working Ages Don't Have Jobs." *Wall Street Journal*. <http://online.wsj.com/news/articles/SB10001424052702304027204579334610097660366>. Accessed July 22, 2014.

Pew Center for the People and the Press. December 12, 2012. "After Newtown, Modest Change in Opinion about Gun Control." Washington, DC: The Pew Charitable Trusts. <http://www.people-press.org/2012/12/20/after-newtown-modest-change-in-opinion-about-gun-control/>. Accessed May 20, 2014.

Pew Center for the People and the Press. March 12, 2013a. "Why Own a Gun? Protection Is Now Top Reason." Washington, DC: The Pew Charitable Trusts. < http://www.people-press.org/2013/03/12/why-own-a-gun-protection-is-now-top-reason/>. Accessed May 20, 2014.

Pew Research Center for the People and the Press. December 20, 2014. "Growing Public Support for Gun Rights." Washington, DC: Pew Charitable Trusts. <http://www.people-press.org/2014/12/10/growing-public-support-for-gun-rights/> Accessed January 3, 2015.

Pew Research Center's Social & Demographic Trends Project. May 29, 2013b. "Breadwinner Moms." Washington, DC: The Pew Charitable Trusts. <http://www.pewsocialtrends.org/2013/05/29/breadwinner-moms/>. Accessed September 20, 2013.

Pew Center on the States. (2009). *One in 31: The Long Reach of American Corrections*. Washington, DC: The Pew Charitable Trusts.

Pilkington, Ed. June 24, 2014. "US Police Departments are Increasingly Militarised, Finds Report." London, UK: *The Guardian*. <http://www.theguardian.com/law/2014/jun/24/military-us-police-swat-teams-raids-aclu>. Accessed July 1, 2014.

Platzer, M. D., and G. J. Harrison. (2009). *The U.S. Automotive Industry: National and State Trends in Manufacturing Employment*. Washington, DC: Congressional Research Service. <http://digitalcommons.ilr.cornell.edu/key_workplace/666>. Accessed April 16, 2014.

Porter II, James. October 23, 2013. "NRA President on the Job of Police: No Duty to Retreat." *The Daily Caller*. <http://www.nranews.com/cam/video/nra-president-james-porter-on-the-job-of-police-no-duty-to-protect/list/cc-presidents-report>. Accessed May 2, 2014.

Provine, Doris Marie. (2007). *Unequal under the Law: Race in the War on Drugs*. Chicago, IL: University of Chicago Press.

Putnam, Robert. (2001). *Bowling Alone*. New York, NY: Simon & Schuster.

Reaves, Brian A. (2012). "Hiring and Retention of State and Local Law Enforcement Officers, 2008–Statistical Tables." Washington, DC: US Department of Justice.

Rios, Victor. (2011). *Punished: Policing the Lives of Black and Latino Boys*. New York, NY: New York University Press.

Roman, John. (2013). "Race, Justifiable Homicide, and Stand Your Ground Laws: Analysis of FBI Supplementary Homicide Data." Washington, DC: The Urban Institute.

Rose, William. (2002). "Crimes of Color: Risk, Profiling, and the Contemporary Racialization of Social Control." *International Journal of Politics, Culture, and Society*, *16*(2), 179–205.

Rosenfeld, Richard, and Steven Messner. (2013). *Crime and the Economy*. London, UK: SAGE Publications.

Ross, Andrew. August 14, 2011. "Jennifer Granholm, Ex-Michigan Governor, on Jobs." San Francisco, CA: *San Francisco Chronicle*. <http://www.sfgate.com/business/article/Jennifer-Granholm-ex-Michigan-governor-on-jobs-2335327.php>. Accessed April 25, 2014.

Ross, P. Luevonda. (2007). "The Transmogrification of Self-Defense by National Rifle Association–Inspired Statutes: From the Doctrine of Retreat to the Right to Stand Your Ground." *Southern University Law Review*, *35*(1), 1–46.

Saad, Lydia. October 25, 2013. "US Remains Divided Over Passing Stricter Gun Laws." Washington, DC: Gallup. <http://www.gallup.com/poll/165563/remains-divided-passing-stricter-gun-laws.aspx>. Accessed May 20, 2014.

Sagar, Andrew, and Janet Schofield. (1980). "Racial and Behavioral Cues in Black and White Children's Perceptions of Ambiguously Aggressive Acts." *Journal of Personality and Social Psychology*, *39*(4), 590–598.

Sampson, Robert. (2012). *Great American City: Chicago and the Enduring Neighborhood Effect*. Chicago, IL: University of Chicago Press.

Sampson, Robert, and Dawn Jeglum Bartusch. (1998). "Legal Cynicism and (Subcultural?) Tolerance of Deviance: The Neighborhood Context of Racial Differences." *Law and Society Review*, *32*, 777–804.

Sanburn, Josh. December 18, 2012. "America's Gun Economy, By the Numbers." New York, NY: *Time Magazine*. <http://business.time.com/2012/12/18/americas-gun-economy-by-the-numbers/>. Accessed May 21, 2014.

Schultz, Howard. September 17, 2013. "An Open Letter from Howard Schultz, CEO of Starbucks Coffee Company." Seattle, WA: *Starbucks.com*. <http://www.starbucks.com/blog/an-open-letter-from-howard-schultz-ceo-of-starbucks-coffee-company/1268>. Accessed May 7, 2014.

Scott, James. (1987). *Weapons of the Weak: Everyday Forms of Peasant Resistance*. New Haven, CT: Yale University Press.

Seitz, Steven Thomas. (1972). "Homicides, and Gun Control Effectiveness." *Law and Society Review*, *6*(4), 595–614.

Shaiko, Ronald G., and Marc A. Wallace. (1998). "Going Hunting Where the Ducks Are: The National Rifle Association and the Grass Roots." In Clyde Wilcox and John M. Bruce (Eds.) *The Changing Politics of Gun Control*, 155–171. New York, NY: Rowman & Littlefield Publishers.

Shapira, Harel. (2013). *Waiting for Jose: The Minutemen's Pursuit of America*. Princeton, NJ: Princeton University Press.

Shearing, Clifford, and Philip Stenning. (1983). "Private Security: Implications for Social Control." *Social Problems*, *30*(5), 493–506.

Shearing, Clifford, and Jennifer Wood. (2003). "Nodal Governance, Democracy, and the New 'Denizens.'" *Journal of Law and Society*, *30*(3), 400–419.

Shearing, Clifford, and Monique Marks. (2011). "Being a New Police in the Liquid 21st Century." *Policing: A Journal of Policy and Practice*, *5*(3), 210–218.

Sherman, Jennifer. (2009). *Those Who Work, Those Who Don't: Poverty, Morality and Family in Rural America*. Minneapolis, MN: University of Minnesota Press.

Simon, Jonathan. (2004). "Gun Rights and the Constitutional Significance of Violent Crime." *William and Mary Bill of Rights Journal*, *12*, 335–356.

Simon, Jonathan. (2007). *Governing through Crime: How the War on Crime Transformed American Democracy and Created a Culture of Fear*. New York, NY: Oxford University Press.

Simon, Jonathan. (2010). "Consuming Obsessions: Housing, Homicide, and Mass Incarceration since 1950." *The University of Chicago Legal Forum*, *165*, 141–180.

Skocpol, Theda, and Vanessa Williamson. (2012). *The Tea Party and the Remaking of Republican Conservatism*. New York, NY: Oxford University Press.

Smith, Douglas A., and Craig D. Uchida. (1988). "The Social Organization of Self-Help: A Study of Defensive Weapon Ownership." *American Sociological Review*, *53*(1), 94–102.

Soss, Joe. (1999). "Lessons of Welfare: Policy Design, Political Leaning, and Political Action." *American Political Science Review*, *93*(2): 363–380.

Soss, Joe, Richard C. Fording, and Sanford F. Schram. (2011). *Disciplining the Poor: Neoliberal Paternalism and the Persistent Power of Race*. Chicago, IL: University of Chicago Press.

Spierenburg, Pieter. (1998). "Masculinity, Violence, and Honor: An Introduction." In Pieter Spierenburg *Men and Violence: Gender, Honor, and Rituals in Modern Europe and America* (Ed.), 1–29. Columbus, OH: Ohio State University Press.

Stabile, Carol A. (2006). *White Victims, Black Villains: Gender, Race, and Crime News in US Culture.* New York, NY: Routledge.

Stack, Steven, and Liqun Cao. (1998). "Political Conservatism and Confidence in the Police: A Comparative Analysis." *Journal of Crime and Justice, 21*(1), 71–76.

Statistics Canada. (2006). "Firearms and Violent Crime." Ottawa, ON: Statistics Canada. <http://www.statcan.gc.ca/pub/85-002-x/2008002/article/10518-eng.htm>. Accessed July 12, 2004.

Stein, Arlene. (2002). *The Stranger Next Door.* Boston, MA: Beacon Press.

Stein, Arlene. (2005). "Make Room for Daddy: Anxious Masculinity and Emergent Homophobias in Neopatriarchal Politics." *Gender & Society, 19*(5), 601–620.

Steinmetz, George. (2009). "Detroit: A Tale of Two Crises." *Environment and Planning: Space and Society, 27*(5), 761–770.

Steinmetz, Kevin, and Howard Henderson. (2012). "Hip-Hop and Procedural Justice: Hip-Hop Artists' Perceptions of Criminal Justice." *Race and Justice, 2*(3), 155–178.

Stevens, Richard. (1999). *Dial 911 and Die.* Hartford, WI: Jews for the Preservation of Firearms Ownership.

Stroud, Angela. (2012). "Good Guys with Guns: Hegemonic Masculinity and Concealed Handguns." *Gender & Society, 26*(2), 216–238.

Sugarman, Josh. (1992). *National Rifle Association: Money, Firepower & Fear.* Washington, DC: National Press Book.

Sugrue, Thomas J. (2005). *The Origins of the Urban Crisis: Race and Inequality in Postwar Detroit.* Princeton, NJ: Princeton University Press.

Swidler, Ann. (1986). "Culture in Action: Symbols and Strategies." *American Sociological Review, 51*(2), 273–286.

Swift, Art. October 28, 2013. "Personal Safety Top Reasons Americans Own Guns Today." Washington, DC: Gallup. <http://www.gallup.com/poll/165605/personal-safety-top-reason-americans-own-guns-today.aspx>. Accessed May 20, 2014.

Target Corporation. (2013). "Forensics Overview." Minneapolis, MN: Target Corporation. <http://pressroom.target.com/backgrounders/forensics-support>. Accessed May 21, 2014.

Tark, Jongyeon, and Gary Kleck. (2014). "Resisting Rape: The Effects of Victim Self-Protection on Rape Completion and Injury." *Violence Against Women 20*(3), 270–292.

TASER International. (2014). "About TASER." Scottsdale, AZ: TASER International. <http://www.taser.com/about-taser>. Accessed May 21, 2014.

Taylor, Carl. (1990). *Dangerous Society.* Lansing, MI: Michigan State University Press.

The Telegraph. May 14, 2010. "Sarah Palin Calls on 'Mama Grizzlies' to Help Republicans Win Election." London, UK: *The Telegraph.* <http://www.telegraph.co.uk/news/worldnews/sarah-palin/7725912/Sarah-Palin-calls-on-mama-grizzlies-to-help-Republicans-win-election.html>. Accessed May 2, 2014.

Time Magazine. November 26, 1984. "Crime: Teen Violence in Detroit." New York, NY: *Time Magazine*. <http://www.time.com/time/magazine/article/0,9171,926983,00.html>. Accessed April 25, 2014.

Tonry, Michael. (1995). *Malign Neglect: Race, Crime, and Punishment in America*. New York, NY: Oxford University Press.

Tonry, Michael. (2011). *Punishing Race: A Continuing American Dilemma*. New York, NY: Oxford University Press.

Van Wolputte, Steven. (2004). "Hang onto Your Self: Of Bodies, Embodiment, and Selves." *Annual Review of Anthropology, 33,* 251–269.

Vernick, Jon, James Hodge Jr., and Daniel Webster. (2007). "The Ethics of Restrictive Licensing for Handguns: Comparing the United States and Canadian Approaches to Handgun Regulation." *The Journal of Law, Medicine & Ethics, 35*(4), 668–678.

Violence Policy Center. (2013). "Gun Deaths Outpace Motor Vehicle Deaths in 12 States and the District of Columbia in 2010." Washington, DC: Violence Policy Center. <http://www.vpc.org/studies/gunsvscars13.pdf>. Accessed July 11, 2014.

Wacquant, Loïc. (2001). "Deadly Symbiosis: When Ghetto and Prison Meet and Mesh." *Punishment & Society, 3*(1), 95–134.

Wacquant, Loïc. (2008). *Urban Outcasts: A Comparative Sociology of Advanced Marginality*. Malden, MA: Polity Press.

Wacquant, Loïc. (2009). *Punishing the Poor: The Neoliberal Government of Social Insecurity*. Durham, NC: Duke University Press.

Wacquant, Loïc. (2012). "The Wedding of Workfare and Prisonfare in the 21st Century." *Journal of Poverty, 16*(3), 236–249.

Waldman, Michael. (2014). *The Second Amendment: A Biography*. New York, NY: Simon & Schuster.

Warren, Donald I. (1975). *Black Neighborhoods: An Assessment of Community Power*. Ann Arbor, MI: University of Michigan Press.

WCHB. March 27, 2012. "Detroit 300 Raphael Johnson and Angelo Henderson Speak at Justice for Trayvon Martin." Detroit, MI: WCHB Radio 1200 AM. <http://www.youtube.com/watch?v=N69LI66WVYc>. Accessed May 20, 2014.

Webb, Vincent, and Chris Marshall. (1995). "The Relative Importance of Race and Ethnicity on Citizen Attitudes Toward Police." *American Journal of Police, 14,* 45–66.

Weber, Max. (2002). *The Protestant Ethic and the "Spirit" of Capitalism and Other Writings*. New York, NY: Penguin Books.

Weisburd, David, Rosann Greenspan, and Edwin Hamilton. (2000). *Police Attitudes toward Abuse of Authority: Findings from a National Study*. Washington, DC: US National Institute of Justice.

West, Candace, and Don H. Zimmerman. (1987). "Doing Gender." *Gender & Society, 1*(2), 125–151.

Western, Bruce. (2006). *Punishment and Inequality in America*. New York, NY: Russell Sage Foundation.

Williams, Timothy. June 4, 2014. "NRA Backs Away from Article Criticizing Advocates of Carrying Guns in Public." New York, NY: *The New York Times*. <http://www.nytimes.com/2014/06/05/us/nra-backs-away-from-criticism-of-open-carry-advocates.html?_r=0>. Accessed July 1, 2014.

Wilson, Reid. September 19, 2013. "Household Incomes Stabilize, but Still Below 2000 Levels." *The Washington Post*. <http://www.washingtonpost.com/blogs/govbeat/wp/2013/09/19/household-incomes-stabilize-but-still-below-2000-levels/>. Accessed April 16, 2014.

Winkler, Adam. (2013). *Gunfight: The Battle over the Right to Bear Arms in America*. New York, NY: W.W. Norton & Company.

Young, Iris Marion. (2003). "The Logic of Masculinist Protection: Reflections on the Current Security State." *Signs: Journal of Women in Culture and Society*, 29(1), 1–24.

Zedner, Lucia. (2006). "Policing Before and After the Police: The Historical Antecedents of Contemporary Crime." *British Journal of Criminology*, 46(1), 78–96.

Zimring, Franklin E. (2011). *The City that Became Safe: New York's Lessons for Urban Crime and Its Control*. New York, NY: Oxford University Press.

INDEX